ROYAL INSTITUTE OF PHILOSOPHY LECTURES

VOLUME TWO · 1967–1968

TALK OF GOD

ROYAL INSTITUTE OF PHILOSOPHY LECTURES
VOLUME TWO · 1967–1968

TALK OF GOD

MACMILLAN
London · Melbourne · Toronto
ST MARTIN'S PRESS
New York

© The Royal Institute of Philosophy 1969

First published 1969 by
MACMILLAN AND CO LTD
Little Essex Street London WC2
and also at Bombay Calcutta and Madras
Macmillan South Africa (Publishers) Pty Ltd Johannesburg
The Macmillan Company of Australia Pty Ltd Melbourne
The Macmillan Company of Canada Ltd Toronto
St Martin's Press Inc New York

Library of Congress catalog card no. 68–10755

Printed in Great Britain by
ROBERT MACLEHOSE AND CO LTD
The University Press, Glasgow

CONTENTS

FOREWORD

In his lecture on Hell, Ian Ramsey, the Bishop of Durham, refers to theologians who are anxious to remain in full flight and never touch down. One way of 'touching down', which Ramsey recommends, is to say how talk of 'God' – and associated talk of 'faith', 'prayer', 'sin', 'repentance', 'judgement', 'heaven', 'hell', 'eternal life' – is to be understood. 'Too often have men talked as if the way to solve theological problems was by great familiarity with God, when what was needed was a patient and thorough examination of the language being used about him.'

What does such 'a patient and thorough examination' reveal? Does it reveal, for example, that utterances like 'I believe in God the Father Almighty' belong with utterances whose function is exclusively 'performative' or 'prescriptive'? In other words, is what is peculiar to religious utterances precisely that they are 'statements which are devoid of any claim to truth and which function in a different way from statements which do lay claim to truth'? This is one of the questions N. H. G. Robinson, Professor of Systematic Theology at the University of St Andrews, asks in the first paper in this volume of the 1967–8 Royal Institute of Philosophy lectures. Is religious language 'non-truth-claiming'? Has it no 'correspondence to independent reality', no 'objective reference'? To Robinson it seems that this question, 'the issue between subjectivism and objectivism', is one that can be put quite significantly. (I am not so sure. I know what it means to call a particular empirical statement, such as 'It is raining', 'true', but this does not help me when it comes to understanding what it means to call empirical statements, in general, 'truth-claiming'; or non-empirical, grammatically similar, statements, in general, 'non-truth-claiming'. Is 'Empirical statements are truth-claiming' itself truth-claiming, or is it prescriptive, a persuasive definition of

vii

'truth-claiming'?) Once this question, of subjectivism or objectivism, is accepted as meaningful it may seem that to avoid 'the elimination of religious *belief*' (and 'Does what is recognisably religion remain when religious belief has been eliminated?'), some way must be found of showing that religious language is, in general, truth-claiming. It is to this problem that Robinson turns in the final part of his paper, in which he propounds a solution which, he thinks, is suggested by the idea 'of encounter, of revelation and response'.

John Hick, H. G. Wood Professor of Theology at the University of Birmingham, distinguishes, in a way Robinson does not, between the question as to what faith is, phenomenologically, and the question as to whether it is 'veridical'. About the latter, he says: 'My own view is that it is as rational for the religious man to treat his experience of God as veridical as it is for him and others to treat their experience of the physical world as veridical.' If he means that one can no more have a reason for questioning religious experience in general, than one can have a reason for questioning sense perception in general (*pace* Descartes), then I would agree.

In his phenomenological account of faith, Hick draws on the same idea 'of encounter, of revelation and response' that suggests to Robinson a solution to the problem of how to show that religious language, in general, is truth-claiming. He remarks on how, whereas the Bible is 'full of men's encounters with God and men's personal dealings with the divine Thou', the dominant systems of Christian theology see faith as an assent to certain theological propositions rather than as 'a religious response to God's redemptive action in the life of Jesus of Nazareth'. This, he believes, is wrong; and in his paper he tries to show how 'the cognition of God by faith is more like perceiving something that is present before us than it is like believing a statement about some absent object'. Different people, or the same person at different times, may see what is objectively the same thing, differently. For example, a drawing of a cube can be seen as a cube viewed from below, or as one viewed from above. Hick expands this notion of 'seeing-as', to which Wittgenstein drew attention in his *Philosophical Investigations*, II xi, into that of 'experiencing-as', and then, by applying it to events instead of objects, comes to talk of 'experiencing the events of our lives and of human history, on the one hand as purely natural events and on the other as mediating the presence and activity of God'.

He considers an objection to this expansion. 'Just as it would be impossible for one who had never seen rabbits to see anything *as* a rabbit, so it must be impossible for us who have never seen an undeniable act of God, to see an event *as* an act of God.' He thinks that the objection collapses if *all* experiencing is experiencing-as. I am not sure about this. Consider the case of the cube seen as a cube viewed from below. Could I not understand 'The cube was viewed from below' without knowing what a cube so viewed looks like? And is not understanding this a logical condition of my having the experience of seeing a cube as a cube viewed from below? Similarly, must I not first understand 'The event was an act of God' to be able to experience an event as an act of God?

This last question leads on, naturally, to another: How am I to come to understand such statements as 'The event was an act of God'? A prior question might seem to be: What is it to understand such statements?

W. D. Hudson, Senior Lecturer in Philosophy at the University of Exeter, says that one thing understanding such statements involves is seeing the logical connection between what is said and a 'picture' (e.g. 'God the Father'). But this would seem to be merely a matter of what Robinson calls the 'internal logical coherence' of the religion, and Hudson himself says that he is sure that there is far more to understanding a religion than this.

He is primarily concerned with the answers given in Wittgenstein's *Lectures and Conversations on Aesthetics, Psychology and Religious Belief* to three questions: (*i*) What training is required in order to participate in religious belief? (*ii*) Is it reasonable, or unreasonable, to do so? and (*iii*) What is the essential difference between those who do participate in it and those who do not?, and their bearing on the question: (*iv*) To what extent can religious belief be regarded as a logically self-contained universe of discourse? In connection with the second question he makes a revealing comment. He remarks that

Wittgenstein was right to insist on what has been called the commissive force of religious beliefs, and then adds that ' "There will be a Judgement Day" appears to have constative force also – to assert that a certain event will, as a matter of empirical fact, occur'. I call this 'revealing' because it suggests that he identifies 'having constative force' (being 'truth-claiming', in Robinson's terminology) with being, or involving, what he calls 'an ordinary empirical assertion'. There is no need to make this identification. We can say, for example, that the truths of geometry are no less truths for not being, covertly, empirical. The idea that we *have* to choose between a view of religion as 'merely subjective' (a matter of 'bliks' or 'onlooks') and one of it as essentially characterised by superstitious beliefs like that of a child in Jack Frost or Santa Claus, may be attractive to the non-religious, who do not like to think that there are meanings they do not grasp, forms of life in which they do not share, but has no basis in sound philosophy.

What Paul M. van Buren, Professor of Religion at Temple University, Pennsylvania, says in the last part of his paper is very much to the point here. The choice between saying that faith and theology are non-cognitive and saying that they are so much nonsense, he says, 'can be forced upon us only on the assumption that understanding and saying how things are are of one sort only'. He goes on:

> I find that the distinction 'cognitive/non-cognitive' is not help-ful in getting clear about how Christian faith is a matter of how the world is, and I regret having once been seduced into picking up that stone axe as an appropriate tool for opening up this delicate bit of watch-works. The issue is not, as that distinction leads us to suspect, that we have an agreed frame of reference, an agreed way of carving up the world into tables and chairs on the one hand, and our attitudes or dispositions towards tables and chairs on the other. Christian faith, on the contrary, proposes another way to do the carving up in the first place.

Perhaps the difference between van Buren (faith is, in some way, a matter of how the world is) and Hick (faith is a matter of how the world is experienced, it being a further question as to

whether that experience is veridical or illusory) on the nature
of faith reflects a difference in their attitude to describing their
faith in terms of 'God'. For Hick an example of faith is experiencing events 'as mediating the presence and activity of
God'. Van Buren says that 'theology is that activity of men
struck by the biblical story, in which they undertake to revise
continually the ways in which they say how things are with
their present circumstances in the light of how they read that
story'; he likens the Church's attempts to capture, for all time,
the significance of the biblical story in some image, or way of
talking, to the attempts, reported in that story, of the chosen
people to realise the promise of Jahweh in one or another of a
succession of different forms; and he gives, as an example of just
such an image, that of 'the eternal, unchangeable and immovable God of Augustinianism'. For van Buren, talk of God is
only one way of responding to the biblical story, a way, moreover, that has had its day, to be replaced now by a language
which allows us to express what we recognise 'in the story of the
utterly faithful Jew of Nazareth', namely, that 'men are made
for each other'. (Incidentally, I am not sure that in some talk of
God – e.g. 'God is love' – this is not amply recognised.) It is
easier to understand it being said of this, that it gives 'a leading
in life which those who follow find, in an odd sort of way, to
be right' (so that a *further* question of its being true does not
arise) than it is to understand it being said of the proposition that some events 'mediate the presence and activity of
God'.

I am reminded by this of something Dietrich Bonhoeffer said,
in a letter dated 5 September 1943,[1] about 'how closely our
lives are bound up with other people's, and in fact how our
centre is outside of ourselves and how little we are individuals'.
He went on to say that 'it is a literal fact of nature that human
life extends beyond our physical existence'. I suppose van
Buren would say that this is nonsense as a statement in the
language of tables and chairs but could be a truth in a possible
language of a theologian – and, if it was, would be something
we simply found to be so. Finding it to be so, it would make no
sense for us to go on to ask 'And does human life in fact extend

[1] *Letters and Papers from Prison*, Fontana Books, 1959, p. 27.

beyond our physical existence?' It would be like asking, when we had found, by using our senses, that there are tables and chairs in the world, 'And are there really tables and chairs, or are there only ideas in our minds?' The fact that some philosophers have asked this very question does not make it a sensible question to ask. Van Buren says: 'Christians have to remember ... that the story by which they have been struck allows them to help free their neighbours and themselves from the tyranny of tables and chairs.'

In the language in which it makes sense to talk of how little we are individuals, perhaps it makes sense to talk of people deliberately turning their backs on what, in one sense, makes them individuals. 'I have been crucified with Christ; it is no longer I who live, but Christ who lives in me; and the life I now live in the flesh I live by faith in the Son of God, who loved me and gave himself for me' (Gal. 2: 20). There is no place in the language of tables and chairs for the Christian idea of dying to the self, or, for that matter, of life as a gift of God. The latter is an idea that determines the Christian's attitude to suicide.

R. F. Holland, Professor of Philosophy at the University of Leeds, touches on the different attitudes to suicide of Schopenhauer and the Christian. He remarks that Schopenhauer condemned suicide because it is a phenomenon of strong assertion of will, and that in this he was not far distant from the Christian. He writes: 'A Christian perhaps might speak, not so much of conquering, but rather of dying to the self, and the most spiritual expression of the idea for him would be in prayer – particularly in such a prayer as "Thy will, not mine, be done".' His point, I take it, is the twofold one, that just as suicide was not what Schopenhauer would regard as self-conquest so it is not what the Christian would regard as 'dying to the self', and that 'dying to the self' is not regarded by the Christian as a case of conquest by a person's unaided efforts of his own evil will. Without the grace of God, he is powerless (Eph. 2: 8, Tit. 2: 11–14). What faith is subjectively, grace is objectively.

Schopenhauer was a pessimist. So is W. W. Bartley III, Professor of Philosophy at the University of Pittsburgh, whose paper is entitled 'The Soul's Conquest of Evil'. What Bartley is pessimistic about is the extent to which there exists what he regards as a necessary condition of acting morally, namely, self-knowledge.

He argues, in the early part of his paper, that the sharp distinction made between religion and morality cannot stand. The argument seems to run as follows. (*i*) Religion involves self-awareness (he quotes, with seeming approval, Keynes, who defined 'religion' as 'one's attitude towards oneself and the ultimate'; he instances, as 'what Keynes called the "religious aspects" ' of Moore's philosophy, 'the love of beauty, and the development of inward consciousness'; and he says that there is nothing 'unenlightened' about calling quests which involve heightened self-awareness 'religious'). (*ii*) 'Our interpretation of our external situation is subject to distortion by our failures in achieving a heightened self-awareness.' (*iii*) Acting morally and making moral evaluations require the interpretation referred to in (*ii*). Therefore, (*iv*) religion is essential to morality. In keeping with this approach, he treats the Christian's 'quest for what is called salvation' as one among a number of possible routes to the same end, the soul's conquest of evil.

In striking contrast to this is what Paul Ricoeur, Professor of Philosophy at the University of Paris, says. For the moralist, evil is characterised by its twofold relation to obligation and to freedom.

Religion uses another language about evil. And this language keeps itself entirely within the limits of the perimeter of the promise and under the sign of hope. First of all, this language places evil *before* God. 'Against you, against you alone have I sinned, I have done evil in your sight.' This invocation which transforms the moral confession into a confession of sin, appears, at first glance, to be an intensification in the consciousness of evil. But that is an illusion, the moralising illusion of Christianity. Situated before God, evil is installed again in the movement of the promise; the invocation is already the beginning of the restoration of a bond. . . . Repentance, essentially directed toward the future, has already cut itself off from remorse which is a brooding reflection on the past.

Next, religious language profoundly changes the very content of the consciousness of evil. Evil in moral consciousness is essentially transgression, that is, subversion of the law; it is in this way that the majority of pious men continue to consider sin. And yet, situated before God, evil is qualitatively changed; it consists less in a transgression of a law than in a pretension of man to be master of his life. The will to live according to the law is, therefore, also an expression of evil – and even the most deadly, because the most dissimulated: worse than injustice is one's own justice. Ethical consciousness does not know this, but religious consciousness does. But this second discovery can also be expressed in terms of promise and hope.

Bartley would seem to be in disagreement, not only with Ricoeur, but also with Hick. If the soul's conquest of evil is regarded as of value only in so far as it makes possible acting morally and competently evaluating the actions of others (and there is nothing in what Bartley says to suggest an alternative view) then we have a reversal of what Hick says is suggested by his analysis of faith in terms of 'experiencing-as'. Hick says that his analysis suggests 'a view of the Christian ethic as the practical corollary of the distinctively Christian vision of the world'. In other words, the morality *follows from* the religion. For Bartley, the religion ('development of inward consciousness', etc.) seems to be *for the sake of* the morality. But perhaps the conflict is only apparent, Hick meaning one thing by religion, Bartley another. That is, perhaps for Bartley the language of religion is the language of Freud and Jung, and not the language in which there is talk of a promise, of hope and of the Kingdom of God.

I said, a little earlier, that it is easier to understand it being said of the proposition 'men are made for each other' that we can simply find it to be right, than it is to understand this being said of the proposition that some events 'mediate the presence and activity of God'. The explanation, I think, is that talk of 'mediation' implies that there is something which is not directly accessible, something 'transcendent', and the question can then be asked 'Does the alleged transcendent being really exist?' The contemporary Death of God theology could thus be represented as a way of escape from a problem of verification. With more historical warrant, Frederick C. Copleston, Professor of the History of Philosophy at Heythrop College, sees it as the spiritual heir of Hegelianism, which in turn is a way of escape from an ontological rather than an epistemological problem.

Copleston distinguishes between a synthesis – an overcoming of the estrangement of man from God – which is *lived*, and one which is *thought*. In Christian love the synthesis is lived; in the philosophy of Christianity an attempt is made to think it. It is in trying to think it that the difficulty lies. Copleston's own view is that it is an essential characteristic of the language in which there is talk of God that the relation between the world and God cannot be adequately grasped and stated; it 'can only be dimly apprehended through the use of analogies and symbols'.

Philosophers have traditionally expressed the problem as that of stating the relation between the infinite (God) and the finite (the world, including man). In these terms, it may be argued that the infinite would not be infinite if there was something outside it, the finite; and that if the finite is set over against the infinite it is 'absolutised, with the result that the infinite becomes a superfluous hypothesis'. Hegel's solution is in terms of a theory about the infinite (the 'Absolute'), known as Absolute Idealism, according to which, Copleston says, 'the essence of the Absolute . . . is not actualised in concrete reality except in the sphere of spirit which requires the sphere of Nature as its necessary presupposition'. In such a theory, Aquinas' idea of God as a transcendent reality of such a kind that we know of him what he is not rather than what he is, can have no place.

According to Hegel, Copleston says, philosophy presents 'the truth of the fundamental unity between the finite spirit and the divine spirit [which] finds expression in the Christian religion in such doctrines as those of the historic Incarnation, the indwelling of the Holy Spirit in the Church, the Eucharist and

the communion of saints . . . as following from the nature of the
Absolute instead of presenting it in the form of contingent
propositions, depending for their truth on historic events which
might or might not have occurred'. Such a programme undoubtedly has attractions for the philosophic spirit, but it has
one overwhelming disadvantage, namely, 'that the fall of
absolute idealism would entail the fall of Christianity'. One can
understand Copleston's reluctance to tie Christianity to any
particular metaphysical system, and in general, his doubts
about the wisdom of trying to capture the at-one-ment of man
with God in the web of a philosopher's abstract terminology,
whether this includes the word 'God', or not.

Judging from what C. de Deugd, Reader in Comparative
and General Literature at the University of Utrecht, says about
him, Paul Tillich would seem to have much in common with
Hegel. Both see the problem in terms of the infinite and the finite.
Both reject the idea of God as 'a personal transcendent being
"out there", over against the world and man' (Copleston on
Hegel) or '*a* being alongside or above other beings' (de Deugd
on Tillich), and for similar reasons (Hegel: if the infinite is set
over against the finite, so as to exclude it, it cannot properly be
described as infinite; Tillich: if God were *a* being alongside or
above others he would be subjected 'to the categories of
finitude'). Both try to preserve the distinction between the
finite and the infinite. Both may be regarded as trying to give
expression in philosophical terms to a mystical experience of
union or immanence. De Deugd, however, is concerned with
the resemblance of Tillich to an earlier philosopher than Hegel,
Spinoza. He likens Tillich's concept of 'the ground of being' to
Spinoza's 'substance', and Tillich's 'power of being' to Spinoza's
'*conatus*'.

In the last part of his paper de Deugd invites us to compare
the way in which the philosopher of religion expresses, in his
chosen terminology, the experience of the mystic, with the
way in which the symbolist poet imparts a meaning other than
the one his words appear to have if taken literally – a point
perhaps not unrelated to what Copleston says about things
which cannot be adequately grasped and stated but only
dimly apprehended through the use of analogies and symbols.

Whereas for Copleston the use of analogies is a means whereby we may dimly apprehend in thought, in philosophising about
Christianity, a relation which is lived, in Christianity, for
Charles Hartshorne, Ashbel Smith Professor of Philosophy at
the University of Texas, analogy is an essential part of a
plausible philosophical theory about how we come to mean
anything by talk about what we do not directly experience.
This is the empiricist theory of meaning, that words have
meaning by virtue of a connection with experience (Hartshorne:
'After all, human terms must acquire their meaning through
human experiences'), and that when words are used for what is
not directly experienced (other people's feelings, the causal
action of one event on another, and so on) they are meaningful
for us by virtue of an analogy which we posit between what
we do experience and what we do not experience (hence, the
argument from analogy for the existence of other minds, the
activity theory of causation, and so on). An example of Hartshorne's use of the theory is his argument that the relation of
God to the universe must be like that of a human mind to a
body. God is spiritual (mental), and so the mind–body analogy
is

> indispensable; for only in the mind–body relation do we
> have an instance of mind dealing directly with physical – by
> which I here mean visible, tangible – reality. All other ex-
> periences of influence between mind and physical things –
> apart from abnormal and controversial cases of table-lifting
> and the like – are indirect, and operate through the mind–
> body relation.

Hartshorne does not mention that the empiricist theory of
meaning, though plausible, has its critics. I do not think it is too
much of an exaggeration to say that it is the main target in all
of Wittgenstein's later works. Philosophers influenced by Wittgenstein,[1] of whom there are a number among the contributors
to this volume, would say that a 'language-game', to be used,

[1] On the so-called 'Other Minds' problem reference might be made to a
short paper, 'Knowledge of Other Minds', by Norman Malcolm, *The Journal
of Philosophy*, vol. LV, No. 23, November 6 1958, and to the book, *Other Minds*,
by John Wisdom, Oxford: Blackwell, 1952.

and so to be meaningful, does not have to be founded on a supposed language in which terms are 'connected' with 'experiences'. They would say that to employ the empiricist theory of meaning in talking about religion is to play into the hands of those who want to dismiss religion either as nonsense or as having only a behaviour-regulating function.[1]

Hartshorne holds the person-analogy (God is personal) to be an essential trait of religion, and hence, since 'there can be no analogy between something wholly absolute, self-sufficient, infinite, or immutable, and persons', that God cannot be any of these things. He holds in particular, that the notion that 'there is but a one-way street between worshipper and worshipped, only God being giver and only creatures receivers of value', 'if taken literally and absolutely, destroys the religious idea of God'. God takes pleasure in our welfare, and so derives benefit from us. He differs from us in that whereas we influence, and are influenced by, only a limited number of our fellows, he influences, and is influenced by, all of us. He is infinite as no one else is, but also finite as no one else is. In this he is 'dually transcendent'.

Hartshorne holds that the analogy which gives meaning to talk of immortality must be that of our living on in the memory of our friends. We are immortal in the sense that God remembers us: God 'will continue to know and cherish us no matter how long we have been dead. If we will have value in the memories of friends and admirers who survive us, much more can we have value in the consciousness of God, who endures forever, and who alone can fully appreciate all that we have been, felt, or thought.' The reasons Hartshorne gives for rejecting the more common doctrine of immortality which 'attributes to man an infinity of individual duration in the future' are (i) that his own view involves no assumptions beyond the mere belief in God, and (ii) that if we were everlasting we could not stop short of being as everlasting as God, and 'where does one stop short in posing as rival to deity?' I can understand the first of these reasons; it is a reason for looking for some other meaning for talk of 'eternal life' than that of immortality in the sense of life

---

[1] See *An Empiricist's View of the Nature of Religious Belief*, by R. B. Braithwaite, C.U.P., 1955.

continuing after death for ever (see below). But I cannot understand the second; I cannot see how rivalry can come in unless
one is thinking of God in human terms.

Hartshorne refers to Martin Buber as one of a number of
philosophers to whom what he calls the idea of 'dual transcendence' has occurred. I am not sure about this. I find it hard to
see what can correspond, in what Buber says in the context of
his distinction between the 'I-It' and the 'I-Thou' relations,
about God being the one Thou who by his very nature cannot
become an It, to what Hartshorne says, in terms of 'finite' and
'infinite', about God transcending us in finiteness as well as
infiniteness.

H. D. Lewis, Professor of the History and Philosophy of
Religion at the University of London, criticises Buber for
expressing himself in a manner which might seem to involve the
denial of something Lewis holds to be true. He is afraid that
what Buber says about the Thou in the I-Thou situation not
being viewed as an It, so that no knowledge of the other's
character, needs, and so forth, enters into the I-Thou relation,
may mean that the other is not recognised as other. 'It may lead
to a conflation in which no one properly takes his stand in
relation to the other, a merging such as we find in some forms of
mysticism.' Such a 'conflation' or 'merging' would contradict
what Lewis claims each person knows about himself, namely
that he is 'a distinct and ultimate being'.

This seems to involve two questions, one of them about what
Buber meant, the other about what is necessary for a relationship to continue as a relationship. On the first of these perhaps
it is worth noting that Michael Wyschogrod, in the article on
Buber in *The Encyclopedia of Philosophy*, ed. Paul Edwards,
Collier–Macmillan, 1967, writes: 'In contrast to much of
mysticism that aims at the obliteration of the abyss between
the self and the Absolute in the ecstasy of mystical union, the
essence of Biblical religion, as conceived by Buber, is the
dialogue between man and God in which each is the other's
Thou.' Evidently Wyschogrod does not see the danger Lewis
sees. I find the second question very puzzling, perhaps because
I do not know what would constitute 'conflation' or 'merging'
of persons.

Although many of Hartshorne's principal tenets can be traced to his unquestioning acceptance of the empiricist theory of meaning, he holds that God is 'analogous to a person' for no other reason than that 'without this analogy, religion loses an essential trait'. That God is in some way like a ruler or parent 'forms part of the very meaning of the religious term God'. Hartshorne does not argue for this; rather, he presents it as an obvious historical fact about what people have meant by 'God'. He is no more concerned to argue that, for some reason, we must *think* of God as a person, than he is concerned to argue that God *is* a person.

Peter Bertocci, Parker Bowne Professor of Philosophy at Boston University, on the other hand, *is* concerned to argue that God is a person. His argument, in Sections 2 and 3 of his paper, may be summarised as follows:

            (*i*) There is regularity in nature;
Therefore (*ii*) There is something which makes nature regular;
           (*iii*) We can learn what the regularities in nature are;
Therefore (*iv*) What makes nature regular must be like ourselves.

In this summary a great deal is left out. But enough is left in to make it evident that Bertocci, like Hartshorne and Lewis (though one would have to refer to Lewis' other works, such as *Philosophy of Religion*, English Universities Press, 1965, to realise this), sees the task of the philosopher of religion as being that of locating talk of God by reference to talk of the world. He describes his argument as a 'way of expressing the meaning of God in relation to man and Nature'.

Hudson says that the overall question that arises from Wittgenstein's lectures on religious belief is: 'To what extent can religious belief be regarded as a logically self-contained universe of discourse?' He says that the basis of some of the things Wittgenstein says 'does certainly seem to be that religious belief is logically distinct from any other universe of discourse'. I assume that by a distinction between universes of discourse Hudson means something like the distinction between the language in which we make contingent statements about actual triangles, squares, and so on, and the language of geometry.

(This assumption was the basis of my remark that utterances do not have to be empirical to be truth-claiming.) Recognition of the distinction between empirical and geometrical statements involves forgoing any attempt to ground the latter in the former. One does not, if one has seen the point of the distinction, suppose the triangles, squares, and so on, of which the geometer speaks, to be in the empirical world, but strangely invisible, or related to the visible triangles, squares, and so on, as causes to effects, or anything like that. In short, one does not try to locate the geometer's talk by reference to talk of what is in the world. Should we regard the language of religion, similarly, as logically distinct from what van Buren calls 'the language of tables and chairs'?

Some have felt the test case to be provided by religious talk about eternal life, heaven, and hell. (Wittgenstein takes the example of belief in the Last Judgement.) As it has sometimes been put, in talk of 'eternal life' does 'eternal' mean 'that always will exist', or does it mean 'not conditioned by time'? And if the latter, how are we to *think* of eternal life?

These are questions which are to the fore in the last three papers in this volume, by Ian Ramsey, the Bishop of Durham; Ninian Smart, Professor of Religious Studies at the University of Lancaster; and John Wisdom, Professor of Philosophy at the University of Oregon.

In his opening paragraph, Wisdom says that 'between those who when they speak of a way to eternal life are thinking of a life after death which endures for ever, and those who when they speak of eternal life give to their words a meaning which carries no implication as to whether there is life after death, there is a link, in that both are seeking a remedy against a sort of despair which comes not merely from the thought of death but from a disappointment with life together with the thought that it ends in death'. He contrasts despair, disappointment, depression, and misery, on the one hand, with contentment, joy, happiness, and cessation of misery, on the other, and says that those who have said 'There is a way to eternal life' have sought to combat despair 'by presenting a view of things which they regard as a truer view than any which generates despair'. Without some indication of the sort of disappointment Wisdom has in mind it

is hard to see whether he is concerned with what is meant by
religious talk of eternal life. He may be thinking of the despair
which afflicts the bereaved, simply because those they love are
no longer with them.

Smart contrasts 'ordinary concerns and those encouraged by
religion'. He writes:

> Ordinary folk want to meet their loved ones in the beyond,
> even if they are not specially concerned with religion, wor-
> ship, piety or contemplation. There is indeed often a tension
> between religion and ordinary hopes: ordinary hopes may be
> pointed towards simple continuation of life in company, but
> not particularly the company of God.

Perhaps what some people would call 'religion' flourishes on
'disappointment with life'. But is it the religion of the Bible? Is
Christianity a religion of salvation in that sense? That it is has
been questioned. Bonhoeffer, for instance, writes (27 June
1944):

> Salvation means salvation from cares and need, from fears
> and longing, from sin and death into a better world beyond
> the grave. But is this really the distinctive feature of Chris-
> tianity as proclaimed in the Gospels and St. Paul? I am sure it
> is not. The difference between the Christian hope of resurrec-
> tion and a mythological hope is that the Christian hope sends
> a man back to his life on earth in a wholly new way which is
> even more sharply defined than it is in the Old Testament.

Is this 'wholly new way' one which is best thought of in terms
of having a new 'view of things'? Does not this way of putting it
neglect the intimate connection between the Christian's faith
and his manner of living in society, his morality?

Ramsey considers three major difficulties about the concept
of Hell as the place, in a life after death, of endless punishment
(its moral repugnance, its logical inconsistency with other doctrines, and cosmological difficulties, particularly about its temporal location), and goes on to ask why, in view of them, anyone
ever upheld the doctrine. One of the reasons he mentions is 'the
permanent significance which men have often felt was attached

to moral choice, in the sense that men have believed that their social actions had some kind of abiding significance, involving God as he who abides'.[1] (Later, he refers to 'the permanent significance of moral behaviour and the need to see our responses to the moral demands of society as an acceptance or rejection of Christ', and 'the cosmic significance of moral decision, the view that the taking of moral decisions involves an attitude to God'.) But how does moral choice having an 'abiding significance, involving God as he who abides' provide a reason for 'the attractiveness and centrality of a doctrine of Hell'? In this way, Ramsey argues. 'Wrong-doing always seems to involve some kind of separation between the wrong-doer and the person wronged. Wrong-doing, in other words, creates some kind of gulf, and separation, between persons. Such a state of separation . . . would seem very likely to be a state leading to personal disintegration and destruction.' This separation, which otherwise would be merely a fact of our psychology, a matter for remorse, is transmuted, with the recognition of the significance of our social actions as involving God as he who abides, into something for which a fitting symbol is that of hell as a place of separation from God, and of punishment. But the recognition at the same time provides the occasion for repentance, for the restoration of the bond. (I am conflating Ricoeur and Ramsey, here.) And what of eternal life? ' "Eternal" is that hint, that signpost, that reminder that in talking e.g. about punishment – "eternal punishment" – we are using a model, viz. "punishment", in such a way as to aim at a revelation of God; that we are using a model by which to point to that loneliness, despair, separation, and so on, in whose agony and anguish it is the claim of the Christian Gospel that God speaks.'

What, then, of eternal life as it is conceived in the language of tables and chairs, a life after death which endures for ever and ever?

In the course of the discussion which followed his lecture Smart said that he would regard some sort of heavenly survival after death as an 'unexpected bonus'. He did not rule out the

---

[1] In Buber's I-Thou terms this would be the point, to which Lewis refers, that the relation of I to other finite Thou's involves the relation of I to the eternal Thou.

possibility. Does Ramsey rule it out? Under 'cosmological difficulties' in the doctrine of hell, he writes: 'Death would seem to be such a major spatio-temporal discontinuity, judging from what happens to the body at death, that there seems little reason to suppose that life after death is in a time series continuous with the present.'

Does he mean that if there is an everlasting life after death then it is unlikely that we enter into it immediately we die? I hardly think so. I think he is hinting at a way of accomodating, in terms of a philosophical theory about different time series, what many feel to be a natural corollary of anyone's having that life which is the knowledge of the only true God (John 17: 3), viz. that it cannot be destroyed by death. If I am right, then we have what would be his answer to our earlier question. If eternal life, if it means everlasting life, is not life in the same time series as our worldly life, then talk of eternal life is not talk in the language of tables and chairs.

But whether what is felt to be a corollary is in fact a corollary, and what can be meant by talk of different time series, are further questions – questions to which I do not know the answers.

G. N. A. VESEY

Honorary Director
Royal Institute of Philosophy

1

THE LOGIC OF RELIGIOUS LANGUAGE

N. H. G. Robinson

By 'the logic of religious language' I understand both a problem: What is the correct account of the logic of religious language? and a theme, a recurrent theme in the modern philosophical discussion of religion, which raises a related but distinguishable question: Is the approach to religion of linguistic analysis an adequate approach? Can we do justice to the logic of religious language by attending to the recognition and analysis of different linguistic forms?

In this latter connection two points ought to be admitted right at the outset. The first is that by the nature of the case much of the theologian's attention and that of the philosopher of religion is bound to be taken up with religious language, and that unless it were, there would be a very poor prospect of any substantial outcome to their investigations. It is true that Dr Alan Richardson once defined Christian apologetics as 'the study of Christian existence in history and to-day';[1] but I imagine that he himself would agree that, while there are such things as religious buildings and religious customs and practices, the student of religion would not get very far in the understanding of his subject if he did not bring into view the language and the literature of religion. Indeed it is only here that he can come to grips with the reality of religion, it is only here that, as it were, he can enter the city rather than be content to glimpse something of its sky-line from a great distance.

The other preliminary point that ought at once to be allowed

---

[1] *Christian Apologetics* (London, 1947), p. 50.

is that the recent concentration upon religious language has been the source of considerable clarification. When, for example, the religious believer declares 'I believe in God the Father Almighty' or 'We acknowledge Thee to be the Lord', it is clear that whatever he is doing he is not simply giving his assent to a proposition. His words have something of a performative character comparable to that which attaches to the words of a returning officer at a parliamentary election when he declares a particular candidate to be the duly elected member of parliament for the constituency, or to the words of the Queen when she ennobles one of her subjects, although neither of these cases offers an exact parallel and to acknowledge God to be God indeed has none of the character of making one to be God who previously was not God. None the less the cases are not entirely dissimilar, for the words of the believer do have the effect, if the believer is not fundamentally misled, of taking to be God for the believer him who is really God independently of all human acknowledgement of the fact. In an epistemological sense or, perhaps more accurately, in a responsive sense, they do make him God who ontologically was already God; and if it were not so the believer would consider himself guilty of idolatry. The immediate point, however, is that this clarification is made available to us by the work of linguistic analysis, whether it is done by a philosopher or by a theologian.

More broadly, linguistic analysis has been of service to the systematic theologian by making him more acutely aware of the problematical character of his accustomed language which, perhaps by reason of his main preoccupation, he may be prone to use without a due sense that it is a very odd language indeed. It may be that linguistic analysis has performed this service in one particular direction more than any other, namely, by reminding the theologian that at the centre of all his varied utterances there is language about God, which at best is radically analogical or symbolic in character and which at worst may be entirely groundless or even altogether meaningless.

On the other hand, if this realisation may reasonably be regarded as one of the major contributions of modern philosophy to religious and theological thought, it must in fairness be said that theology too, by its own inherent movement, has itself come within view of much the same insight. This in fact is one of the most promising features of the present situation in religious studies, the curious and intriguing confluence of two diverse movements of thought, one strictly philosophical and the other predominantly theological. For just as the philosophical school of linguistic analysis has underlined the analogical, the parabolic and, at the same time, the problematical character of religious language, so theology under its own impetus, and usually apart from any influence by linguistic trends in contemporary philosophy, has undergone a vast revolution in the last thirty years, which may be variously described as, for example, the replacement of a dogmatic standpoint by an apologetic one, or as the substitution of an anthropocentric system of thought for a theocentric one, but which in any case has led those theologians most influenced by it to speak much of the place of symbol and myth in religious thought and language and has inclined them virtually to define religious reality in terms of human response and attitude.

My present concern, however, is with the philosophical attempt to understand religion by means of linguistic analysis; and if one keeps in view the historical context which gave birth to this movement one can appreciate the sense of release which it brought and the vigour with which it was pursued. Its predecessor, logical positivism, had no alternative, on its own presuppositions, but to reject as quite meaningless the characteristic statements of religion and theology as well as those of metaphysics, since they could be regarded neither as empirical statements open to the accepted methods of empirical verification nor as belonging to the same class as the necessary statements of logic and mathematics, sometimes described as tautologies. No doubt such iconoclasm – if I may religiously characterise the so-called elimination of metaphysics and theology – is immediately impressive and perhaps persuasive, throwing overboard as it does the burden of belief; but on second and more sober thoughts it was never really plausible to dismiss as merely meaningless both sides to the long and heated controversy between theism and atheism. Some explanation seems required which would help the enlightened modern to understand how the protagonists in that long debate deluded themselves into believing that they were confronting a genuine issue. The fact that their statements were usually made in accordance with the rules of grammar is scarcely an adequate explanation; and just as the case for atheism itself was greatly strengthened by the adumbration of the psychological explanation of religion as working by means of deep-seated subjective projections, so the elimination of metaphysics and theology, of atheism as well as theism, urgently required that some light be thrown on an almost universal self-delusion.

The recognition, then, that language may be meaningful in more ways than one – or two – according to the various uses which men have for the words they employ, rendered the philosophical approach to religion and theology both more flexible and more adequate. Nor was religion the only subject-matter to gain from this broader philosophical approach. So too did morals, for although some logical positivists had regarded moral statements as expressions of a particular emotion it was an advance to realise quite clearly that when we use words to express an emotion we give the words a meaning. Moreover, there are many other uses which confer a meaning on the statements we make, as when we use words to tell a story, or to give a command, or to express not just an emotion but an attitude, or a disposition, or an intention to act in a certain way; and when all these varieties of meaning are kept in view the possibility is opened up that the logic of moral and religious statements may be understood in terms of one of them or in terms of more than one. Certainly in recent years not a few attempts have been made to give substance and form to this possibility.

It is not my purpose to examine any of these attempts in detail but rather to try to extract from the various attempts that have been made some general conclusion regarding the validity and adequacy of the linguistic approach itself. To raise this question of the final adequacy of linguistic analysis in dealing with the logic of religious belief is not of course to question the value of this analysis. Any comprehensive view of religious statements is bound to reveal that some of these statements function as fiction and perform their allotted task no worse because of that. In most sermons there are illustrations which embody in concrete form some religious insight, and the effectiveness of the illustration very often depends on its logical relationship to the insight in question and not on its correspondence with actual fact, past or present. Its effectiveness may even be all the greater because it achieves an entry into a larger realm of related illustrative material all of which is freely acknowledged to be fictional. Indeed it seems to be the case that much of the historical narrative of the Old Testament, without being discredited as history either by the preacher or by his hearers, frequently functions in sermons as illustration. It does its work, not by reason of its accuracy as historical record (even if this is not doubted), but by virtue of its illustrative power. Moreover, as there are fictional elements in religious language, so there are examples of almost all the other linguistic forms that analysis has painstakingly distinguished. There are prescriptions, there are expressions of emotion, there are declarations of intent, and there are, as we have seen, statements the force of which is performative, that is to say, statements which add something to the situation, do something in it, and are not simply content to report what is otherwise done or happens in that situation.

In the interests of an adequate account of the logic of religious language it is clearly valuable that these discriminations should be made; and further the making of them may save the student of religion from other errors. Thus, while the theologian may not be prone to transplant a given proposition from a severely theological context to one of prayer or devotional writing, he may find that in his use of Scripture he has been guilty of the reverse operation which may be no less improper. For example, it is plainly inappropriate that in prayer the religious person should list his various virtues and virtuous activities, like the pharisee in the parable who was not as other men are 'or even as this publican'; but to transpose what is proper in prayer into theology and a fully articulated doctrine of total depravity is manifestly to confuse one use of religious language with another.

There is, however, one feature of the various linguistic forms so far distinguished, from the fictional to the performative, which they all seem to have in common and which may yet

prove to be an important, even a decisive, factor in the final
assessment of the treatment of religion by the linguistic analyst;
and this feature is the absence from all these uses of language of
any claim to truth. Plainly, a prescription is neither true nor
false, and a declaration of intent, while it may be sincere or
insincere, is likewise neither true nor false. Similarly a performative, whether effective or ineffective, does not try to say
something true of things as they are but rather to make some
change in things as they are. It is true that some fictional statements do not seem to have a different linguistic form from other
non-fictional statements which claim to be true; but the
apparent claim to truth of some fictional statements is a
pretence and is understood to be a pretence both by speaker
and by hearer, so that when the claim to truth is not understood
as a pretence the statements are so far misunderstood.

Thus there comes into view in outline one type of account
that can be given of the logic of religious language. It may allow
that here and there throughout the broad expanse of religious
language there are to be found empirical statements that do
claim to be true and of which the claim to be true can be tested
in ordinary ways, precisely as in the case of other empirical
statements that do not normally occur in a religious context,
in terms of the canons of critical historiography, by observation
or on the basis of reliable testimony. But, according to this kind
of understanding of religious language, such empirical statements are incidental, and the characteristic statements of
religion are not empirical and, further, it is not their function to
make any claim to truth at all. Perhaps they prescribe a way of
life, or they express an intention to follow a way of life, or they
express an attitude towards life and the world. It may even be
that they also narrate stories, as Professor R. B. Braithwaite has
alleged, which are not straightforward empirical statements to
be empirically verified like any other empirical statement but
which, by being merely entertained rather than believed,
provide psychological or imaginative backing for the way of life
intended. In any case, according to this kind of view, statements
which bring out the peculiar character of religion are statements
which are devoid of any claim to truth and which function in a
different way from statements which do lay claim to truth; and

it is because in the past these different functions were not carefully distinguished that the dispute between theism and atheism was for long thought to be in the last resort a dispute regarding what is or is not the case, regarding truth and error.

It is at this point that doubts and questions begin to arise regarding the ability of linguistic analysis to uncover the logic of religious language. The possibility which these doubts and questionings expose for investigation is that by concentrating upon linguistic forms we unwittingly put ourselves in blinkers and prevent ourselves from understanding the logic of religious belief. The suggestion is – and at this stage it is no more than a suggestion and a question – the suggestion is that if we attempt to correct the elimination of theological or of religious language by a method which certainly involves the elimination of religious *belief* we are simply defeating our own ends. The elimination of religious belief is for all practical purposes the elimination of religious language and of religion. The answer, of course, which proponents of the general type of theory we have been considering are likely to give is that, for all practical purposes, it is nothing of the kind. That, however, is precisely the question: Does what is recognisably religion remain when religious belief has been eliminated? No doubt to believe in God is to do much more than to believe that certain propositions are true of God, and it may require all the refinements of linguistic analysis to make plain what that something more is; but none the less, is not belief that certain propositions are true of God the indispensable undergirding so that without it religion has ceased to exist? In other words, although belief *in* God is not just belief *about* God, no matter how fully articulated, is it not in and through belief about God that one believes in him, so that without the former either the latter is altogether empty and vacuous or else religion becomes something other than itself, a declaration of moral intent or a number of inspiring stories or both, but not religion? It is the elimination of religious belief that can be true or false that arouses the suspicion – at this stage no more than the suspicion – that the linguistic analyst's account of religious language is doomed to be reductionist in character.

This suspicion is equivalent to the suspicion that justice has not been done to the rationality of religious belief; and this way of putting the point enables us to deal more precisely with the suspicion by allowing us to tackle it in two stages. For when we speak of the rationality of religious belief (or of religious language) we may have in mind one or other (or both) of two alleged characteristics of religious belief, its internal logical coherence and, secondly, its correspondence with, or its grasp of (so far as it does grasp it), independent reality.

So far as the former characteristic is concerned, what I have called internal logical coherence, it does appear to be beyond all denial that religious statements are not just isolated statements but, if uttered by the same mature person or group of persons, tend to hang together with some degree of logical coherence. Thus one can distinguish different types of what is called religious experience and, corresponding to that, of religious language, so that logically one type diverges from another, while within each type the diverse affirmations are held together by a logical thread of compatibility. One type of theory of the atonement, for example, may be more congenial to a given type of Christological thought than another; and this relationship of congeniality is a logical relationship, so that by careful analysis one can trace the logical links. Even when the believer's thought ends in paradox there seem to be logically compelling reasons for holding the two sides of the paradox together, rather than casting them asunder and throwing in his lot with the one side or the other. By no stretch of the imagination is the Bible an argumentative book or anything like an academic treatise; but it shows unmistakable signs of internal logical coherence. 'If ye then, being evil', said Jesus on a famous occasion, 'know how to give good gifts unto your children, how much more shall your Father which is in heaven give good things to them that ask him?'[1] Indeed many of the parables are arguments which underscore either the character of God or the way of the Christian. It matters little whether we begin the parable of the lost sheep with St Matthew's version, 'How think ye? if a man have an hundred sheep . . .',[2] or with St Luke's version, 'What man of you, having an hundred

[1] Matt. 7: 11; cf. 1 John 4: 20.
[2] Matt. 18: 12.

sheep . . .';[1] both versions clearly foreshadow an argument, not a formal argument, rather one which appeals to the heart as much as to the head, but an argument which proceeds none the less by logically coherent steps.

To this aspect of the rationality of religious belief, however, the interpretation of distinctively religious language in terms of non-truth-claiming sentences can do some sort of justice, for part of the linguistic analyst's task has been to explore the logical relationships which obtain among non-truth-claiming state-ments of this sort or of that. As yet there may be a considerable uncertainty how this kind of analysis is to be applied to religious language; but encouragement may legitimately be drawn from the example of ethics and from the attempt therein to explicate the internal logical relationships of moral language, when that language is understood as non-truth-claiming, as, for example, in Professor R. M. Hare's words, 'one sort of prescriptive language'.[2] Professor Hare himself has been eminently successful in clarifying the kind of internal logical coherence which may obtain within a variety of moral utterances when understood in this way. In particular, he has shown how a specific piece of moral advice may be rationally justified by reference to broader practical principles and these in turn by reference to a total way of life which they exemplify. In this manner the understanding of morality in terms of one kind of non-truth-claiming statement, namely prescriptions, may prove itself much more resourceful than the understanding of morality in terms of another kind of non-truth-claiming statement, namely expressions of emotion, in exhibiting, and in doing justice to, what might be called the rationality of the moral judgement; and there is no reason to doubt that a similar resourcefulness is available to the philo-sopher who would interpret religious language in the same general way.

It is important therefore to acknowledge the extent to which justice can be done to the rationality of religious belief by the interpretation of religious language as basically consisting of non-truth-claiming statements. None the less, at precisely this point two critical questions arise. In the first place, since it is

[1] Luke 15: 4.
[2] *The Language of Morals* (Oxford: Clarendon Press, 1952), p. 1.

scarcely plausible either to treat religious language as wholly different from moral language or to treat it as nothing but moral language, the linguistic account of religious language is almost bound to follow Professor Braithwaite's example in recognising within religious language at least two different linguistic types; and then the question is acute as to what logical relationship obtains or may obtain between statements of the one type (e.g. Braithwaite's stories) and statements of the other type (Braithwaite's moral policies). Moreover, if the treatment by linguistic analysis is, as often seems to be the case, committed to the view that there is no such logical relationship between statements of different linguistic types, the rationality of religious belief, even in the sense of internal logical coherence, has been called in question; and it seems to me a device of despair to say with Professor Braithwaite that the connection is not logical but psychological and causal, as if one fed into the machine raw material that could not be used in a certain way and extracted at the other end something which could be used in that way.

Unless I am mistaken, however, this critical question is swallowed up by the other which is even more far-reaching. It is: Even if justice can be done to the rationality of religious belief in the sense of internal logical coherence, by the interpretation of religious language in terms of non-truth-claiming statements, can justice also be done to the rationality of religious belief in the other sense of the phrase, namely its correspondence to, or its grasp of, independent reality; in other words, its objective reference? It is here that the suspicion of reductionism which the linguistic treatment of religion sometimes arouses comes to its head, for the suspicion in the end is precisely this, that subjectivism has been affirmed and objectivism denied or rejected; and it is difficult to believe the suggestion that is sometimes made, both in ethics and in the philosophy of religion, that on the contrary the issue between subjectivism and objectivism simply does not arise. Psychologically that may be so, for attention may have been distracted from it; but logically it is not so for the question can be put quite significantly. Or so at any rate it would seem.

It may indeed be argued that since the issue between subjectivism and objectivism is one of truth or error it cannot arise in connection with a discussion of morality or religion, since what is distinctive of these is one or more peculiar linguistic forms, such that statements of one of these forms can be logically related only to statements of the same form, and such that, further, distinctively moral and religious statements, whatever their peculiar form or forms, are *ex hypothesi* not of the form characteristic of truth-claiming assertions. This is a perfectly intelligible argument; but it does rest upon the assumption that the different linguistic forms are rigidly separable and that each form, corresponding to a distinguishable use of language, is governed by its own logic. It assumes too that the distinctive character of morality and religion can be exhaustively exhibited in terms of one or several of the non-truth-claiming linguistic forms. If this assumption is to be accepted, justice can be done, at any rate up to a point, to the rationality of religious belief and the moral judgement, in the sense of internal logical coherence; but the question I am now raising is whether this assumption is valid, whether the rationality of religious belief and the moral judgement is restricted in this way to internal logical coherence or rather involves also some element of objective reference. In other words, is there at the spring-head of morality a decision, so that as Professor Hare has said,[1] 'in the end everything rests upon . . . a decision of principle', a decision so general and comprehensive that nothing more general and comprehensive can be envisaged as its logical justification, but a decision, a declaration of intent which logically is nothing other than that, as if in this sphere the human will were altogether sovereign? Or is that decision and declaration at the same time an apprehension and a response and consequently something of a logical complexity? Likewise, at the spring-head of religion is there a commitment only or a commitment which is also a response and a distinctively religious apprehension?

In these questions we bring out into the open the suspicion of reductionism which the account of religious language in terms of non-truth-claiming statements is apt to arouse; but it is well to recognise that these questions in turn may be countered by another suspicion or fear, in the case of morality that of the

[1] *The Language of Morals*, p. 69.

naturalistic fallacy, and in the case of religion that of sheer meaninglessness. Thus, at this stage, the discussion may be thought to issue in a rather tentative dilemma: either reductionism in ethics and the philosophy of religion or else the naturalistic fallacy and meaninglessness. Is there any way out of this dilemma?

It will be noticed that in indicating some sort of alternative to the understanding of moral and religious language in terms of non-truth-claiming statements I have used such words as 'apprehension' and 'response' both of which reintroduce the claim to truth. The statements which sum up an apprehension may be true or false in relation to that which is apprehended, for in the very act of apprehending I may to some extent misapprehend; and, although in the first instance a response may be thought to be appropriate or inappropriate rather than true or false, the response itself involves an apprehension which may in turn be something of a misapprehension. Thus when we say 'We acknowledge Thee to be the Lord' no doubt the immediate question is whether the acknowledgement is genuine or only apparent and a pretence; but it is difficult to believe that the acknowledgement does not involve a propositional element which may be true or false. It is because this is so that we were able to say that to acknowledge God to be God is to take to be God for the believer him who is really God independently of all human acknowledgement of the fact. No doubt to take God to be God in this way is to commit oneself to a certain manner of life, and the acknowledgement may well be associated with a fairly extensive range of story; but the connection between the stories and the commitment is not simply a causal and psychological one. On the contrary, the stories appear to bear a complex logical relationship to other elements in the acknowledgement, for, while they serve to illustrate the way of life, they also provide analogical material for the affirmative element in the acknowledgement of God; and this affirmative or propositional element in religious belief may well be deemed assessable on the score of its truth or error.

It is with this propositional content of belief that much theology is concerned, and the theologian finds congenial the ideas which pave the way for it and introduce it, the ideas of apprehension and response. Many theologians are themselves accustomed to speak of response and of what they call revelation to which the response is a response; and some go on to develop what has come to be known as a theology of encounter. There is indeed much to be said for the view that this idea of encounter, of revelation and response, is in the last resort the axis around which a great deal of recent, specifically theological controversy has revolved; and certainly it helps to provide a useful intellectual framework which facilitates the development of various theological themes.

None the less it is important to recognise that, although the idea of encounter has proved itself an eminently fruitful one within the field of contemporary theology, it does not of itself offer an immediate solution to the specifically philosophical problem in the discussion of religion and its language, and it does not directly point a way out of the dilemma already formulated: either reductionism both in ethics and in the philosophy of religion or else the naturalistic fallacy and the threat of meaninglessness. On the one hand, the treatment of the statement 'I ought to tell the truth' as through and through a prescription with no propositional or affirmative element represents it as arbitrary and wilful and allows the objective claim and challenge of morality to escape from its net; and likewise the treatment of the statement 'We acknowledge Thee to be the Lord' as through and through a performative, a statement the whole point of which is to do something, or as some other kind of non-truth-claiming statement, loses the indefeasibly objective reference which permeates the language of religion, and not the language only but its activity as seen, for example, in the posture of prayer. On the other hand, to allow an affirmative or truth-claiming element in moral and religious language, other than empirical statements of fact, is at the present time to expose oneself as a target for criticism; so far as morality is concerned that one has committed the naturalistic fallacy of deriving moral judgements from non-moral ones, and also, so far as religion is concerned, that one has begun to use language totally devoid of meaning, language which claims to have an objective reference where ostensibly there is none.

If, then, the idea of encounter offers no immediate way of escape from this predicament and is not itself a solution to this philosophical problem, the question arises whether none the less, when examined explicitly in relation to this problem, it does not suggest a solution. Is there, in other words, an inroad into the philosophical problem from the side of theology and, in particular, from what is sometimes called the theology of encounter? To this question the answer is, I think, that there is. In particular, the idea of encounter draws our attention to the fact that a language, treated as a self-contained totality or as a self-contained source of a wide diversity of meaningful statements in a variety of linguistic forms, is an abstraction. Language appears, and linguistic analysis takes place, within a social context. Language is a means of communication between persons; and the picture of an impersonal language, however rich in linguistic possibilities, hovering over the world of ordinary experience, of tables and chairs and so on, is, when drawn clearly, a quite incredible one. Language which is ultimately ownerless and anonymous has no more meaning than 'the creaking of a door in an empty house'. This means, however, that to use language is to take part in dialogue, for although a monologue is an obvious possibility it is so only within an ultimate context of dialogue. Monologue made absolute becomes nonsense; it depends upon that which it disowns. Moreover, when attention is thus directed, not to a self-contained language, but more comprehensively and realistically to the linguistic situation, it is open to the theologian of encounter to claim that his basic idea is an analogy dictated by that situation, since dialogue is a form of meeting and encounter.

The recognition of the linguistic situation does not permit the philosopher of religion to play fast and loose with the logic of this or that area of language, but it may enable him to see where a given account of the logic of moral or religious language, for example, is too narrow and has become something of a strait-jacket in which neither religion nor morality can breathe freely. This, I suggest, is precisely what has happened in the treatment of morality as consisting of nothing other than prescriptions and in the treatment of religion as a combination of expressions of intent, performatives and fictional elements; and it has happened because the linguistic situation has been ignored or discounted, and because accordingly it has been assumed that the almost impersonal idea of a self-contained language, ownerless and anonymous, is perfectly adequate and not in the least misleading. It is not to be thought that the linguistic situation and the social context of language have been completely ignored. It is more likely that they have been immobilised by being given a place within the language. I who speak to you and you who listen to me have become 'he' and 'she' and 'they' within the language. We have become what might be called logical subjects, and we function within the language as logical subjects. It is clear, however, that this is not, and cannot be, the whole story. We who function as logical subjects within a language are those who create and use the language, and inevitably therefore stand outside and above it; and we stand outside and above it, not in isolation, but in personal relationship – otherwise there would be no language. By the very nature of the case I am not just a possible 'he' in the language which I use, nor are you; and the first- and second-personal pronouns effectively break through the barrier which a self-contained interpretation of language would erect.

What this implies is that the linguistic situation posits and presupposes by the nature of the case a community of persons, of metaphysical subjects who transcend all possible logical subjects within the language which they employ. This statement amounts to an affirmation of the supernatural, not of the contranatural, but of the supernatural in the sense in which as Professor H. H. Farmer put it, 'the personal is the true supernatural'.[1] Moreover, the force of the prefix 'super' in this use of the word 'supernatural' is not to signify something that is indefinitely more or beyond, as perhaps in 'supernumerary', something which might trail off into blank mystery, but to signify something that is above and in control, a *present* centre of thought, awareness and action – and this in the plural as a community of present centres of communicating thought, mutual awareness and interaction. This, however, is not an esoteric doctrine nor the affirmation of the ineffable. What is affirmed is a presupposition of the linguistic situation to which

[1] *The World and God* (London, 1935), p. 6.

we are none the less tied, and it reveals itself in language by the peculiar behaviour of the first- and second-personal pronouns. In a sense they establish, in another sense they report, a system of personal relationships to which, primarily, moral and religious language refers; and we are seriously handicapped in understanding this aspect of our linguistic situation if our thinking is governed by the assumption that everything of which we are aware is either purely private, like the feeling of distaste we may express, or plainly public as the matters of which we speak in empirical statements of fact. The community of persons in relation, on the contrary, which the linguistic situation presupposes, provides a sphere no less objective than the world of ordinary experience and empirical fact, which yet requires for its understanding a more forthcoming and sympathetic approach than that of the mere observer no matter how careful and painstaking he may be, a sphere where frequently thought articulates itself by means of analogy and symbol, and where from the beginning the interpersonal relationships are moral in character.

If we think faithfully of the community of persons posited by the linguistic situation, strictly in relation to that situation and, in particular, to the first- and second-personal pronouns, we are aware of a dimension of depth and mystery radiating from a plurality of present centres; and it is this dimension which moral and religious language seeks to probe and out of which it takes its rise. It appears in language as the expression of insight, which may resemble to some extent expressions of emotion or attitude in being expressive of personality and which may even have some performative force, but which also grapples with a reality much larger than the speaker's own centre of consciousness and may consequently constitute a more or less adequate apprehension of truth. Thus expressions of insight cut across the distinctions drawn by linguistic analysis when it deals with an impersonal or third-personal and self-contained conception of language; and they seem largely concerned to clarify something which we already know or of which we are aware. Perhaps that is why the theologies and philosophies of the past are not discarded like outworn hypotheses but play their part in a continuing dialogue, having still some light to shed upon the dimension of depth and mystery. Doubtless that too is why there seems no prospect of finality, whether as a final moral code or as a final theology. None the less the task of clarification is a logical one, matching one ultimate conviction with another; and even the most ordinary language of everyday life holds us to it, when we allow ourselves to grasp the linguistic situation and the condition of intersubjectivity, as some existentialists call it, which that situation necessarily posits.

I have mentioned the peculiar behaviour of first- and second-personal pronouns, and by that I mean, primarily, the fact that they indicate what transcends all merely logical subjects. If Mr P. F. Strawson is right in fixing on completeness as the significant characteristic of logical subjects, then these first- and second-personal pronouns, as logical subjects, are essentially incomplete, in pointing to what transcends, because it creates and uses, language. To fail to see this is to fall into absurdity. It is absurd, for example, to treat human actions as non-explicit performatives, as if actions were to be understood in terms of performatives and not performatives in terms of actions. It is absurd to suggest that one prediction as a performative logically entails another as a performative. It is true that what I predict in general terms (for example, that it will rain on every Saturday in November) may logically entail what I might predict in more particular terms (for example, that it will rain tomorrow); but my general prediction as a performative does not logically entail my particular prediction as a performative. For good reasons or bad I may decline to make the latter prediction, refusing to spell it out to my hearers and leaving them to draw their own conclusions.

Similarly, if we regard what Professor Braithwaite has called 'a mysterious gap . . . between the moral judgment and the intention to act in accordance with it'[1] as a logical gap which a better linguistic analysis may close, for example by holding that 'there is no such gap if the primary use of a moral assertion is to declare such an intention', we fall into an elusive but genuine self-contradiction, both positing and in effect denying the metaphysical subject, since clearly there is a gap between

[1] I. T. Ramsey (ed.), *Christian Ethics and Contemporary Philosophy* (London, 1966), p. 61.

the moral judgement and the intention to act in accordance with it, but it is not a logical gap, it is a gap in personal life which is not closed by linguistic analysis but filled by responsible decision.

Positively and constructively, the first- and second-personal pronouns not only burst through the barriers which a self-contained view of language as ultimately ownerless and anonymous would impose, but they also yield admission to a sphere of personal relationships and of personal knowledge where the passive observer, so far as I can see, is out of place. So far as religion is concerned it was an Old Testament psalmist who declared that 'the secret of the Lord is with them that fear him'; and in a famous sermon on a similar text from the New Testament, 'If any man will to do his will, he shall know of the doctrine, whether it be of God, or whether I speak of myself', the nineteenth-century preacher, F. W. Robertson of Brighton, contended that obedience is the organ of spiritual knowledge. Similarly, on the human level, it might be equally affirmed that sympathy and obligation are the organ of personal knowledge; and certainly these factors seem inseparable from genuinely personal knowledge which falls within the 'I-thou' dimension of dialogue and encounter and is not simply a knowledge of subjects as objects, assimilated to, and immobilised within, an ultimately self-contained, ownerless and anonymous language.

Moreover, just as I do not infer the meaning of a statement from the words that comprise it,[1] but rather comprehend it in and through the latter, so I do not seem to infer the 'thou' who means what is said in the statement but rather come up against him as having a point of view comparable, positively and negatively, with my own. Nor can I see that in the last resort, so far as its ultimate grounding is concerned, religious language is essentially different from moral language in this respect. In both we are dealing with a genuine supernatural whose presence (and this is simply the other side of a genuine supernaturalism) is sacramentally conveyed.

In the context of the present discussion I am content to try to

---

[1] I would have to understand the meaning of statements in order to make the inference!

indicate the objective reference of moral language and of religious language together, although clearly there is a logically subsequent problem concerning their mutual differentiation and the understanding of their relationship. As for the former question, which is quite fundamental, it is reported in the New Testament that Jesus claimed to be 'the way, the truth, and the life',[1] and that is a declaration congenial to the kind of argument I have been trying to unfold. On the other hand, the Wittgenstein of the *Tractatus* took a quite different turning when he spoke of the metaphysical subject in the singular[2] and contended that 'everything that can be thought at all can be thought clearly. Everything that can be said can be said clearly.'[3]

[1] John 14: 6.   [2] Op. cit., 5. 641.   [3] Ibid., 4. 116.

2

RELIGIOUS FAITH AS EXPERIENCING-AS

John Hick

THE particular sense or use of the word 'faith' that I am seeking to understand is that which occurs when the religious man, and more specifically the Christian believer, speaks of 'knowing God' and goes on to explain that this is a knowing of God by faith. Or again, when asked how he professes to know that God, as spoken about in Christianity, is real, his answer is 'by faith'. Our question is: what does 'faith' mean in these contexts? And what I should like to be able to do is to make a descriptive (or if you like phenomenological) analysis that could be acceptable to both believers and non-believers. A Christian and an atheist or agnostic should equally be able to say, Yes, that is what, phenomenologically, faith is – though they would of course then go on to say radically different things about its value.

The modes of cognition have been classified in various ways. But the distinction that is most relevant to our present purpose is that between what I shall call cognition in presence and cognition in absence; or acquaintance (using this term less restrictedly than it was used by Russell) and holding beliefs-about. We cognise things that are present before us, this being called perception; and we also cognise things in their absence, this being a matter of holding beliefs about them. And the astonishing fact is that while our religious literature – the Bible, and prayers, hymns, sermons, devotional meditations and so on – confidently presuppose a cognition of God by acquaintance, our theological literature in contrast recognises for the most part only cognition in absence. That is to say, whereas the Bible itself, and other writings directly expressing the life of faith, are full of men's encounters with God and men's personal dealings with the divine Thou, the dominant systems of Christian theology nevertheless treat faith as belief, as a propositional attitude. In the Catholic tradition deriving from St Thomas, and no less in the Protestant Orthodoxy that supervened upon the Reformation movement, faith has been quite explicitly defined as believing on God's authority certain truths, i.e. propositional truths, that he has revealed. Thus faith, instead of being seen as a religious response to God's redemptive action in the life of Jesus of Nazareth, has been seen instead as primarily an assent to theological truths. For good or ill this was a very major and radical step, taken early on in the Church's history and displaying its implications over the centuries in many different aspects of the life of Christendom. I believe that it was a wrong step, which the Reformers of the sixteenth century sought to correct. If this is so, we want to find a viable way, or perhaps even ways (in the plural), of thinking of faith as a form of cognition by acquaintance or cognition in presence. Instead of assimilating faith to propositional belief – whether such belief be produced by reasoning or act of will or both – we must assimilate it to perception. I therefore want to explore the possibility that the cognition of God by faith is more like perceiving something, even perceiving a physical object, that is present before us than it is like believing a statement about some absent object, whether because the statement has been proved to us or because we want to believe it.

But surely – if I may myself at once voice an inevitable protest – the cognition of God can no more be like sense perception than God is like a physical object. It is true that Christian tradition tells of an ultimate beatific vision of God, but we are not now speaking of this but of the ordinary believer's awareness of God in our present earthly life. And this is not a matter of perceiving him, but of believing, without being able to perceive him, that he nevertheless exists. It is in fact, as it has traditionally been held to be, a case of cognition in absence, or of holding beliefs-about.

However the hypothesis that we want to consider is not that

religious faith *is* sense perception, but that as a form of cognition by acquaintance it is *more like* sense perception than like propositional belief. That propositions may be validly founded upon the awareness of God, and that they then play an indispensable and immensely valuable part in the religious life, is not in question. But what we are interested in now is the awareness of God itself; for this is faith – that is to say, distinctively religious cognition – in its primary sense.

It is today hardly a contentious doctrine requiring elaborate argumentation that seeing – to confine ourselves for the moment to this one mode of perceiving – is not a simple straightforward matter of physical objects registering themselves on our retinas and thence in our conscious visual fields. There are complexities, and indeed a complex variety of complexities. The particular complexity that concerns us now was brought to the attention of philosophers by Wittgenstein's discussion of seeing-as in the *Philosophical Investigations*. Wittgenstein pointed to puzzle pictures and ambiguous diagrams of the kind that are found in abundance in some of the psychological texts – for instance the Necker cube, Jastrow's duck-rabbit, and Köhler's goblet-faces. The cube diagram, for instance, can be seen as a cube viewed either from below or from above, and the perceiving mind tends to alternate between these two perspectives. The goblet-faces diagram can be seen as the outline of a goblet or vase or as the outlines of two faces looking straight into each other's eyes. The duck-rabbit can be seen as the representation of a rabbit's head facing to the left or of a duck's head facing to the right. In these cases every line of the diagram plays its part in both aspects (as Wittgenstein called them) and has equal weight in each: these may accordingly be called cases of total ambiguity. Another sort, artistically more complex, might be called cases of emergent pattern; for example, those puzzle pictures in which you are presented with what at first seems to be a random and meaningless scattering of lines and dots, but in which as you look at it you come to see, say, a face; or again, as another example, the well-known 'Christ in the snow' picture. And in between there are various other sorts of intermediate cases which we need not however take account of here. We speak of seeing-as when that which is objectively there, in the sense of that which affects the retina, can be consciously perceived in two different ways as having two different characters or natures or meanings or significances; and very often, in these two-dimensional instances, we find that the mind switches back and forth between the alternative ways of seeing-as.

Let us at this point expand the notion of seeing-as into that of experiencing-as. The elements of experiencing-as are the purely visual seeing-as which we have thus far been discussing, plus its equivalents for the other senses. For as well as seeing a bird as a bird, we may hear it as a bird – hear the bird's song as a bird's song, hear the rustle of its wings as a bird in flight, hear the rapping of the woodpecker as just that; and so on. Again, a carpenter may not only see the wood as mahogany but also feel it as mahogany; he may recognise it tactually as well as visually. Or again, we may taste the wine as Burgundy and smell the cheese as Gorgonzola. Not of course that the different senses normally function in isolation. We perceive and recognise by means of all the relevant senses co-operating as a single complex means of perception; and I suggest that we use the term 'experiencing-as' to refer to the end-product of this in consciousness.

The next step is from these two-dimensional pictures and diagrams to experiencing-as in real life – for example, seeing the tuft of grass over there in the field as a rabbit, or the shadows in the corner of the room as someone standing there. And the analogy to be explored is with two contrasting ways of experiencing the events of our lives and of human history, on the one hand as purely natural events and on the other hand as mediating the presence and activity of God. For there is a sense in which the religious man and the atheist both live in the same world and another sense in which they live consciously in different worlds. They inhabit the same physical environment and are confronted by the same changes occurring within it. But in its actual concrete character in their respective 'streams of consciousness' it has for each a different nature and quality, a different meaning and significance; for one does and the other does not experience life as a continual interaction with the transcendent God. Is there then any true analogy or parallel between, on the one hand, these two ways of experiencing human life, *as* an encounter with God or *as* an encounter only with a natural order, and on the other hand the two ways of seeing the distant shape, *as* a rabbit or *as* a tuft of grass?

An immediate comment might be: if there is any such analogy, so much the worse for religious cognition! For does not the analogy between seeing a puzzle picture in a certain way and experiencing human life in a certain way underline once again the purely subjective and gratuitous character of religious knowledge-claims in contrast with the compelling objectivity of ordinary sense perception?

So far as the argument has thus far gone, perhaps it does. But the next point to be introduced must considerably affect the upshot of what has gone before. This is the thesis that *all* experiencing is experiencing-as – not only, for example, seeing the tuft of grass, erroneously, as a rabbit, but also seeing it correctly as a tuft of grass. On the face of it this sounds paradoxical. One might put the difficulty in this way: we may if we like speak of seeing the tuft of grass *as* a tuft of grass because it is evidently possible to misperceive it as a sitting rabbit. But what about something utterly familiar and unmistakable? What about the fork on the table? Would it not be absurd to say that you are seeing it *as* a fork? It must be granted that this particular locution would be distinctly odd in most circumstances. However we have more acceptable names for ordinary seeing-as in real life; we call it 'recognising' or 'identifying'. Of course we are so familiar with forks that normally we recognise one without encountering even enough difficulty to make us notice that we are in fact performing an act of recognition. But if the fork were sufficiently exotic in design I might have occasion to say that I can recognise the thing before me on the table as a fork – that is, as a man-made instrument for conveying food into the mouth. And, going further afield, a Stone-Age savage would not be able to recognise it at all. He might identify it instead as a marvellously shining object which must be full of *mana* and must not be touched; or as a small but deadly weapon; or as a tool for digging; or just as something utterly baffling and unidentifiable. But he would not have the concept of a fork with which to identify it as a fork. Indeed to say that he does not have this concept and that he cannot perform this act of

recognition are two ways of saying the same thing. That there is
no ambiguity or mystery about forks for you or me is simply due
to the contingent circumstance that forks are familiar parts of
the apparatus of our culture. For the original nature or meaning
of an artefact is determined by the purpose for which it has
been made, and this purpose necessarily operates within a
particular cultural context. But simply as a physical object of a
certain size and shape an artefact does not bear its meaning
stamped upon it. To recognise or identify is to experience-as in
terms of a concept; and our concepts are social products having
their life within a particular linguistic environment.

Further, this is as true of natural objects as it is of artefacts.
Here, too, to recognise is to apply a concept; and this is always
to cognise the thing as being much more than is currently
perceptible. For example, to identify a moving object in the
sky as a bird is not only to make implicit claims about its present
shape, size, and structure beyond what we immediately observe
but also about its past (for instance, that it came out of an egg,
not a factory) about its future (for instance, that it will one day
die), and about its behaviour in various hypothetical circumstances (for instance, that it will tend to be frightened by loud
noises). When we thus equate experiencing-as with recognising
it is I think no longer a paradoxical doctrine that all conscious
experiencing is experiencing-as.

But – if I may raise a possible objection – is it not the case that
'He recognises x' entails that the thing recognised is indeed x,
while 'He is experiencing a as x' does not entail that a is indeed
x: and must we not therefore acknowledge a distinction between
recognising and experiencing-as? As a matter of the ordinary
use of these words the objection is, I think, in order. But what it
indicates is that we lack a term to cover both recognition and
misrecognition. We are accordingly driven to use 'recognition'
generically, as 'knowledge' in 'theory of knowledge' is used to
cover error as well as knowledge, or as 'morality' in 'theory of
morality' is used to cover immorality also. I have been using
'recognition' here in an analogous way to include unjustified as
well as justified identification assertions.

I proceed, then, from the proposition that all conscious
experiencing involves recognitions which go beyond what is

given to the senses and is thus a matter of experiencing-as. This means that ordinary secular perceiving shares a common epistemological character with religious experiencing. We must accordingly abandon the view – if we ever held it – that sense perception at the highly sophisticated human level is a mere automatic registering by the mind of what is on the retina, while religious perception is, in contrast, a subjective response which gratuitously projects meanings into the world. We find instead that all conscious perceiving goes beyond what the senses report to a significance which has not as such been given to the senses. And the religious experience of life as a sphere in which we have continually to do with God and he with us is likewise an awareness in our experience as a whole of a significance which transcends the scope of the senses. In both cases, in a classic statement of John Oman's, 'knowing is not knowledge as an effect of an unknown external cause, but is knowledge as we so interpret that our meaning is the actual meaning of our environment'.[1] And, as Oman also taught, the claim of the religious believer is that in his religious commitment he is relating himself to his total environment in its most ultimate meaning.

The conclusion that *all* experiencing is experiencing-as enables us to meet a fundamental objection that might be made against the analogy between experiencing-as in ordinary life and in religious awareness. It might be pointed out that it is only possible to see, let us say, a tuft of grass as a rabbit if one has previously seen real rabbits; and that in general to see *A* as a *B* presupposes acquaintance with *B*s. Analogously, in order to experience some event, say a striking escape from danger or a healing, as an act of God it would seem that we must first know by direct acquaintance what an act of God is like. However all that has ever been witnessed in the way of divine actions are earthly events which the religious mind has seen as acts of God but which a sceptical observer could see as having a purely natural explanation. In other words, we never have before us unambiguously divine acts, but only ambiguous events which are capable of taking on religious significance to the eyes of faith. But in that case, it will be said, we have no unproblematic

[1] *The Natural and the Supernatural* (Cambridge, 1931), p. 175.

cases of divine actions available to us, as we have in abundance unproblematic instances of rabbits and forks; and consequently we can never be in a position to recognise any of these ambiguous events *as* acts of God. Just as it would be impossible for one who had never seen rabbits to see anything *as* a rabbit, so it must be impossible for us who have never seen an undeniable act of God, to see an event *as* an act of God. This seems on the face of it to be a conclusive objection.

However the objection collapses if, as I have been arguing, *all* experiencing, involving as it does the activity of recognising, is to be construed as experiencing-as. For although the process of recognising is mysterious, there is no doubt that we do continually recognise things, and further that we can learn to recognise. We have learned, starting from scratch, to identify rabbits and forks and innumerable other kinds of thing. And so there is thus far in principle no difficulty about the claim that we may learn to use the concept 'act of God', as we have learned to use other concepts, and acquire the capacity to recognise exemplifying instances.

But of course – let it at once be granted – there are very obvious and indeed immense differences between the concept of a divine act and such concepts as rabbit and fork. For one thing, rabbits and forks are objects – substances, if you like – whereas a divine act is an event. This is already a considerable conceptual contrast. And we must proceed to enlarge it still further. For the cognition of God recorded in the Bible is much wider in scope than an awareness of particular isolated events as being acts of God. Such divine acts are but points of peculiarly intense focus within a much wider awareness of existing in the presence of God. Indeed the biblical cognition of God is typically mediated through the whole experience of the prophet or apostle after his call or conversion, even though within this totality there are specially vivid moments of awareness of God, some of which are evoked by striking or numinous events which thereby become miracles or theophanies. However, we are primarily concerned here with the wider and more continuous awareness of living within the ambience of the unseen God – with the sense of the presence of God – and this is surely something very unlike the awareness of forks and rabbits.

But although the sense of the presence of God is indeed very far removed from the recognition of forks and rabbits, it is already, I think, clear that there are connecting links in virtue of which the religious awareness need not be completely unintelligible to us. In its epistemological structure it exhibits a continuity with our awareness in other fields.

In seeking further to uncover and investigate this continuity we must now take note of another feature of experiencing-as, namely the fact that it occurs at various levels of awareness. By this I mean that as well as there being values of x and y such that to experience A as x is incompatible with experiencing it as y, because x and y are mutually exclusive alternatives, there are also values of x and y such that it is possible to experience A as simultaneously x and y. Here y is supplementary to x, but on a different level. What is meant by 'levels' in this context? That y is on a higher level than x means that the experiencing of A as y presupposes but goes beyond the experiencing of it as x. One or two examples may be useful at this point. As an example, first, of mutually exclusive experiencings-as, one cannot see the tuft of grass simultaneously as a tuft of grass and as a rabbit; or the person whose face we are watching as both furiously angry and profoundly delighted. On the other hand, as an example of supplementary experiencings-as, we may see what is moving above us in the sky as a bird; we may further see it as a hawk; and we may further see it as a hawk engaged in searching for prey; and if we are extremely expert bird watchers we may even see it as a hawk about to swoop down on something on the far side of that low hump of ground. These are successively higher-level recognitions in the sense that each later member of the list presupposes and goes beyond the previous one.

Now let us call the correlate of experiencing-as 'significance', defining this by means of the notion of appropriate response. That is to say, to recognise what is before us as an x involves being in a dispositional state to act in relation to it in a certain distinctive way or range of ways. For example, to recognise the object on the table as a fork is to be in a different dispositional state from that in which one is if one recognises it as a fountain pen. One is prepared in the two cases for the object to display different characteristics, and to be surprised if it doesn't; and one is prepared to use it in different ways and on different occasions, and so on; and in general to recognise something *as* a this or a that (i.e. as significant in this way or in that way) involves being in a certain dispositional state in relation to it.

Our next step must be to shift attention from isolated objects as units of significance to larger and more complex units, namely situations.

A situation is composed of objects; but it is not simply any random collocation of objects. It is a group of objects which, when attended to as a group, has its own distinctive significance over and above the individual significances of its constituent members. That is to say, the situation evokes its own appropriate dispositional response.

As in the case of object-significance there can be different levels of situational significance, with higher levels presupposing lower. An example that is directly relevant is the relation between the ethical significance of a human situation and its purely natural or physical significance. Think of any situation involving an element of moral obligation. Suppose, for example, that someone is caught at the foot of a steep cliff by an incoming tide and I at the top hear his cries for help. He asks me to run to the nearest telephone, ring the police and ask them to call out the lifeboat to rescue him. Consider this first at the purely natural or physical level. There are the cliff and the sea, a human creature liable in due course to be submerged by the rising tide, and his shouted appeals for help. And, morality apart, that is all that there is – just this particular pattern of physical events. However as moral beings we are aware of more than that. As well as experiencing the physical events as physical events we also experience them as constituting a situation of moral claim upon ourselves. We experience the physical pattern as having ethical significance; and the dispositional response that it renders appropriate is to seek to help the trapped person in whatever way seems most practicable. We can, however, conceive of someone with no moral sense at all, who simply fails to be aware of the ethical significance of this situation. He would be interpreting or recognising or experiencing-as only at the physical level of significance. And there would be no way of proving to someone who was thus morally defective that there is any such thing as moral obligation. No doubt an amoral creature could be induced by threats and promises to conform to a socially desirable pattern of behaviour, but he could never be turned by these means into a moral being. In the end we can only say, tautologously, that a person is aware of the ethical significance of situations because he is a moral being; he experiences in moral terms because he is built that way.

The ethical is experienced as an order of significance which supervenes upon, interpenetrates, and is mediated through the physical significance which it presupposes. And if on some occasion the moral character of a situation is not at first apparent to us, but dawns upon as we contemplate it, something happens that is comparable to the discovery of an emergent pattern in a puzzle picture. As the same lines and marks are there, but we have now come to see them as constituting an importantly new pattern, so the social situation is there with the same describable features, but we have now come to be aware of it as laying upon us an inescapable moral claim.

Now consider religious significance as a yet higher level of significance. It is a higher level of significance, adding a new dimension which both includes and transcends that of moral judgement, and yet on the other hand it does not form a simple continuation of the pattern we have already noted. As between natural and ethical significance it is safe to say that every instance of the latter presupposes some instance of the former; for there could be no moral situations if there were no physical situations to have moral significance. But as between ethical and religious significance the relationship is more complex. Not every moment of religious awareness is superimposed upon some occasion of moral obligation. Very often – and especially in the prophetic type of religion that we know in Judaism and Christianity – the sense of the presence of God does carry with it some specific or general moral demand. But we may also be conscious of God in solitude, surrounded only by the natural world, when the divine presence is borne in upon us by the vastness of the starry heavens above or the majestic beauty of a sunrise or a mountain range or some lake or forest scene, or other aspect of earth's marvellously varied face. Again, the sense of the presence of God may occur without any specific environmental context, when the mind is wrapt in prayer or meditation; for there is a contemplative and mystical awareness of God which is relatively independent of external circumstances. And indeed even within the prophetic type of religious experience there are also moments of encounter with God in nature and through solitary prayer as well as in the claims of the personal world. But on the other hand even when the sense of the presence of God has dawned upon us in solitude it is still normally true that it leads us back to our neighbours and often deepens the ethical significance of our relations with them. Thus the dispositional response which is part of the awareness of God is a response in terms of our involvement with our neighbours within our common environment. Even the awareness of God through nature and mystical contemplation leads eventually back to the service of God in the world.

Let us then continue to think here primarily of the prophetic awareness of God, since although this is not the only form of religious cognition it is the typically Judaic-Christian form. And let us test the notion of faith as religious experiencing-as by applying it to the particular history of faith which is reflected in the biblical records.

The Old Testament prophets were vividly conscious of Jahweh as acting in relation to the people of Israel in certain of the events of their time. Through the writings which recall their words and deeds we feel their overwhelmingly vivid consciousness of God as actively present in their contemporary history. It was God who, in the experience of Amos, was threatening selfish and complacent Israel with Assyrian conquest, while also offering mercy to such as should repent. It was God in his holy anger who, in the experience of Jeremiah, was bringing up the Babylonian army against Jerusalem and summoning his people to turn from their greed and wickedness. It is equally true of the other great prophets of the Old Testament that they were experiencing history, as it was taking place around them, as having a distinctively religious significance. Humanly explicable events were experienced as also acts of God, embodying his wrath or his mercy or his calling of the Jewish nation into covenant with him. The prophets experienced the religious significance of these events and declared it to the people; and this religious significance was always such that to see it meant being conscious of a sacred demand to behave in a new way towards one's neighbours.

It is, I think, important to realise that this prophetic interpretation of Hebrew history was not in the first place a philosophy of history, a theoretical pattern imposed retrospectively upon remembered or recorded events. It was in the first place the way in which the great prophets actually experienced and participated in these events at the time. Hosea did not *infer* Jahwah's mercy; second Isaiah did not *infer* his universal sovereignty; Jeremiah did not *infer* his holy righteousness – rather they were conscious of the Eternal as acting towards them, and towards their nation, in his mercy, in his holy righteousness, in his absolute sovereignty. They were, in other words, experiencing-as.

Again, in the New Testament, the primary instance of faith, the rock on which Christianity is based, consisted in seeing Jesus as the Christ. This was the faith of the disciples, epitomised in Peter's confession at Caesarea Philippi, whereby their experience of following Jesus was also an experience of being in the presence of God's personal purpose and claim and love. They may or may not at the time have used any of the terms that were later used in the New Testament writings to express this awareness – Messiah, Son of God, divine Logos. However, these terms point back to that original response, and the faith which they came to express must have been implicit within it. And once again this primary response of the first disciples to Jesus as Lord and Christ was not a theory about him which they adopted, but an experience out of which Christian language and theory later grew. That he was their Lord was a fact of experience given in their personal dealings with him. And the special character of their way of seeing and responding to him, in contrast to that of others who never found him to be their Lord, is precisely the distinctive essence of Christian faith.

The experiencing of Jesus of Nazareth as Lord – Jesus of Nazareth, that is to say, not as a theological symbol but in his historical concreteness, including his teaching concerning God and man – meant coming to share in some degree both his experiencing of life as the sphere of God's redemptive activity and his practical response to God's purposes in the world. What that involved for Jesus himself, as the one in whom men were to see the divine Logos made flesh, is spelled out in his life, and especially in the drama of his death. What it involves for Christians – for those who have begun to share Jesus' vision of the world in its relation to God, – is indicated in his moral teaching. For this is simply a general description, with concrete examples drawn from the life of first-century Palestine, of the way in which someone tends spontaneously to behave who is consciously living in the presence of God as Jesus has revealed him.

I have now, I hope, offered at least a very rough outline of a conception of faith as the interpretative element within our cognitive religious experience. How is one to test such a theory, and how decide whether to accept or reject it? All that can be done is to spell out its consequences as fully as possible in the hope that the theory will then either founder under a weight of implausible corollaries, or else show its viability as it proceeds and float triumphantly on to acceptance. I have already tried to indicate its epistemological basis in the thesis that all experiencing is experiencing-as, and the way in which this thesis is relevant to the stream of distinctively religious experience recorded in the Bible. Let me now in conclusion sketch some of its lines of implication in other directions.

It suggests, as I have already mentioned, a view of the Christian ethic as the practical corollary of the distinctively Christian vision of the world. Taking a hint from the modern dispositional analysis of belief we may say that to experience the world as having a certain character is, among other things, to be in a dispositional state to live in it in the manner which such a character in our environment renders appropriate. And to experience it in a way derived from Christ's own experience is accordingly to tend to live in the kind of way that he both taught and showed forth in his own life.

Another implication of this theory of faith concerns the nature of revelation. For in Christian theology revelation and faith are correlative concepts, faith being a human response to the divine activity of self-revelation. If faith is construed as a distinctively religious experiencing of life as mediating God's presence and activity, this clearly fits and even demands a *heilsgeschichtliche* conception of revelation as consisting in divine actions in human history. God is self-revealingly active within the world that he has made. But his actions are not overwhelmingly manifest and unmistakable; for then men would have no cognitive freedom in relation to their Maker. Instead God always acts in such a way that man is free to see or fail to see the events in question as divine acts. The prophets were conscious of God at work in the happenings of their time; but many of their contemporaries were not. Again, the disciples were conscious of Jesus as the Christ; but the scribes and pharisees and the Romans were not. Thus revelation, as communication between God and man, only becomes actual when it meets an answering human response of faith; and the necessity for this response, making possible an uncompelled cognition of God's presence and activity, preserves the freedom and responsibility of the finite creature in relation to the infinite Creator.

This in turn suggests an understanding of the special character of the Bible and of its inspiration. The Bible is a record of the stream of revelatory events that culminated in the coming of the Christ. But it differs from a secular account of the same strand of history in that the Bible is written throughout from the standpoint of faith. It describes this history as it was experienced from within by the prophets and then by the apostles. And the faith of the writers, whereby they saw the revelatory events *as* revelatory, is their inspiration. The uniqueness of the Bible is not due to any unique mode or quality of its writing but to the unique significance of the events of which it is the original documentary expression, which became revelatory through the faith of the biblical writers. As such the Bible mediates the same revelation to subsequent generations and is thus itself revelatory in a secondary sense, calling in its own turn for a response of faith.

This theory of faith can also be used to throw light on the nature of the miraculous. For a miracle, whatever else it may be, is an event through which we become vividly and immediately conscious of God as acting towards us. A startling happening, even if it should involve a suspension of natural law, does not constitute for us a miracle in the religious sense of the word if it fails to make us intensely aware of being in God's presence. In order to be miraculous, an event must be experienced as religiously significant. Indeed we may say that a miracle is any event that is experienced as a miracle; and this particular mode of experiencing-as is accordingly an essential element in the miraculous.

Finally, yet another application of this theory of faith is to the sacraments. In the sacraments some ordinary material object, bread or wine or water, is experienced as a vehicle of God's grace and becomes a focus of specially intense consciousness of God's overshadowing presence and purpose. A sacrament has in fact the same religious quality as a miracle but differs from other miracles in that it occurs within a liturgical context and is a product of ritual. In themselves, apart from the sacramental context of worshipping faith, the bread and wine or the water are ordinary material things; they have no magical properties. What happens in the sacramental event is that they are experienced as channels of divine grace. They thus invite a peculiarly direct moment of religious experiencing-as, fulfilling for subsequent believers the faith-eliciting and faith-nourishing function of the person of Christ in the experience of the first disciples.

Now in conclusion may I repeat something that I said near the beginning. What I have been attempting to formulate is an epistemological analysis of religious faith, not an argument for the validity of that faith. Faith, I have been suggesting, is the interpretative element within what the religious man reports as his experience of living in the presence of God. But whether that experience is veridical or illusory is another question. My own view is that it is as rational for the religious man to treat his experience of God as veridical as it is for him and others to treat their experience of the physical world as veridical. But that requires another argument, which I have not attempted to supply here.

3

SOME REMARKS ON WITTGENSTEIN'S ACCOUNT OF RELIGIOUS BELIEF

W. D. Hudson

PUPILS' notes of some lectures on religious belief which Wittgenstein gave in 1938 have recently been published,[1] and what I have to say is set against the background of these lectures. My title may suggest that there is a distinctive and precise account of religious belief which can be extracted from them and stated clearly for consideration. But I do not think that this is so. It is evident from these lectures that, in the subject of religious belief, Wittgenstein's prodigious capacity for puzzlement, in which Moore recognised the marks of genius, found full scope. But, at many points, it is not clear to me, at any rate, just how he is resolving – or would resolve – the puzzlement. So I am most certainly not setting myself up to explain 'what Wittgenstein really meant'. However, like every-thing which we have from him, these lectures are fascinating, suggestive, provocative. And, at some hazard, I am going to offer a few observations on one or two of the points which he was, or appears to have been, making.

The overall question which arises from – or perhaps I ought to say with which one comes to – these lectures is: to what extent can religious belief be regarded as a logically self-contained universe of discourse? I have not found a completely satisfying answer to this question in Wittgenstein, nor indeed anywhere

[1] L. Wittgenstein, *Lectures and Conversations on Aesthetics, Psychology and Religious Belief* (Oxford, 1966). Throughout this lecture the page-references enclosed in brackets are to that work.

else, but there are three related questions, on each of which Wittgenstein had something to say, and a consideration of these will, I think, help us to see more clearly what is involved in that overall question. The three questions are: (i) What training is required in order to participate in religious belief? (ii) Is it reasonable, or unreasonable, to do so? (iii) What is the essential difference between those who do participate in it and those who do not?

I

Wittgenstein said that before we can participate in religious belief we need to have been trained in the technique of using the appropriate picture or pictures. According to him, acquiring this technique means learning what conclusions are drawn from the picture and what are not. In any given case, it will be found that religious believers draw some you might expect but not others. The conclusions which they draw determine what does, or does not, make sense in their religion. Take Wittgenstein's example, the picture, 'God's eye sees everything'. Theists, who use this picture, would be prepared to discuss the question: does God see what is going to happen as well as what is happening now? To raise that question would not be out of line with their use of the picture. But, as Wittgenstein asked rhetorically: 'Are eyebrows going to be talked of, in connexion with the Eye of God?' (p. 71). No: it would strike theists as silly to discuss the shape or shagginess of the divine eyebrows. That is not how they use the picture.

So, learning to be a religious believer is being trained in how to use the picture. There are, however, two points which, I think, have an important bearing on this training.

(i) There is a difference between simply saying and doing the correct things in religion and saying or doing them with understanding. Suppose you coached somebody to say and do all the right things in the liturgy so that he was word-perfect in the creeds, prayers and responses, knew exactly when to stand or to kneel or to go to the altar, and so on. Would that be sufficient to make him a religious believer? No: it is perfectly

E

possible to say and do all the right things in religion without knowing what they mean. We are probably all in that condition to some extent as children. However, to be a religious believer one must have some understanding of what is being said or done. And so it is a necessary condition of effective training in religion that it should not merely acquaint the trainee with what to say or do but give him this understanding of the use to which the picture is put.

(ii) By 'the use to which the picture is put' two somewhat different things may be meant: (*a*) the use of it which is given in, or definitive of, the religion in question; and (*b*) the use which is made of it by adherents of the religion in question, when they are reflecting upon their beliefs or interpreting new situations in the light of them. For example, on the one hand, it is given in, or definitive of, Christianity that, from the picture, God the Father, the conclusion should be drawn that he regards all men with goodwill, but not the conclusion that he is their physical progenitor. And, on the other hand, it is characteristic of Christians that, within such given limits, individually and collectively, they continue to think, and indeed to disagree, about what follows, or does not follow, from the Fatherhood of God. The training, therefore, which is a necessary condition of religious belief, must initiate the trainee into both these uses of the picture. After undergoing it, he must know what conclusions it is constitutive of his religion to draw, or not to draw, from the picture; and also how to participate in that continuing consideration of what the picture does, or does not entail, which constitutes religious reflection and discussion.

Now, in order to see what training will meet these requirements, we must be clear what it is to use the picture, in either of our two senses, *with understanding*. I think this is a hard thing to be clear about; the notion of understanding religion is not a simple one. However, for our purposes at the moment, I think it will be enough to see one thing which using the picture with understanding must mean. It must, surely, be a matter of recognising what is said or done in a religion as logically connected with what is there taken to be fundamental, namely the picture in use. To take first the use which is given or definitive: if, for example, I, as a Christian, have not merely learned to say 'God loves us' but to say it with understanding, then, at a minimum, I recognise it as logically entailed by the picture, God the Father (assuming that picture to be fundamental to Christianity). And to take the other use: if I reflect upon, or discuss, petitionary prayer, let us say, with understanding, then I shall have in mind the logical connection between whatever is being thought or said about it and this picture, God the Father. I shall see the point of the view, for instance, that petitionary prayer is unnecessary, when I recognise that this is being said for some such reason as that, God being Father, we do not need to ask him to do us good; or, alternatively, of the view that petitionary prayer is essential, when I recognise this as being said for some such reason as that, God being Father, we need to effect our side of a personal relationship with him and petitionary prayer is the way to do it. What I wish to say then is this: understanding the use of the picture which is definitive of a religion, or the use to which it is put in continuing reflection or discussion within that religion, is in both cases a matter of seeing the logical connection between what is being said and what is logically fundamental, namely the picture itself. I am sure that there is far more to understanding a religion than this. All I want to say is that there is at least this.

In order to participate in religious belief, then, one needs to know two things. First of all, one must know how the use to which certain expressions are being put *differs* from the use to which they are normally put in non-religious contexts. For example, that, though God has an eye, one does not ask questions about the divine eyebrows. But, more fundamentally, one needs to know how the use to which expressions are being put in religion *resembles* the use to which they are put in non-religious contexts. Obviously, one cannot know how they differ from that norm unless one knows what that norm is. And when one is using the picture, in either of our two senses, with understanding, one is recognising conclusions which follow from the ordinary use of the words which give the picture.

From all this, it follows that, in so far as religious belief consists in using the kind of picture which Wittgenstein instanced, the training which is required, in order to participate, must include training in two things:

(i) In the ordinary use, in non-religious contexts, of the expressions which give the picture. 'A Last Judgement', 'The Eye of God', 'God the Father' etc. – such pictures mean nothing to you unless you know what 'judgement', 'eye', 'father' etc. mean in non-religious contexts. However varied, complicated or abstract the pictures become, I think this point is sustained. What you are always inquiring into, or arguing about, in religion is whether, and how, in the light of a more general use than the specifically religious, such expressions as 'eye', 'father', etc. are applicable to God. If you have not learned these more general uses, you cannot participate.

(ii) The training must include training in certain rules or notions of logic, e.g. what it is to contradict oneself. It may well be (as we shall see in a moment), Wittgenstein said, that the reasons given for using pictures in religion are not like those given for uttering propositions in other universes of discourse; but, in so far as using the picture means drawing conclusions from it, one needs to have learned what it is to do this. One has to bring this knowledge to religious discourse in order to engage in it.

So what it comes to is this: the training to be a religious believer necessarily includes training in how to use language more widely. The language used in religion is the same as that used in other universes of discourse. It is not a special sort of language, but just ordinary language put to a particular use. I am not, of course, suggesting that there is an entity, ordinary language, which is logically distinct from all the language games in which it is used; but merely pointing out that, in the case of some at least of the expressions used in religion, the meaning of what is said is not logically altogether distinct from the meaning, or meanings, which these expressions may have in other contexts. What it makes, or does not make, sense to say in religion is, therefore, to some extent determined by what constitutes sense or nonsense in other contexts. To this extent, at any rate, religious discourse is not logically self-contained.

II

Is it reasonable or unreasonable to participate in religious belief? In trying to get at, and assess, what Wittgenstein thought about that, we must first consider rather more carefully what he had to say about the nature of religious belief. The following are some of the relevant points which he made, taking belief in a Last Judgement as a paradigm case.

(i) There is an enormous gulf between believer and unbeliever in religion which is not paralleled in, say, science or commonsense. 'Suppose', he said, 'someone were a believer and said: "I believe in a Last Judgement", and I said: "Well, I'm not so sure. Possibly." You would say that there is an enormous gulf between us. If he said "There is a German aeroplane overhead," and I said "Possibly. I'm not so sure," you'd say we were fairly near.' (p. 53) And again: '. . . you don't get in religious controversies, the form of controversy where one person is *sure* of the thing, and the other says: "Well, possibly." ' (p. 56)

(ii) This enormous difference between believer and unbeliever in religion, however, is not simply that the believer thinks the evidence for such a happening as a Last Judgement well-established, while the unbeliever does not. You could have two men, *A* and *B*. *A* believes that the evidence shows that there will be a Judgement Day in, say, two thousand years' time, but his 'belief in this happening wouldn't be at all a religious belief'. (p. 56) *B*, on the other hand, sees that this belief in a Last Judgement is not as well established by the evidence given for it as some other beliefs, but it is for him nevertheless 'the firmest of all beliefs'. (p. 54)

(iii) What, then, *is* religious belief? This is the sort of answer which Wittgenstein gave: 'Suppose somebody made this guidance for this life: believing in the Last Judgement. Whenever he does anything, this is before his mind . . . he has what you might call an unshakeable belief. It will show, not by reasoning or by appeal to ordinary grounds for belief, but rather by regulating for all in his life.'(pp. 53–4)

(iv) 'Belief', in the case of religion, then, means something rather different from what it normally means in other contexts.

'There is', said Wittgenstein, 'this extraordinary use of the word "believe". One talks of believing and at the same time one doesn't use "believe" as one does ordinarily. You might say (in the normal use) "You only believe – oh well . . .". Here [*sc.* in religion] it is used entirely differently: on the other hand it is not used as we generally use the word "know".' (pp. 59–60) That is so. Of course, religious people do sometimes claim to know the content of their beliefs (e.g. 'I know that Christ has saved me') but the difference between what is called belief in religion and in other contexts is certainly not that religious belief is what we normally call knowledge. In the ordinary use of the word, the claim to *know* implies that we can cite evidence which entitles us to be sure. Religious believers do frequently offer evidence for their beliefs – that of their own experience, of historical events, etc. – but there are two comments at least which must be made about this putative evidence. (*a*) Some of it is, to say the least, pretty odd. Wittgenstein's instance of a man who said he believed in a Last Judgement because he had seen it in a dream, is perhaps not typical of sophisticated believers. Nevertheless, it is undeniable that what passes for evidence in religion would frequently not do so anywhere else. (*b*) But even if the evidence offered for a religious belief were such as would carry weight in science or history, and even if it were weighty enough to put a hypothesis beyond all reasonable doubt, it would never be enough to establish a religious belief. Why? 'Because', said Wittgenstein, 'the indubitability wouldn't be enough to make me change my life.' (p. 57) There is a logical gap between the belief that something will happen, however well-established, and that all-or-nothing commitment which Wittgenstein took religious belief to be.

Against the background of this account of the nature of religious belief the question remains: is it reasonable to participate in it? About that, Wittgenstein's cryptic conclusion was as follows:

Here we have people who . . . base things on evidence which taken in one way would seem exceedingly flimsy. They base enormous things on this evidence. Am I to say they are unreasonable? I wouldn't call them unreasonable.

I would say, they are certainly not *reasonable*, that's obvious. 'Unreasonable' implies, with everyone, rebuke.

I want to say: they don't treat this as a matter of reasonability.

Anyone who reads the Epistles will find it said: not only that it is not reasonable, but that it is folly.

Not only is it not reasonable, but it doesn't pretend to be. (pp. 57–8)

What are we to make of this? The basis of Wittgenstein's position here does certainly seem to be that religious belief is logically distinct from any other universe of discourse. In his remarks which follow the last quotation, he comes down very heavily on apologists, both for and against religion, whom he considers guilty of failing to see this. Referring to those who argue that religious beliefs can be treated as though they were scientific hypotheses, he says: '. . . if this is religious belief, then it's all superstition.' (p. 59) But he is careful to add that they deserve ridicule, not because their beliefs are based on insufficient evidence, but because they are cheating themselves. On the other hand, any unbeliever who thinks that he can refute religion by showing that the evidence adduced for its beliefs, if compared with anything in science which we call evidence, is not good enough, will be overlooking the fact, as Wittgenstein put it, that 'for a blunder that's too big'. He explained: 'If you suddenly wrote numbers down on the blackboard, and then said: "Now, I'm going to add", and then said: "2 and 21 is 13", etc. I'd say: "This is no blunder".' (p. 62) Wittgenstein's point is that in such a case you would be up to some queer arithmetic, not making mistakes in the ordinary variety; or at least one would be wise to suspect that you were. The 'blunders' in religion are too big for it to be simply bad science.

A number of issues arise from all this and I should like to comment on one or two of them.

1. I think Wittgenstein was perfectly right to insist on what has been called by others the commissive force of religious beliefs. When a believer says 'There will be a Judgement Day', part of what he is doing, in saying that, is committing himself

to a norm by which to evaluate his own deeds and those of other men, namely, how we may suppose that they will appear to the Divine Judge. But, of course, it is one thing to hold that this commissive force is part, another that it is the whole, of the illocutionary force of religious beliefs or their expression. 'There will be a Judgement Day' appears to have constative force also – to assert that a certain event will, as a matter of empirical fact, occur. Now, the fact that one has had certain dreams, or experienced terror, in connection with some norm, may be quite respectable as reasons for holding it in the forefront of one's mind. To do so may be, for instance, the only alternative to neurosis. But it does not follow that these are therefore good reasons for any other element in what is being said by one who professes belief in a Last Judgement. Of course, Wittgenstein did not say explicitly that they were. But what he seems to me at times to have come near to suggesting is that, because religious beliefs have commissive force, that somehow entitles us to by-pass the troublesome problem of their constative force.

II. Let us, then, turn to that problem. What kind of an assertion, on the lips of a believer, is 'There will be a Last Judgement'? It is certainly not just a prediction that a certain spatio-temporal event will occur, comparable to, for example, 'There will be a World War by 1970'. You remember Wittgenstein's point that one man can believe it probable that there will be a Judgement Day, without this making him a religious believer; and another can have a religious belief in a Last Judgement, while thinking the evidence for it not particularly good. The difference, he said, is that the unbeliever does not use the picture at all; whereas, in the case of the believer, 'it will show, not by reasoning or by appeal to ordinary grounds for belief, but rather by regulating for all in his life'. (p. 54) We have seen that it regulates in the sense that it provides the believer with a norm for guiding, or judging, conduct. The question now is: does it regulate in any other sense? I think it does. A religious belief – or at any rate a picture which is taken to be logically fundamental in any system of religious belief – exercises a regulative function over the things which the believer says, or hears said, in the sense that it determines which of these, for him *qua* religious believer, are intelligible (i.e. have any meaning, afford any explanation) and which are unintelligible. It is, in effect, his standard of sense and nonsense. So that, for instance, 'This is a punishment' explains illness for him, *qua* religious believer, as 'This is pneumonia' would not.

Now, it is a familiar line of argument that propositions which exercise this regulative function do not need to fulfil the conditions of meaningfulness which apply to ordinary assertions of empirical fact. They register 'bliks' or 'onlooks'; they are 'end-statements'.[1] Did Wittgenstein take this view? Some of his remarks may suggest that he did. For example: 'What we call believing in a Judgement Day – or not believing in a Judgement Day – The expression of belief may play an absolutely minor role' (p. 55) – where 'the expression of belief' can, I think, be taken to mean the assertion that there will be such a Day. 'Believing in a Judgement Day' – this seems to be the point – is not thinking true the assertion that there will be such a Day, but adopting a criterion of meaning or explanation.

Attractive as this line of argument may be, it is difficult to quell altogether at least two doubts about it. (i) Does, or can, the religious believer, as such, rest content with this account of his beliefs? (ii) It could be said of everybody, madmen included, that there is one proposition, or more, which may look like an ordinary assertion but constitutes for them the standard of sense and nonsense. Surely, we cannot just lump all these standards together indiscriminately. Must there not be a super-standard by reference to which the madmen are recognised as such? And if there is, must not religious belief, in order to pass as reasonable, conform to it?

III. What, then, can be taken to constitute this norm of rationality? That has been the subject of much learned controversy; most notably of late between Professors Winch and MacIntyre. What I have to say about it will, I fear, strike you as, at best, inconclusive and, at worst, quite unhelpful. Broadly speaking, however, there are, I think, two main views of the

---

[1] See R. M. Hare, 'Theology and Falsification' in *New Essays in Philosophical Theology* (ed. Flew and MacIntyre) (London, 1955); D. D. Evans, *The Logic of Self Involvement* (London, 1963); P. van Buren, *The Secular Meaning of the Gospel* (rev. ed. London, 1965).

matter, which may be described as the 'closed' and 'open' views respectively. According to the former, or as I call it, closed view, the norm of rationality is necessarily, in the last analysis, the standard of sense and nonsense which is generally accepted in our twentieth-century, scientific and technological culture. What it is reasonable or unreasonable to say is determined by the use, or uses, of language which constitute this form of life. According to the second, or open, view of the norm of rationality, the rational man is, by definition, always free to acquire new standards of sense or nonsense from cultures other than his own or universes of discourse with which he has not hitherto been acquainted. The importance of this open view for religious belief is, according to some exponents, that it shows there to be no standard of ordinary usage which determines, in any ultimate way, what it does or does not make sense to say in religion.

Wittgenstein would, presumably, have favoured the open view. That, at any rate, is what his cryptic remarks on the reasonableness and unreasonableness of religious belief suggest.

Now, I can see that there are dangers in the closed view. At least two: (i) It may lead those who hold it to misinterpret religious belief: to suppose, for examples, that religious believers mean by the Last Judgement a future spatio-temporal event, or that they use petitionary prayer simply as a way of getting what they want; when in fact they do not mean, or do not do, these things, or not solely. (ii) Exponents of the closed view may claim for their norm of rationality an absoluteness or logical necessity which it does not possess. It is just a contingent fact that science and technology predominate in our culture as they do; and if, as is logically possible, any alternative universe of discourse were taken as the norm of rationality, they would appear irrational.

Is the open view more satisfactory? One thing which I find worrying about it is this. Those who maintain that religious belief can be rendered intelligible quite apart from the standard of sense and nonsense embodied in ordinary language do not seem to me to be able to carry their programme through consistently and successfully. May I take as an example of what I have in mind, the treatment of petitionary prayer in Mr

D. Z. Phillips' interesting and provocative book *The Concept of Prayer*? According to this author, if we have regard only to what 'petition' means in ordinary discourse – asking an agent to produce effects in the natural world – we cannot understand petitionary prayer. We must look and see the *quite distinct* sense which 'petition' has in a truly religious context. Mr Phillips sets about showing us what this is. I quote from his book:

> When deep religious believers pray *for* something they are not so much asking God to bring this about, but in a way telling Him of the strength of their desires. They realise that things may not go as they wish, but they are asking to be able to go on living whatever happens. In prayers of . . . petition, the believer is trying to find a meaning and a hope that will deliver him from the elements in his life which threaten to destroy it: . . . his desires.[1]

The author emphasises more than once that he is concerned only with the meaning of petition in the case of prayer, and so that must be what these remarks are intended to elucidate. I have these comments to make. (*a*) Phillips says that, when the deep religious believer prays for something, he is not so much asking God to bring this about, but in a way telling Him of the strength of his desires. Well, yes; the proposition 'Smith said "Give me X" ' certainly does imply that Smith wanted X, provided he knew the meaning of the words which he was using and did not intend to deceive. In *that* sense a petitioner who prays 'God give me X' is telling God of the strength of his desires, but only in that sense. 'P implies q' is not logically equivalent to 'P means q'. (*b*) The justification which the author offers for saying that the deep religious believer is, in petitionary prayer, trying to find deliverance from his desires is that, *qua* deep religious believer, he will always add '. . . if it be Thy will'. We are told that we must not think that, by this condition, he is either making the anthropomorphic assumption, or offering the theoretical explanation, that God may have reasons for answering the prayer or for not answering it. We must not thus identify God's will with anything natural. We must not think of petitionary prayer as asking Him to produce effects in the

[1] *The Concept of Prayer* (London, 1965) p. 121.

natural world. By '. . . if it be Thy will', we are told, the believer
is not recognising how the world is or may be, but that it is.
And what such recognition apparently comes to is this: 'meeting
the possibility of things going either way in God'. Now, I can
see that it makes sense to say that *in effect* this is what the deep
religious believer does in petitionary prayer – that, when he
adds sincerely '. . . if it be Thy will' to his petitions, he thereby
subordinates his desires to God's will, and, in effect, will not
thereafter be consumed by them. But what I find it hard to
swallow is that 'This deep religious believer said "God give
me *X*" ' *means* 'This deep religious believer asked to be able to
go on living whatever happens'. But, let's suppose it does. How,
then, does the deep religious believer differ from a mere fatalist?
We are assured that he does: that he is not merely saying 'Ah
well, that's the way things are'. He is, rather, 'asking that his
desires will not destroy the spirit of God within him'. Presumably, 'asking' here means something different from merely
expressing the wish that; and presumably, since this is prayer
and not simply auto-suggestion, the one being asked to see
that desire does not destroy the spirit of God within is God.
The spirit of God within presumably means, among other
things, certain psychological conditions, e.g. that 'joy and
peace in believing' of which St Paul speaks (Rom. 15: 13).
But doesn't this explanation of the difference between deep
religious believer and fatalist, therefore, take the former to be
asking God to produce an effect in the natural world? The
fact that the effect is the preservation of a certain psychological
condition within the petitioner himself does not make it any
less an effect in the natural world. But we were told that we
have got it wrong if we think of God as an agent who produces
effects in the natural world or of petitionary prayer as asking
Him to do so. Personally, I think that we have not got it
wrong, if we do so, or not necessarily. But I am not concerned
here to argue that, only to point out that this attempt to
explain what 'petition' means in religion falls back in the end
on what it means in ordinary use. It means asking an agent
to do something for you – to produce an effect in the natural
world.

I have certainly not answered the question: Is it reasonable or unreasonable to participate in religious belief? But what perhaps I have done is show that this cannot, at any rate, be answered simply by taking the 'open' view of the norm of rationality – by treating religious belief as a logically self-contained universe of discourse which is intelligible quite apart from canons of sense and nonsense embodied in a wider use of language.

III

What is the essential difference between those who participate in religious belief and those who do not? Wittgenstein appears to have thought that there is an impassable logical gulf between them. He said:

> If you ask me whether or not I believe in a Judgement Day, in the sense in which religious people have belief in it, I wouldn't say: 'No. I don't believe there will be such a thing.' It would seem to me utterly crazy to say this.
> And then I give an explanation: 'I don't believe in . . .', but then the religious person never believes what I describe. I can't say. I can't contradict that person. (p. 55)

His point here appears to be this. Normally, in a difference of belief, *A* says 'I believe *X*' and *B*, 'I don't believe *X*', where *X* is some statement of the belief in dispute, which is acceptable to both of them. But, in the case of the religious believer and unbeliever, no such statement is possible: 'And then I give an explanation: "I don't believe in . . .", but then the religious person never believes what I describe.' For example, suppose the unbeliever shows conclusively that the probability of a Last Judgement as a future spatio-temporal event is not well-established, the believer may say 'Well, I know it's not. That isn't what I mean'. In some such way, the religious believer always does appear to be elusive to contradiction by the unbeliever.

Wittgenstein went on to make the point which we have already noted: that the expression of religious belief is not like ordinary assertion of empirical fact. Those who reject it are not merely denying the assertion that, for example, there will be a Judgement Day. They are rejecting a whole way of thinking. All this talk of a Judgement Day makes no sort of sense to them; the denial that there will be one is as absurd as the assertion that there will. As Wittgenstein put it:

> Suppose someone is ill and he says: 'This is a punishment', and I say: 'If I'm ill, I don't think of punishment at all.' If you say: 'Do you believe the opposite?' – you can call it believing the opposite but it is entirely different from what we normally call believing the opposite.
>
> I think differently, in a different way. I say different things to myself. I have different pictures. (p. 55)

Religious belief is sometimes criticised because its assertions do not pass tests for meaningfulness which apply to ordinary empirical assertions. It is legitimate, I think, to object that this criticism misses the point. That is not what they are meant to be. There may be all sorts of grounds for rejecting religious belief but it is invulnerable to attacks which misconceive its nature.

Are we, then, to say that believers and unbelievers do not understand one another? There is a long history to the view that, in religion, in order to understand one must first believe, and it seems to be back in favour with some modern philosophers. But Wittgenstein does not appear to have held it, not, at least, in any clear or straightforward way. He said:

> You might say: 'Well, if you can't contradict him [the religious believer] that means you don't understand him. If you did understand him, then you might.' That again is Greek to me. My normal technique of language leaves me. I don't know whether to say they understand one another or not. (p. 55)

In one sense – that which I put forward when discussing what it is to say things in religion with understanding – the unbeliever certainly can understand the believer. If he is told that it is definitive of a religion to draw such-and-such conclusions from a picture, he can understand that; and he can recognise other conclusions as entailed, or not entailed, by the picture thus defined. So, if it means anything to say that the unbeliever does not understand the believer, it must mean that the former in some other way, does not fully enter into the game as the believer does. I think Wittgenstein was after this, when he said that, in religious belief, 'a number of ways of thinking and acting crystallize and come together', and went on: 'A man would fight for his life not to be dragged into the fire. No induction. Terror. That is, as it were, part of the substance of the belief.' (p. 56) It would make sense, would it not, to say that if you do not feel the believer's terror about Hell Fire, you do not really understand what he believes?

IV

Summarising, we may say that there are at least three elements constituting the logical gap between religious believer and un-believer, taking 'I believe in a Judgement Day' as a paradigm case:

(i) the commissive force of this utterance on the lips of the believer;
(ii) the regulative function which it exercises in determining what for him constitutes an explanation and what does not;
(iii) the specific emotions, of awe, terror, or whatever, which for him are part of the substance of the belief.

The unbeliever, as such, is necessarily excluded from all three. If this is what it means to say that religious belief is logically self-contained, I agree.[1]

---

[1] I discuss some other aspects of the relationship between Wittgenstein's philosophy and religion in my small book, *Ludwig Wittgenstein: The Bearing of His Philosophy Upon Religious Belief* (London, 1968).

4

ON DOING THEOLOGY

Paul van Buren

THAT a theologian has been asked to contribute a lecture to this series on the philosophy of religion is, I assume, not an invitation to him to play amateur philosopher, but to offer, for what it is worth, what he can. I have conceived it my responsibility, therefore, both to those to whom I owe the honour of the invitation to be here, and to the furtherance of honest discussion between philosophers and theologians, to take as my task a clarification of what theology is, what a theologian is up to when he is doing theology.

The title of this paper, 'On Doing Theology', is meant to draw attention to a fact which everyone knows already but may not sufficiently notice: theology is a human activity. It is done by particular people; you can name theologians by name and point them out. They talk and argue with each other, write papers and books. But as a human activity, as something which certain people do, theology is a historical enterprise, a temporal affair, like any other human activity in this respect. Like politics, literature, even doing philosophy, it has a past and a present. And like so many other human activities, it seems, at least to us today, to have had a particularly interesting modern history. As is true of so many things men do today, theology is not always done now in the way it used to be done.

I begin with this historical observation because theology is itself an activity in a historical context, an aspect of how some men face life in their particular circumstances; how, to be more specific, Christians wrestle with the question of what it

52

means for them to be men in their own time. Theology is therefore a deceptively general name for what is in each case as particular, time-bound and relative an undertaking as being a human being. So if someone were to ask, what is theology, it would be misleading to begin by saying, for example, that theology is systematic reflection upon man's language about God. Such a definition would not help us to understand Christian theology as it has been done in the West and as it is done today. Reflection on man's language about God is more properly to be placed under the heading of cultural history than under that of theology, as for example the observation that men seem in fact to have spoken more of God a thousand years ago than they do today, and also used the word 'God' in some ways which few would today. Such approaches to theology omit what as a theologian I cannot omit without forgetting what I seek to understand: the particular men in their particular time out of which theology comes and to whom it is addressed. Theology as I know it has never been, and I do not see how it can ever be, neglectful of its particular circumstances.

As a way of getting started, I shall give what I take to be a less misleading definition of theology, although this definition will require considerable elaboration in order to make it clear just what theologians are up to. So as a starter, let me say that *theology is that activity of men struck by the biblical story, in which they undertake to revise continually the ways in which they say how things are with their present circumstances, in the light of how they read that story.*

I should like at once to call attention to a tension which I have purposely built into this definition at every possible point, a dynamic that I have also tried to stress in calling this paper 'On Doing Theology'. I call theology an activity, and an activity of men who have been struck by, impressed by, influenced by the biblical story. I use the expression 'struck by' to indicate that on the one hand those who do theology have always to reckon with this story, that this story is for them unavoidable in what they are up to. But this expression is not the same as 'dominated by', 'defined by', or some such phrase, which would suggest that that is all that determines men who do theology. They are struck by the biblical story, but in doing theology, they are just men, like any others in their time, and therefore many other influences are at work in their lives and thought and work. A theologian is also a man of his time, a man in history, and the definition is meant to draw your attention to this tension in theology between the biblical story and the other human story or stories within which theology takes place.

This same tension accounts for the way I concluded the definition, saying that the revisionary work of theology is undertaken in the light not simply of that story, as though the story could be abstracted from those who read, share and interpret it. The biblical story which is fundamental for doing theology is the story as it is read and understood by the theologian, which means, of course, the story as it is read and understood among those in his time who are also struck by that story. If it is the same story that is read from generation to generation, yet it is read with the eyes of men who read other things as well, which means that the story has also been read in sometimes slightly, sometimes seriously, different ways in different times and circumstances. Here too is a tension to be noticed.

Finally, theology aims to say how things are, yet to say this with respect to contemporary circumstances. Theology is therefore in a constant state of being revised and rewritten. Since the world it speaks of is our experienced world, the world of history, in which we live, and the way we live in that world, it is an activity of change and in the midst of change, relative always to the circumstances in which it is done. It is, for reasons which we shall have to develop, always on the move, so that I am tempted to say that it is concerned about how things are in the sense of how they are becoming, where they are going. The apparent stability of the expression 'how things are' is therefore qualified fundamentally by the flexibility of continual revision, so that what is said about present circumstances is left open toward the future.

Perhaps I should add, before turning to a closer look at the sources of these tensions in theology, that I have ascribed an unfinished, always-to-be-revised character to theology not in order to justify or ensure future employment for myself or other theologians. That theologians be paid for their activity is by no means guaranteed by the nature of their work. That condition is as relative to our present circumstances as anything could be. Nor do I wish to imply that as long as history continues, there will always be a theological task to perform. No, theology will presumably be done only as long as there are men who in their contemporary circumstances are struck by the biblical story. If that should no longer be found anywhere to be the case on this earth, then the time for doing theology would be over. And the tension that pervades the work of theology only reflects the tension arising out of the fact that men who have also been struck by that ancient story, seek to understand their circumstances.

The principal element of continuity in the whole history of theology, the thread which runs through it and gives it what unity it has, is the fact that those who do theology and those who read it with concern are men who have been struck by the same story, the story which is spread out in the many books which together we call the Bible. If anyone cares to know what theology is about, what sort of activity it is, not to speak of any who would care to do theology, he must not take it for granted that there exists this particular book, the Bible, or that it is read, and above all that there exist men and women who not only read it but are struck by it, such that it becomes for them not just one more book, but in an odd way, *their* book. If others choose to take this book for granted, certainly no theologian can, for theology stands and falls with the fact that there is this book and that it is read in this way. The theologian cannot even begin to consider the question why it should be this book which is decisive for his work, why it should be this rather than some other book, for that would be to consider as a serious question of theology whether there ought to be theology at all. Others may regard Christian faith as an illusion and theology a waste of time, if not a fraud, but obviously neither the believer nor the theologian can take these as matters of serious concern. The starting point for theology is the fact that there is this book, for better or worse, that it is read by men and women who read it as in some sense their own story, and the theologian can not give a foundation to or a justification of this point of departure. He can analyse it, explore its implications and consequences, unfold its content, but the fact of this book read in this way is not one he can account for as a theologian.

If theologians and any who care to understand theology are unable to justify this fact which is the foundation of theology, they should also not take the fact for granted. It is difficult but not quite impossible to imagine the continuation of human life in some form in a world from which all traces of the Bible had been destroyed. It is less difficult to imagine a future condition of human life in which men might still have but no longer read the Bible, or read it and no longer be struck by it. It has happened in individual lives, and there is no reason in principle, no logical contradiction in the supposition, that this could conceivably be the case universally. If the existence of this book, and the existence for thousands of years of men and women who have read it as their own story, is what gives continuity to theology, yet this in no way leaves theology a less contingent activity. The continuity, wide distribution, and ready availability of the Bible can mislead us as to its character and as to the character of theology. But these qualifications of the apparent stability and continuity of theology, of the fact that it is the same book which has been read throughout the history of Christianity, are as nothing compared to the qualifications arising from the story itself which is told in that book.

In this connection it is important to recall that for at least the first century of its existence, the Bible, the book of sacred scripture of the Christian churches, was the Book of Israel, the Old Testament. Moreover, it took apparently another century before there was a consensus among Christians about which writings should be bound together with the Book of Israel to form our present Bible. Christianity, in short, has existed without the New Testament as we know it, but it has never existed without the Old Testament. I do not say this to devalue the New Testament, but simply to remind you that when I speak of the biblical story or of the character of that story, I have in mind a story unfolded in the whole Bible, not just that story of the Jew of Nazareth and his disciples, which would hardly be the story it has been for Christians if it were cut loose from its foundations and background, the larger story of Israel.

The character of the story presented by the Bible qualifies the continuity and stability of the fact that it is this same story which has always been the starting point for Christian faith and for theology. It does so because the story is itself one of discontinuity. It is a story largely about and exclusively by one people, of course, from beginning to end, although at both beginning and end it widens out in a universal way, and of and by a people who understood themselves to be led on in the hope of one promise, or one series of promises. But as the story developed, each attempt to realise the promise, each formulation of the hope, every concrete image of the fulfilment of the promise was in turn shattered, and only out of that shattering was the promise renewed and hope reawakened. Discontinuity and brokenness mark the whole history of the people who wrote this story. Convinced that their kingdom was the fulfilment of the promise which they believed was given to their fathers, they saw the kingdom divided and finally crushed. Sure of their security as a chosen people among all the nations, they suffered defeat and exile in order to learn a new meaning of their election. With political hopes crushed, they placed all their confidence in their Law, and the Law was in turn overturned by one who showed its fulfilment in love. And when this one was by at least some of them hailed as the messiah who was to restore Israel, he was killed by the Roman occupation forces. Such is the discontinuous story which has been continually read by Christians.

The most cursory reading of the history of Christianity will show that the Church has fared no better than Israel with this story. It too has tried to make the story more stable than the story will allow, and it too has had to suffer the same sort of breaking and discontinuity as a result of reading this story as its own. Like Israel, the Church has tried again and again to forget the discontinuity of its past and to fix the promise and above all the promiser, that illusive strange one named Jahweh, in formulas, conceptions and creeds. Even as the empire it had conquered was crumbling, it put its trust in a conception of Jahweh as the eternal, unchangeable and immovable God of

Augustinianism, and if it took time to break that image, because of its apparent unassailability, yet the evidence of the past
few centuries is that this too has had its day. Whatever else
can be said about that illusive figure of Jahweh in that story, he
is surely one who hands out no guarantees, and it seems to
have been the case that each guarantee which Israel or the
Church has tried to write for itself or for him has been torn to
shreds.

A second qualification to the continuity of what is read by
believers and therefore the continuity of theology arises from
the fact that the story has been always a story read with human
eyes and told with human words. That means that it has been a
continually changing story. What in modern biblical studies
seems so clear, the brokenness which characterises the story,
for example, has not always seemed so evident. Indeed, under
the long reign of Augustinianism, still not without its representatives, the brokenness was hardly seen at all. If the same pages
have been read for thousands of years, yet the fact remains that
the story read therein seems to have been read rather differently
in different times and places. Indeed, there have been times
in which it seems to us today to have been read not as a story at
all, but as a collection of propositional truths, eternal and unchanging. The continual reading of this one book, therefore,
has given theology a continuity of a most ambiguous sort.

I said that theology is an activity of men who have been
struck by this story. I mean by that that there are men who not
only read the story, but find that having read it, it sticks with
them, if I may put it so. They find the story to be their own
story, the story of their own past. How this can be so for the
Jew is evident, or at least more evident than it is for the Christian. For the Christian, the story can be read as his own history
or past only by seeing himself claimed by the story, adopted, as
it were, as a son of Abraham. As an adopted son he is aware
of his natural condition, but he finds himself unable to shake
off this further determination or qualification of himself, that
this is also his story, that he is heir to this promise with all its
attendant threat of discontinuity and insecurity. No one has
to take up this burden, but if he calls himself a Christian and if
he engages in the task of theology, he will find that not by

choice, nor by preference, but as an inescapable part of his experience of the world, he has been so struck by this story that he cannot easily get himself free of it.

I have described theology as an activity of men struck by this story, rather than as an activity of the Church, which would be a more traditional description. I have done so because of certain changes which have come about in our use of the word 'church', which make that older description somewhat misleading today. In our ordinary usage the word has become so tied to buildings and institutional structures, so static, so clearly marking off a 'we' from a 'they', that it seems almost necessary, in order to see what theology is, to substitute a phrase, such as 'men struck by the biblical story'. The substitution is made all the more necessary by factors in our present circumstances which are also to be taken into account in doing theology today. I want to turn to our present circumstances, not just for this reason, but especially to make clear what I have in mind in speaking of men as struck by the biblical story, and more particularly, how it goes with such men's understanding of things. When this is clearer, we shall be in a better position to see why it is that such men, or some among them, do theology.

In the sense in which it is true that our knowledge is founded on experience, in the sense in which we believe that we are able to learn from experience, our knowledge or understanding may be said to be pluralistic or multiform in so far as our experience is pluralistic or multiform. The plurality of our experience produces a plurality of ways of understanding. We inhabit our world in a variety of ways, and we understand our world in as many ways. This is the point which Wittgenstein made so much clearer by speaking of the multiplicity of 'language-games' which we play, but which William James had made, if less sharply, just as strongly in making his case for what he called 'radical empiricism' and 'a pluralistic universe', some sixty years ago. What I wish to underscore in this idea is that neither James nor Wittgenstein presented us with the picture of each of us off in our own little corner playing our own little game; rather both have drawn our attention to the ways in which we speak and live as evidence that we are each of us engaged in a multiplicity of language-games. We have learned, or most of us have, to read newspapers as well as novels. We have some idea of the difference between a historical and a mathematical argument. We are involved in politics and economic affairs in varying ways, and in families of various sorts. We have one or another profession, job or occupation. We can shop for food, clothing and books. We can enjoy various hobbies and sports, have friends, acquaintances and enemies, and subscribe to certain ideals and loyalties; and on the whole, we rather seldom get mixed up about what we are doing. One person can and usually is involved at various times of the day and year with a good many of these various activities or patterns of life. If he knows, let us say, the jargon of his profession or trade, he also knows the jargon of his political and economic associations, and of his family, and of his other activities. And it is the same person who does all this, one man who speaks, let us say, English, and therefore is a member of a social community and part of a culture.

Now surely it is no surprise to find that the man who has been struck by the biblical story is not in such different circumstances from those of his contemporaries. He has been brought up in a not so dissimilar home, learned to play the games of his contemporaries, learned with them in school the difference between history, literature, mathematics and physics. He too has to earn a living, pay taxes, and stand in some sort of relationship to a wide variety of elements of our pluralistic culture. His circumstances are to a very large extent the circumstances of us all.

We could say this in other words by saying that we are all of us men, and that we are as men qualified in a wide variety of ways. Some of us are qualified as having had a university education, and further qualified as having studied the humanities. We are all qualified by nationality, occupation, income, and age. We are qualified by aesthetic interests, such as they may be, by special talents, by the literature which we prefer to read. And now, within these circumstances, and without forgetting them, I want to add that some men are also qualified as Christians. I shall in what follows use this somewhat cumbersome phrase, 'man qualified as Christian', in order to help us remember those other qualifications, the circumstances which we all too easily forget when we use the shorter term, 'Christian'.

The point can be made in a way more conformed to the terminology of the theological tradition, by saying that the Christian is first of all a man; in the course of time, theology has developed a doctrine of man, and insofar as it has developed a doctrine of the Christian, it has been a doctrine of what men may be and therefore do in relation to other men. 'Man qualified as Christian' is a way of referring to certain factors in the experience of some men, certain characteristics of their understanding, but man qualified as Christian does not cease to be a man. As a man, he is, at least in our culture and in our time, surely qualified in many other ways, and his experience and therewith his understanding is as multiform as that of any of his contemporaries. He faces the same problem as others of sorting out and arranging the variety of ways in which he is in this world, but he has the particular problem of how he is to sort out and relate to all his other understandings of himself and the world, his understandings arising under his qualification as Christian. He is as liable as his contemporaries to have read at least some of Marx and Darwin and Freud, of natural science and social science and technology. All these in various ways tell him who he is and how he is in his world. He has, however, also read and been influenced by the Bible and by other men who have read and been influenced by the Bible, and these too in their own way tell him who he is and how he is in the world. How he is going to fit these together, how he is to live his qualification as Christian in relation to all the other understandings which he has, this is the problem to which theologians today address themselves.

Theology has been assumed to provide help to men struck by the biblical story and qualified in many other ways as well. In what sense or in what way does it provide help? I shall begin with a general answer, and then pursue it and define it more carefully: theology aims to help men qualified as Christians in how they talk. The theologian considers those to whom he addresses himself as, in a certain sense, linguistic beings. Theology itself is not only a linguistic enterprise in the sense of being something which is done with words; it is linguistic in

that it is written by and for men who have heard and retell as
their own the biblical story. The somewhat ambiguous image
of man which informs Christian theology and faith is man as he
appears in that story, and how men hear and how they respond
is presented again and again in that story as the decisive matter
in human life. The men of that story lived not so much by
inner or mystical experiences as they did by words, and consequently it is the story of a society, a nation, a people. One did
not have to have religious experiences to be part of that society,
but one did have to belong to a community which told a story
of its past and looked forward to a future. Words are so important in that story because of what men did to and with each
other with their words, for the story never isolates language
from the social and political life of those men. They made and
broke contract or covenant with words, they gave thanks or
boasted with words. They came to the aid of some and to the
hurt of others with words, and above all, they both hoped and
remembered with words.

That story shows that men do other things than speak, but
it has no interest in isolating these other things men do from
the fact that they live as they do, relate themselves to each other
as they do, in that form of life which men live because they
are creatures who listen and speak. Again, the story sees that
we are related to our words in a variety of ways. Our commitment to what we say is no trifling matter but is itself one
of the important aspects of what we do when we use words. To
speak with deceit, to speak without care, to speak with conviction, these are distinctions which the men of that story were
well aware of. In this view of man as a linguistic creature, it
makes sense to ask whether a man will be as good as his word.

We may say in sum that the biblical story presents an image
of man in which a privileged status is given to man's linguistic
behaviour only because it is realised how deeply words are the
stuff of our actual human living. This interest in how men use
words is, in other words, pragmatic: words matter in that
story because of what happens when men speak. Talk can, of
course, be just talk, nothing serious. It becomes serious on the
basis of what men do with words, how what men say goes into
the way in which they then move ahead with the business of

human life. Language is important in the biblical story, and therefore to Christianity and to theology, because it is seen as the point of entry into the whole life of man. When you see what a man does with words, you have the clearest picture you are liable to get of how it goes with his life.

These preliminary considerations suggest how it is that some theologians today have come to find the linguistic investigations of some philosophers helpful. Those investigations of language which are aware that it is not finally words which mean something, but that people mean something with their words, that language is not to be understood apart from its use by human beings, and that this use is as broad and as complex as human life into which it is woven; such investigations can help the theologian to see and think more clearly. But of course what we are to say, how we are to use language, what story we tell and whether we tell it as our own, and so how we are to walk ahead in life, such fundamental matters for theology do not receive much direction from investigations into the workings of our language. I want, therefore, to pursue more closely the sort of talk of men struck by the biblical story which is of concern to theology.

Of the many ways in which men qualified as Christian, and as many other things as well, speak, I have singled out as fundamental for theology how they say things are with their present circumstances. Let me expand this to avoid misunderstanding. I should like to avoid the picture of someone simply giving a so-called objective description of the evidence before him. That picture is much too static for what I have in mind. That is of course one of the ways in which any of us may say how things are, one of the many different sorts of conditions under which we should say something to the effect that things are this way and not that. What I have in mind, however, is the sort of case in which we are speaking of what is the case with our present circumstances, where how we say things are is part of how we then proceed to move ahead in these circumstances.

Let us take a simple case to start with: that of a man crossing a dark room at night. If someone has told him to watch out for the chairs in the room, and he doesn't and has a nasty fall over one of them, he will learn by experience, we may hope, to heed his adviser in the future. He was told to watch out for the chairs because there just are chairs in that room, and he comes to accept this view of the room because of the sort of leading in life which such ways of talking produce. Chairs are facts, and facts, as William James liked to say, are what we carve our experienced world up into. We have found it pays to talk of chairs as facts and of watching out for them, that this way of speaking of how things are has considerable pragmatic value, or is, in other words, true.

Until fairly recent times, people used to think that you should watch out for demons, angels, gods, and other mysteriously illusive entities, which could have decisive effects upon how men made their way through life. More recently we have, on the whole, chosen to abandon this way of speaking because in matters of health, for example, we find that medical science provides more satisfactory leading. Cutting the world up into devils and gods does not seem to have provided an adequate way for most of us to deal with, to see, and so to speak of our experienced world.

In that older world in which men watched out for gods and demons, Christian faith led men, at best, to be just a little sceptical of that way of saying how things are. At its best, it resisted the temptation to call Yahweh one of the gods you should watch out for, although it failed rather badly in preventing this idea from remaining with the pagan majority which it baptised. In a world in which gods are not taken so seriously as tables and chairs, Christians have to remember that this world may be spoken of in just as closed a way as the world of gods and demons, and that the story by which they have been struck allows them to help free their neighbours and themselves from the tyranny of tables and chairs. I do not see, however, that Christian faith calls for men to take sides in this cultural shift from the monistic, idealistic world of a past age to the pragmatic, pluralistic age we live in now. If Christians had anything to contribute to others in that past age, they have the same contribution to make now, and it has nothing to do with the choice of circumstances in which our culture finds itself. It has to do with what we make of this culture, how, in speaking of what is the case, including tables and chairs, we are to move ahead in our present circumstances. Moreover, Christians should be the last to protest the pragmatic concern with leading, with making our way through life as we seem to do, for surely the biblical story which Christians have gone on telling has had a good deal to do with nurturing this pragmatic concern. It has kept alive such sayings as that about the fruit being the criteria of a good tree, the importance of a cup of cold water, about taking pragmatic measures to alleviate human suffering and support human life. It has even talked about a welfare state in which peace and justice would be as empirically evident as war and injustice are today. That is not all there is in the story, but it cannot be denied that all that is part of the story. Christian faith and theology have, for better or worse, a considerable investment in pragmatic concerns and judgements.

What the world is like, how things really are, is to a large extent a matter of how we cut up our experienced world into its parts, and the leadings by which we test such cuttings depends in turn on what we want to do. If health is our concern, we come to rely on medical doctors rather than on witch doctors. If crossing a dark room is our goal, we find it useful to talk of tables and chairs. You can, if you wish, argue that that pretty well covers it, that what is not a matter of logic or mathematics is either about such things as chairs and blood circulation, or else is so much nonsense and best committed to the flames. But is the Christian's response to this to say that faith and theology are non-cognitive? Such a choice can be forced upon us only on the assumption that understanding and saying how things are, are of one sort only. But just this assumption is what I wanted to question when I suggested that what was primary in saying how things are is the matter of how we cut up our experienced world, the whole range of our experience, and that we do this in many different ways. Carving up the world into tables and chairs, or into electrons and subatomic particles, or into economic factors, or into political parties, are just a few of the ways in which we determine for ourselves what we are going to call the facts of the case. The choice of carvings is a matter of our purposes, what sort of leadings we choose to follow, and these leadings are as diverse as human life.

For this reason, I find that the distinction 'cognitive/non-cognitive' is not helpful in getting clear about how Christian faith is a matter of how the world is, and I regret having once been seduced into picking up that stone axe as an appropriate tool for opening up this delicate bit of watch-works. The issue is not, as that distinction leads us to suspect, that we have an agreed frame of reference, an agreed way of carving up the world into tables and chairs on the one hand, and our attitudes or dispositions towards tables and chairs on the other, and that faith must lie on one side or the other. Christian faith, on the contrary, proposes another way to do the carving up in the first place. And in so far as how we carve up the universe of our experienced world sets the terms for further speaking and understanding, how we do that carving is fundamental for cognition. Only we do this in more than one way, and in each way in which we do it, we are embarked on a cognitive enterprise, in which questions of truth and questions of matter of fact are very much in order.

Given the variety of ways in which we say how things are and thereby embark on cognitive enterprises, given this variety of ways in which we understand the world for different purposes, it remains to clarify of what sort is the contemporary believer's way of doing this. Professor John Wisdom has argued that religious belief is a matter of truth and a matter of fact in something of the way that determining a case of negligence before the law is a matter of truth and of fact, a matter to be argued after all the evidence is in, still to be settled after all the particular facts of the case have been agreed upon;[1] but surely this is not quite right. If in such a case before the law we have really reached the point at which no further evidence is to be admitted, then the question is how we can fit this case to previously determined cases. What is true or false is whether this case is enough like some recorded case to warrant the same judgement. The arguments of prosecution and defence consist, it is argued, in so putting the facts together that the picture comes out to look like or unlike certain other pictures. Justice, in such a matter, is the product of being as careful as possible about such comparisons, and the determination of

---

[1] *Paradox and Discovery* (London, 1966), pp. 54 ff.

justice in such a case does not take us beyond the careful comparison of cases. But the way in which religious faith is a matter of what is so, is more like the way in which the determination of rules of evidence settles what we are going to count as evidence in a case, and that is not how Wisdom used the example of a court getting at the truth of a matter. In an unfortunately misleading way, a figure out of the distant past is permitted to stand up in Wisdom's trial and say that in his Father's house are many mansions, which sounds very much as if a new piece of evidence were being offered, an additional fact which had not been previously noted. If that is not to wreak havoc with an argument designed to show how there can still be questions of truth after all the facts have been settled, it is necessary to say in what other way that bit of testimony is to be taken. Professor Wisdom once wrote that 'the existence of God is not an experimental issue in the way it was'.[1] We may add to that that faith is not a matter of what is in fact the case in the world in the way in which it was. And yet for all that, I would agree with Wisdom that it is in some way a matter of what is the case, and it is the theologian's business to say what that way is, and to do so without forgetting other ways in which we say this.

Since man is qualified in many ways, since his experience of the world is multiform, there are many ways in which he wants to say what is in fact so in the world. Because of this, there is the possibility of incoherence in what he says and thinks, not only within any one way in which he speaks, but especially between various ways of speaking. In so far as a man is qualified as Christian today, he finds that many of the older, traditional religious ways of saying how things are run into difficulties because of the fact that he agrees with his contemporaries in the pragmatic validity of carving up the world in so many more ways than did his ancestors in the faith. Perhaps the vast majority of Christians today, and for the same pragmatic reasons their neighbours would give, are inclined to follow the leadings which the natural sciences give in their picture of the universe. The origin of the earth, its development and estimates of its longevity, the origin of life and its development to

[1] *Philosophy and Psychoanalysis* (London, 1952), p. 149.

the stage at which we find ourselves, questions about life of some sort existing elsewhere in the universe, these are all matters in which we find that the scientific method is our most useful guide. Many or perhaps most Christians today fail to see that their religion does or ought to throw any light on such matters, except to save them from the conclusion that that is all there is to say about human life.

Within the experienced world of human life, however, in the realm of personal action, attitudes and relationships, we also have to settle what the facts are, how things are really. From matters of war and peace, through matters of social, political and economic justice, and questions of the preservation of human life and euthanasia, to issues of friendship, personal trust and love, we are driven back again and again to the picture or image of man which we are using. What is it to be a man? Or, as it used to be put, what is human nature? Men qualified as Christian today are aware that much can be said to this question by both natural and social sciences that is pragmatically important, which for some purposes provides a helpful leading. In addition, however, sometimes in competition with, at other times complementary to one or another political or social vision of man and human life, there is that way of saying what is the case in human life which is characteristic of Christian faith. A man is qualified as Christian just in so far as he also has within the range of his whole experience of the world the experience of reading and being struck by the Christian story, in its primary biblical form, or in its many derivative forms, and the further experience of knowing and being struck by other men whose view of human life is also informed by this same story. Such a man will say that men are made for each other, that it is not enough to make our way through rooms of tables and chairs, but that we are responsible to one another for how we keep that room, and for the course of others as they try to cross it with us. If we depart from this sort of corporate faithfulness to each other, if we settle for some other idea of justice and mercy and love, then we are being less than human. If you ask him why he says such things, you will usually discover that he has derived this picture of human life in important respects from the biblical images of life in a covenant, as this is brought into focus in the story of the utterly faithful Jew of Nazareth. If you persist with your questions, asking why this picture and this story are to be taken so seriously, or why this story rather than another, he will finally say, because that is how things are. Because, you may ask, because it is true? And the answer will probably be, yes, it is true in the way in which such matters are true, pragmatically true, true because they give a leading in life which those who follow find, in an odd sort of way, to be right. Some such pragmatic considerations appear in a famous remark of Reinhold Niebuhr's, that man is good enough to make constitutional democracy work, and sinful enough to make it necessary. The biblical image of man, according to the Christian, gives a reliable leading. This conviction may be judged to rest on circular reasoning, for that image and story provide their own measure of what sort of leading is satisfactory. I think that judgement is correct, but I do not see how any alternative conviction in this matter can escape the same circularity. In any case, that does not prevent this from being a matter of what is the case, a matter of truth or falsehood. A small piece of its verification would be the fact that we take solitary confinement to be a severe form of punishment.

Christian faith, then, is of little help in many ways in which we carve up our experienced world. It does not bear directly on many ways in which we say what is so in the universe. Its adherents today have grounds in Christian faith to share the pragmatic concern of their contemporaries for many of these other ways of speaking and thinking. But our pragmatic society is not at all of one mind about what is to constitute satisfaction in human life. We are not as a civilisation at all settled about what we mean by the good life and the good society, for we are not of a mind on what it is to be a full human being. Wherever others may turn for their image or ideal or picture of what is the truth about man, men qualified as Christian look to an ancient story of what they take to be the way, the truth and the life for human beings, and from time to time gain from that story the courage and freedom to encourage others to face an uncertain future without fear. And if you ask them, why this one, why not another, they can say no more and no less than that this is how things are.

I hope that my opening definition is now somewhat clearer: theology is that activity of men struck by the biblical story, in which they undertake to revise continually the ways in which they say how things are with their present circumstances in the light of how they read that story. It centres in how things go with men, with the human condition, in what it is to become a man among men in our sort of world. It bears only indirectly on other ways in which we say how things are, in the sense that it protests now, as it has in other ages, whenever men say how things are in such a way that the picture is closed, the future settled, the factor of risk and uncertainty removed. In such cases, the story reminds the theologian of how often men have said such things and of how their assurance has been broken by events. In this way, doing theology is putting one's shoulder to the door of the future, to keep it open for the sake of men, in the conviction that that ancient story is not yet finished, that the last word, promised in that story, has yet to be said.

A final word about the matter of coherence: differences between so-called scientific, historical and political ways of saying how things are can result in tensions in our understanding. Those ways of speaking of man and human activity which take inorganic or even non-human organic models as normative will create even greater tension with ways of speaking of man which take persons as their point of departure. We find we can live with these tensions most of the time because we have what we regard as sound pragmatic grounds for using each of them. If the matter at hand is a tumour in the body, or a defective sewage system, or the development of new forms of providing electric power, impersonal models are quite adequate for diagnostic purposes and are still of great importance in solving the problem. In the development of a marriage, the raising of young children, and in much of our social legislation and policies, personal models seem to many to be more satisfactory. When we are driven back to our root understanding of what it is to be a human being, when it comes to what we mean by love, justice, and mercy, the Christian story has something to say to those who are struck by it. The conceptions of human life and community, and the quality of love, justice and mercy, which are centred in that story around the awesome, mythical figure of the desert God of the Hebrew prophets, can and often do stand in considerable tension with other images of man and society, of love and righteousness, which are portrayed in newspapers, courts of justice, governmental action and personal policy in our society. If theology seeks coherence in the contemporary understanding of Christians, it knows that coherence is not necessarily without friction and tension. In this sense, the man qualified as Christian, and the theology which takes his circumstances seriously, will know a certain tension, a tension between saying how things are in the world in many other ways, and saying what is the case as this is informed by the biblical story. This tension can of course always be called incoherence, but it can also be seen as the ground of hope and the occasion for sacrifice.

5

SUICIDE

R. F. Holland

I AM concerned with the subject as an ethico-religious problem. Is suicide all right or isn't it; and if it isn't, why not?

The question should not be assumed to be susceptible of an answer in the way the question whether arsenic is poisonous is susceptible of an answer (which would be *the* answer to the question). Moreover in the case of arsenic the question what it is, and the question whether it is poisonous, are separable questions: you can know that arsenic is poisonous without having analysed its nature. But to know or believe that suicide is objectionable *is* to have analysed its nature or construed its significance in one way rather than another. So let us not ask at the outset whether suicide is objectionable as though we already knew perfectly well what it was (which we don't), but let us rather approach the problem by asking what it might *mean* to commit suicide – or simply, What *is* suicide? I do not think it is just one thing and I do not expect to get very far with the question.

Durkheim, whose book on suicide is one of the classics of sociology, seems to me not to have understood what suicide is. He believed that in order to avoid being prejudiced the enquirer into human behaviour should never go by what people think ('the confused impressions of the crowd') but should make comparisons and look for the common properties of actions as a botanist or zoologist distinguishes objective common properties among flowers and fruits, fish and insects.[1] Durkheim

[1] *Suicide* (trans. Spaulding and Simpson) (London, 1952), pp. 41–2.

thought it a condition of the possibility of investigation that systems of human behaviour should be capable of being identified and classified as one thing or another quite independently of any reference to the agents' ideas. And since intentions involve ideas, he declined to allow that the question whether a man was a suicide could be settled in the negative by the discovery that he did not intend to take his life:

> . . . if the intention of self-destruction alone constituted suicide, the name suicide could not be given to facts which, despite apparent differences, are fundamentally identical with those always called suicide and which could not be otherwise described without discarding the term. The soldier facing certain death to save his regiment does not wish to die, and yet is he not as much the author of his death as the manufacturer or merchant who kills himself to avoid bankruptcy? This holds true for the martyr dying for his faith, the mother sacrificing herself for her child, etc. Whether death is accepted merely as an unfortunate consequence, but inevitable given the purpose, or is actually itself sought and desired, in either case the person renounces existence, and the various methods of doing so can be only varieties of a single class.[1]

On this account of the matter it looks as if we have to say that a man who exposes himself to mortal danger, for whatever reason and whatever the circumstances, is exposing himself to suicide. Well, why not? Isn't it enough that the man should know what he is doing?

> The common quality of all these possible forms of supreme renunciation is that the determining act is performed advisedly; that at the moment of acting the victim knows the certain result of his conduct, no matter what reason may have led him to act thus. . . . We may say then conclusively: the term *suicide is applied to all cases of death resulting directly or indirectly from a positive or negative act of the victim himself which he knows will produce this result.*[2]

Durkheim here ignores the problem of how the investigator,

[1] Ibid., p. 43. [2] Ibid., p. 44.

especially one who is supposed to be collecting data in the spirit of a botanist, can judge whether or not a man knows what he is doing. And in trying to make the applicability of the term 'suicide' to martyrdom turn upon this, he simply begs the question of *what* it is that the martyr is doing; for of this we are only entitled to say thus far that he goes to his death.

Though the martyr may go willingly to a death which he foresees, it is a death which has been decided upon for him first by someone else. Whether he now makes things easy or difficult for the decider is hardly to the point. He might accept the decision as justice and so in a way concur with it, assisting its implementation out of duty, as Socrates did. Socrates took the cup of hemlock and drank it, and thereby might be said strictly to have died by his own hand. Yet even this cannot make a man a suicide, given the fact that his death was not decreed by him. In the case of the mother who dies while rescuing her child from a blazing building, the death is not decided upon at all, inevitable though her action might cause it to be. Similarly with the soldier facing certain death to save his regiment, of whom Durkheim remarks that he does not wish to die. He would not necessarily be a suicide even if he did wish to die – to die well or just to die. For to wish that death might come, to hope that it will soon come, is still not to decree that one shall die. Socrates had a wish for death and thought it his business as a philosopher to 'practise dying';[1] but not to practise suicide, which he said should be committed by no one.[2]

However I can imagine an objector insisting that there is a logical entailment which I have not got round between 'Socrates knowingly and deliberately drank the poison' and 'Socrates killed himself, i.e. was a suicide'. One way of meeting this objection would be to accept the entailment and invoke the idea that in killing himself a man may be at the same time doing something else. Thus in killing himself by taking hemlock Socrates was also doing something else which belonged to the role of a state prisoner and formed part of the procedure for judicial execution in Athens. And the additional factor makes (so it might be said) a radical difference to the ethico-religious status of the self-slaughter. But although this has an illuminating

---

[1] *Phaedo*, 64A.   [2] *Phaedo*, 62A.

sound the illumination is spurious because the alleged entailment between Socrates' taking of the hemlock and his committing suicide is non-existent. Taking hemlock does not, in the context of an Athenian judicial execution, amount to slaughtering oneself: in this circumstance it is no more an act of suicide than the condemned man's walk to the scaffold in our society.

If the suggestion be that Socrates was a man bent on self-destruction to whom the advent of his execution came in handy, then that is a different matter. But I should think the innuendo impossible to account for save as a misinterpretation of the fact that Socrates did in a certain sense wish to die. Hence he was able to take the poison gladly as the fulfilment of his wish. However, anyone construing that wish as a pointer towards suicide would be taking it for something other than it was through failing to relate it to its surrounds.

Though he did not go in for theology, Socrates thought it well said that mortals are the chattels of the Gods.[1] 'Wouldn't you be angry', he went on, 'if one of your chattels should kill itself when you had not indicated that you wanted it to die?' Socrates, then, did not wish to die before it was time for him to die. He did not wish to run away from anything. And it certainly cannot be said of him that he wished to die because he found no sense in living. On the contrary the sense he found in living was what on the one hand made him reject suicide and on the other hand enabled him to look on death, whenever it should come, as something to be welcomed rather than feared; hence it enabled him to die courageously. To put this another way, the sense he made of death and the sense he made of life were one and the same. A man who decides to commit suicide because he sees no sense in living cannot from this point of view be said to contemplate anything sensible in regard to his situation, for his death must be just as senseless to him as his life.

In contrast with the kind of objection that Socrates had against suicide, some of the objections to be heard against it are only of an external or accidental nature. For instance one reason, and it is a moral reason, which a man contemplating suicide might give for refraining is the fact that he has a wife

[1] *Phaedo*, 62B.

and children who depend on him. However this consideration would be no more a reason against suicide than it would be a reason against his walking out on them and declining to return, so we do not learn from this example whether or not the suicide itself is especially objectionable. It would be likewise with the case of an army officer who cannot pay his gambling debts, so he wants to commit suicide, for which there are precedents anyway; but then he reflects that this would be a reprehensible thing to do because if he kills himself there will be no chance of the debts ever being repaid, whereas his duty is to try to work them off. The objection would be much the same if he were inclined to go off to live in Rhodesia under an assumed name.

I once read of an officer with gambling debts who confusedly thought he had a moral reason, not against, but in favour of shooting himself. The note he left behind contained a remark to the effect that he was choosing death rather than dishonour (at the time of writing he had not yet been found out). Now that great maxim of the military ethic, 'death rather than dishonour', is exemplified by the conduct of the sentry who declines to leave his post when he could run away to safety but stays and carries out his duty although the consequence of doing so is death. Here the death and the dishonour are genuine alternatives – if he escapes the first he incurs the second, and if he embraces the first he avoids the second. But the case of the gambling officer is not like that at all. So far from being an alternative to the disgrace incurred by his inability to pay the debts, his death by suicide is rather a consequence of that disgrace. What he ends up with is both the death and the dishonour. There might or might not have been a way out of the dishonour had he stayed alive, but at least it is clear that killing himself is no way out of it. As Socrates observes in the *Phaedo*, death is not an escape from everything: if it were, it would indeed be a boon to the wicked.[1]

There are situations, though the gambling officer's is not one of them and neither is the sentry's, in which the only way of choosing death rather than dishonour would be to kill oneself – for instance if it is dishonourable to be taken captive

[1] *Phaedo*, 107C.

and the only way of avoiding capture is to kill oneself. In just this situation Greek heroes fell upon their swords. However in regard to dishonour there is a distinction to be drawn between doing and suffering. The captured hero suffers dishonour in being treated as a slave: he does not in his loss of freedom *do* anything dishonourable. He would therefore have been exhorted by Socrates not to commit suicide but to accept what comes, for Socrates believed that harm befell a man through his doing evil rather than through his suffering it.[1]

The choice before the hero on the eve of his capture is, one might say, between suicide and *indignity*. Opting for the former he chooses both nobly and rationally according to a thoroughly serious conception. For a man who is truly a hero cannot consent to live otherwise than as a hero; and above all the servile life is not open to him. Now if a Christian were to make that choice. . . . But then you see for a Christian it could not possibly be *that* choice. The status of the alternatives would not be the same although the Christian also might be described as choosing between suicide and indignity. However, in his case opting for the indignity would not be ignoble, while opting for the suicide would amount to consigning himself to damnation.

Let us now try to explore the idea of a choice between suicide and dishonour not in the sense of suffering but of doing something terrible. Compare the Greek hero with a modern spy who on his impending capture kills himself by swallowing a pill which has been supplied for use in this emergency. I am supposing that he swallows the pill not because of the possible consequences of the capture for himself but because he knows that under torture he will inevitably betray the secrets of his comrades and his country. Though I cannot imagine Socrates saying to a man in this predicament that he must not commit suicide, there is something he might have said to him earlier, namely that anyone who is concerned about his soul should beware of engaging in this sort of spying. For it is to enter into an institution the ethics of which require that in a certain eventuality you poison yourself; and the poisoning is not transformed into something other than suicide by the institutional role as it was in Socrates' own case by the role of being a

[1] *Gorgias*, 469B.

condemned man in process of execution. Still, the fact that the spy's suicide is committed as an act of self-sacrifice gives it a very different flavour from the deed of the financier who does away with himself when his empire starts to totter. The financier 'can't take it'. This is also true, though on a much deeper level, of the Greek hero, who unlike the financier dies nobly. The hero commits suicide because there is something he cannot accept for himself, namely captivity. But the spy (in this particular variant out of many possible cases) is concerned solely with the good of others. Because of this one would like to deny that his is the spirit of a suicide. The difficulty is that he has supposedly entered the spying profession, which is a suicidal game, with his eyes open: he was not compelled to enter into it. But this consideration also means that his case fails to provide me with exactly the example I was looking for: I wanted an example of a completely forced choice between suicide and the doing of something morally terrible.

It might be held by a religious person that no man is ever forced to make such a choice; that it is something a good God would never inflict on a human being. But whether or not it be religiously imaginable, it is logically possible and I can depict a case where there will be no question of the agent's having voluntarily let himself in for the outcome by postulating that he suffers and knows that he suffers from a congenital form of mental instability, as a result of which he is overtaken from time to time by irresistible impulses towards something very horrible, such as raping children. Getting himself locked up is no solution, either because no one will listen to him or because no mental hospital is secure enough to contain him during one of his fits; and his fits come upon him without warning. So he decides to kill himself.

At first it may seem possible to argue that this man is not a suicide. For does he not belong to the category of those who are called upon to sacrifice their lives for the safety of others? Most often in such cases the order of events is: salvation of the imperilled followed by death of the saver, as in shipwrecks, when the men who have made possible the escape of others are trapped on board; or else the two events are concomitant, as at a grenade-throwing practice when one of the grenades is dropped and there is no time to throw it clear, whereupon an N.C.O. falls on the grenade and with his body shields the others from its effects. Either way, what the saver here decrees is another's salvation, with the unavoidable consequence of a death for himself which he does not decree. If, as with my imaginary maniac, the saver's own death has to take place first in order that the peril to others should be averted, the characterisation of what is decreed can remain exactly the same as before. To put it another way, all the man really does is to preserve someone else and his death is encompassed as a consequence of this. The peculiarity of the case is that the death has to be encompassed first and is thus an instance of an effect preceding its cause.

But now I fear that the argument has overreached itself; not in positing an effect that precedes its cause, which I should accept here as a coherent conception, but in gliding over the fact that the man's death is not encompassed *for* him – he encompasses it directly himself. This is manifestly a doing and not a suffering; hence it was false to claim that 'all he really does is to preserve someone else'. That is not all, for he kills himself.

A comparable example, not this time from the imagination, is that of the explorer, Captain Oates. On the day before his death Oates had said that he could not go on and had proposed that the rest of the party should leave him in his sleeping bag. 'That we could not do' says Scott, whose account of the upshot is as follows:

> He slept through the night before last, hoping not to wake; but he woke in the morning – yesterday. It was blowing a blizzard. He said, 'I am just going outside and may be some time.' He went out into the blizzard and we have not seen him since. . . . We knew that poor Oates was walking to his death, but although we tried to dissuade him, we knew it was the act of a brave man and an English gentleman.[1]

What Oates decreed was that his hard-pressed companions should be relieved of an encumbrance: of this there can be little doubt. He had borne intense suffering for weeks without complaint (Scott tells us) but remained cheerful right to the

[1] *Scott's Last Expedition* (London, 1935), vol. i, p. 462.

end. The sentiment that he was entitled to quit, or that anyway he was going to quit, never entered into it. Accordingly I want to deny he was a suicide, as I should have liked to do in the case of the maniac. And there is a feature of Oates's case that enables me to persist in my denial beyond the point to which I could take it in the other case. For if someone objects, 'But he killed himself', in regard to the maniac there was no answer, but in Oates's case I can say, 'No; the blizzard killed him.' Had Oates taken out a revolver and shot himself I should have agreed he was a suicide.

We are back again at the distinction between doing and suffering, which here as elsewhere is fraught with difficulty. For if a man puts his head on a railway line and claims 'I'm not going to kill myself, the train will do it', I shall reject that as a sophistical absurdity; yet I do not consider it absurd to claim that the blizzard killed Oates. But then of course neither is it absurd to claim that he killed himself by going out into the blizzard. And there is much to be said for a description that is midway between the two: 'He let the blizzard kill him.' To call one of these descriptions the right one is to say little more than 'That's how I look at it.'

Still I do not look at it arbitrarily when I say that Oates was killed by the blizzard. The indirectness of what he did in relation to the onset of his death and the entrance of time as a factor are features of the case which help to put it for me in this perspective. Yet do not time and a certain indirectness enter in as factors when a man puts his head on a railway line? They enter in, but not to the same effect because of the difference in the spirit and in the surroundings of what is done. That the blizzard is a natural phenomenon is something that makes a difference. To be sure, a man who out of sorrow drowns himself might also perhaps be said to expose himself to a natural phenomenon, but again the context and the spirit of it are different. Oates simply walks away from his companions – and in the act of doing so becomes exposed to the blizzard: he needs to put distance between himself and them and he cannot do so in any other way. He is concerned only with their relief. And he is well on the way towards death already. Such are the features of the case which in combination make it possible, though not obligatory, to say of him unsophistically what would naturally be said of a martyr, namely that he goes to his death.

The great divide among attitudes towards suicide lies between those in whose eyes this possibility is of special significance and those to whom it would not matter whether a man like Oates were held to be no suicide, or a suicide but an honourable one. The former are upholders of a religious ethics and I should call them that even though they might entertain no theological beliefs and never even mention a deity: the latter I should call humanists.

I am not suggesting that from the standpoint of an ethics untinged with religion it would have been exactly the same if Oates had shot himself. For it would have been ugly, unpleasant and messy, and hence a course to be rejected out of fastidiousness or consideration for the feelings of his companions. From the religiously ethical standpoint, however, the rejection of that course would be bound up with ideas of a different kind, about a man's relation to his life and destiny, or in other words about the soul.

Schopenhauer remarked that if there are any moral arguments against suicide they lie very deep and are not touched by ordinary ethics.[1] An ordinary ethics is for instance one in which the idea of prudence looms large, as it did for Aristotle, or which speaks, as Kant did, about the duty of self-preservation. Schopenhauer saw something vulgar in the idea of duties to oneself no matter what were deemed to be their foundation. But Kant spoke in a different vein when he called suicide the extreme point along the line of *crimina carnis* and when he drew attention to the element of disdain for the world in Stoicism ('leave the world as you might leave a smoky room').[2] Both of these latter considerations of Kant connect with the point which Schopenhauer took to be central about suicide, namely that it is a phenomenon of strong assertion of will.[3] The real reason why suicide must be condemned, Schopenhauer said, had to do with self-conquest. In this idea he was at one with Socrates and not far distant from the Christian religion. A Christian perhaps

[1] *Foundation of Morals.*
[2] *Lectures on Ethics: Suicide.*   [3] *World as Will and Idea,* § 69.

might speak, not so much of conquering, but rather of dying to the self, and the most spiritual expression of the idea for him would be in prayer – particularly in such a prayer as 'Thy will, not mine, be done'.

The sanctity of life is an idea that a religious person might want to introduce in connection with suicide, but if he left the matter there he would be representing suicide as objectionable in the same way and to the same degree as murder. It is only when he thinks of life as a gift that the difference starts to emerge. For the murderer does not destroy a gift that was given *to him*; he destroys something which was given to someone else but which happens to have got in his way. This argues his crime to be from the standpoint of ordinary ethics worse than that of the suicide, of whom at least it may be said that it was his own affair. On the other hand the suicide, unlike the murderer, is – religiously speaking – necessarily an ingrate; and the ingratitude here is of no ordinary kind, for it is towards his Creator, the giver of life, to whom everything is owed. That the destruction of a life should at the same time be the act of extreme ingratitude towards the giver of a life accounts for the special horror attaching to parricide, against which there is something like the same religious feeling as there is against suicide: as if these were two different ways of getting as close as possible to deicide. Or perhaps rather it is parricide which symbolises the destruction of God and suicide the destruction of the universe. Thus G. K. Chesterton: 'The man who kills a man, kills a man. The man who kills himself, kills all men; as far as he is concerned he wipes out the world.'[1] Chesterton took himself there to be expressing the spirit of *all* suicides and in that he was mistaken. But there is no doubt that when a substitute for the end of the world is called for, suicide is the only possible one:

> Dressed in flowing white robes, 26 people sat tense and silent in an upper room of a London house. Leader of the strange group was middle-aged solicitor Peter Shanning. He had given up practising law after experiencing what he called 'an amazing series of dreams'. He claimed it had been

[1] *Orthodoxy: The Flag of the World* (London, 1909).

revealed to him that the world would come to an end on July 23rd, 1887, at 3 p.m. Shanning spent five years travelling the country and preaching. He gained 25 believers and they bought a house in north London. On the fatal day, they were gathered in a room, watching the clock ticking towards 3 p.m. Shanning sat quietly praying. Three o'clock came – and went. It wasn't the end of the world. But it was the end of Shanning. After his followers had left in bewilderment, he shot himself dead. (From a feature in a popular weekly paper.)

The fact that there is about suicide a kind of terribleness that ordinary, i.e. non-religious, ethics fails to touch is a weakness in ordinary ethics not only from the standpoint of religion but from the standpoint of philosophy. However, there is from the standpoint of philosophy a weakness to be discerned in the religious conception of suicide also. For according to the religious conception, all suicides are (unless their minds are unsound) guilty of an identical offence and separated from non-suicides by the same gulf; so that it does not really matter what kind of a suicide a man is so long as he is one.

Now this principle of equal disvalue, as it might be called, is manifestly objectionable to the non-religious conscience, which will either wish to remain silent in the face of suicide or else will wish to attribute to it an enormous range of disvalue, and also sometimes value, in a gamut that resists compression and runs from the squalid and mindless suicides of playboys or film starlets through the pitiful suicides of the oppressed and rejected, the anguished and maddened suicides of those goaded beyond endurance, the Stoic suicides and the heroic suicides, and thence to the self-sacrificial suicides, terminating with cases that religion would doubtless not classify as suicide at all. Ordinary ethics, however, will see no point in any alternative classification because it can descry variety in suicide where religion neglects it. And in this discrimination philosophy must side with ordinary ethics. For philosophy is a distinction-drawing business which emphasises differences and focuses the mind on variant possibilities.

Consider for just a moment some of the alternative possibilities inherent in the case of the gambling officer I mentioned earlier, who thought he was choosing death rather than dishonour. The point was then that suicide could not be the kind of escape he thought it was. But suppose he realised that there were no possibility of escape from the dishonour anyway. If so, he could divide through by the dishonour and consider whether it might not be as well for him to commit suicide in order to put an end to his misery. If that were the idea, it could be objected on the one hand that the misery might pass and on the other hand that, even supposing it did not, the idea of being put out of one's misery is below human dignity and appropriate rather to dogs and horses.

However, it might not be simply a matter of his wanting to put himself out of his misery but rather that he has got himself into an impossible situation. And this is different, for it is now being supposed that the incurring of the dishonour means he can no longer carry on his life as a soldier. This possibility is closed to him, yet no other life is conceivable: soldiering *is* his life. The morality of the society, and the military ethic in particular, might well in all seriousness prescribe suicide for just this type of case.

On this interpretation, the suicide of the gambling officer has come to resemble that of an American journalist named Wertenbaker, who developed cancer in middle age and whose story has been told by his wife. Here too it was not, or not simply, a question of the man's inability to stand misery, but of his finding it impossible to carry on living as the kind of creature he had become. A difference between the two cases is that the officer's life, unlike the journalist's, becomes impossible as the result of something he himself did, and this consideration would be capable of affecting the outcome in more than one way. For on the one hand the knowledge that he has made a mess of his life through his own fault might drive a man to suicide out of sheer self-hatred ('he could murder himself'; and so he does). On the other hand he might be willing to abide by the consequences of his own folly out of a sense of equity which would not be there to sustain him if he thought he were the victim of a cruel and arbitrary fate. Not that Wertenbaker entertained this thought; he wrote as follows:

Problem with death is to recognise the point at which you can die with all your faculties, take a healthy look at the world and people as you go out of it. Let them get you in bed, drug you or cut you, and you become sick and afraid and disgusting, and everybody will be glad to get rid of you. It shouldn't be such a problem if you can remember how it was when you were young. You wouldn't give up something for instance to add ten years to your life. All right, don't ask for them now. You wouldn't give up drinking and love-making and eating – and why should you have given them up? Nothing is ever lost that has been experienced and it can all be there at the moment of death – if you don't wait too long.[1]

What Wertenbaker saw no sense in was prolonging his life beyond a certain point, living on as something different from what he had been before, as a squalid pain-wracked thing, a dying man. It cannot be said that he found life meaningless. Rather, the meaning he found in life was such as to justify, to give him a reason for, doing away with himself in a certain circumstance.

In relation to the example of Wertenbaker, Chesterton's words about wiping out the world have little grip. Wertenbaker did not want to throw back the world in its creator's face – and not just because he had no belief in a creator either: if he had been offered his life over again he would have taken it gladly.

But all of it? No, not all of it: he was not prepared to accept *the whole* of the life that had been given him. Instead he despaired of it, despaired of the existence of any power to sustain him in his predicament. That he should have reviled what his life had become was understandable. The trouble was he did not love what he reviled; he had not 'this primary and super-natural loyalty to things'.

The last few words of that religiously ethical comment are Chesterton's again and they help to make clear the point of the passage I quoted before.[2] But still I do not see how they could be expected to influence a man like Wertenbaker, who after all had his own kind of loyalty to things.

---

[1] Lael Tucker Wertenbaker, *Death of a Man* (New York, 1950), p. 10.
[2] His remark about the suicide wiping out the world might otherwise seem to be no more than a solipsistic muddle.

6

THE SOUL'S CONQUEST OF EVIL[1]

W. W. Bartley III

Behold, I send you forth as sheep in the midst of wolves:
be ye therefore wise as serpents, and harmless as
doves. Matthew 10: 16

In much wisdom is much vexation, and he who
increases knowledge increases sorrow. Ecclesiastes 1: 18

I

IN his autobiography, Mr Leonard Woolf very forcibly protests
Lord Keynes's familiar account of the kind of influence
G. E. Moore had exerted over those who were later to become
members of the Bloomsbury Group. You will remember that
Keynes, writing in 1938 about his early beliefs as an under-
graduate at Cambridge, maintained of himself and his companions: 'We accepted Moore's religion . . . and discarded his
morals . . . meaning by "religion" one's attitude towards oneself
and the ultimate and by "morals" one's attitude towards the
outside world and the intermediate.'[2] In *Sowing*, the first
volume of his memoirs, Woolf calls this a 'distorted picture',
stressing that he himself, Moore, and their companions at

[1] I am much indebted to Professor Donald MacKinnon and to Mr
Stephen Kresge for their most helpful critical comments on an earlier draft
of this essay.

[2] John Maynard Keynes, 'My Early Beliefs', in *Two Memoirs* (New York,
1949), p. 82.

Cambridge were all quite concerned about practical politics and public morality.[1]

If one examines the lives and records of those extraordinary individuals who were to make so famous the squares and streets through which we have passed on our way to this hall tonight, and whose spirits, one likes to think, still haunt this neighbour-hood, one is inclined to think that Keynes did indeed paint a rather romantic picture of their early days in Cambridge, and that Woolf's recollections are nearer to the truth. One's suspicion that Keynes's recollections are somewhat distorted is reinforced by Mr Holroyd's recent biography of Lytton Strachey. But it is not with this question that I wish to deal tonight.

Rather, I should like to call your attention to a point on which Keynes and Woolf appear to be agreed. Both maintain a distinction between one's religion – which is said to concern one's own inner states and one's attitude towards the ultimate – and one's morals – which are said to be directed towards the outside world and what Keynes calls the 'intermediate', which, among other things, are those things which are less than ultimate. This distinction has a venerable heritage in British philosophy, and it is still very much alive today. Interestingly, John Stuart Mill used a distinction very much like this to define his differences with the philosophy of Jeremy Bentham. In effect, Mill accused Bentham of leaving out of his account of human nature those things which Keynes brackets as religious. Bentham's general conception of human nature and life, Mill wrote:

> furnished him with an unusually slender stock of premises . . . [He wantonly dismissed as] 'vague generalities' the whole unanalysed experience of the human race . . . the faculty by which one mind . . . throws itself into the feelings [of a mind different from itself] was denied him by his deficiency of Imagination. Self-consciousness, that daemon of . . . men of genius . . . never was awakened in him . . . he had never been made alive to the unseen influences which were acting

[1] Leonard Woolf, *Sowing: An Autobiography of the Years 1880–1904* (London, 1960), pp. 146 ff.

on himself . . . his recognition does not extend to the more
complex forms of [sympathy] – the love of loving . . . or of
objects of admiration and reverence. . . . Man is never
recognized by him as a being capable . . . of desiring, for its
own sake, the conformity of his own character to his standard
of excellence, without hope of good or fear of evil from other
source than his own inward consciousness. . . . The sense of
honour and personal dignity . . . the love of beauty, the
passion of the artist. . . . None of these powerful constituents
of human nature [so Mill concludes] are thought worthy of a
place among the Springs of Action.[1]

Although Mill did not use the words 'religion' and 'morals' to
define this difference, any more than Moore himself did, it is
clear that Mill was accusing his mentor of having concentrated
his attention on those things which Keynes was later to dub
the 'moral aspects' of Moore's philosophy at the expense of
what Keynes called the 'religious aspects', at the expense of
those things, such as the love of beauty, and the development
of inward consciousness, of which Moore was to write so power-
fully in the famous last chapter of *Principia Ethica*.

This distinction between religion and morals, or, crudely,
between the 'inner' and the 'outer' was, then, present in the
very different forms of utilitarianism championed by Bentham
and by Stuart Mill; it appears in the reaction to utilitarianism
represented by Moore and the Bloomsbury group. And, as I
have suggested, it remains very much alive today – for example
in what has come to be called the philosophy of 'negative
utilitarianism' propounded by Sir Karl Popper. In the course
of developing a Popperian account of ethics, one of his distinguished disciples has written categorically as follows:
'Morality should be understood in an extraverted way as
concerned with our behaviour towards others. I draw a sharp
distinction between a man's morality and his personal religion
and private ideals.'[2]

---

[1] John Stuart Mill: 'Bentham', in, for example, John Stuart Mill, *On Bentham and Coleridge*, intro. F. R. Leavis (New York, 1962), or in John Stuart Mill, *Utilitarianism*, ed. Mary Warnock (London, 1962).

[2] J. W. N. Watkins, 'Negative Utilitarianism', in *Proceedings of the Aristotelian Society, Supplementary Volume* (1963), pp. 96 ff.

II

This venerable distinction between a man's behaviour towards others and his personal religion and private ideals does not, I submit, bear examination. I do not wish to reduce morals to religion or religion to morals; I do wish to maintain that these two, as defined by Keynes, are so intertwined that an attempt to carry through the distinction amounts to something like an attempt to analyse the unanalysable. More important, and more pertinent to the title of my talk, it hinders understanding of the development of either personal or social morality, understanding of the soul's conquest of evil.

I may as well begin by stating several prejudices. The first is that a far larger part of our behaviour towards other persons than we are inclined to admit is a tangled web of guilt, fear, shame, projection, exploitation, ignorance, lack of inner consciousness, and all the other stuff of which evil and arbitrary behaviour is compounded. Man, being in any case by nature a confused animal, and alarmed by these virtually unmanageable forces and states of being, erects various maxims, morals, and wise sayings – indeed, occasionally even codifying them – to help him cope with his social environment. By and large he treats these uncritically, dogmatically, as magic charms against the unknown and unpredictable in himself and in his fellows.

Another prejudice is that we tend to ignore these facts, and the complexities of interpretation that accompany them, and to ignore them perhaps especially when constructing our moral and ethical theories. A third prejudice is that there may indeed be very little one can do about the way people behave towards one another, but that occasionally a few people can with some small measure of success embark on an at least partial conquest of evil. There is no one route to this conquest: the route may be sought, as in the Christian traditions, in the quest for what is called salvation. It may be sought, as for example in the philosophical psychology of the late C. G. Jung, in the quest for individuation, whose goal is 'wholeness'. It may be located, as many philosophers would prefer, in the Socratic tradition of searching for self-knowledge. Whatever the route, almost all such endeavours when successful involve what can be called heightened self-awareness, including some awareness of the evil of which one is capable – a subject to which I shall return. These quests are by and large *inner*; there is nothing 'unenlightened' about calling them *religious*. And without such inner quests, any so-called morality that may crop up in our external, *outer* behaviour is usually either conventional, coincidental, or accidental. For our interpretation of our external social situation is subject to distortion by our failures in achieving a heightened inner self-awareness. This does not imply that we ought to compose ourselves in meditation, withdrawn from the social world, until some such time as we feel able to cope with it in full self-awareness. For paradoxically, our inner awareness develops as we reflect on the way in which our psyches impinge on the outer world, indeed, as we learn to differentiate between the *I* and the *not-I*.

III

It would no doubt be useful at this point to analyse the 'meanings' of the various words and concepts I have been employing. It would be more useful to think about some examples. I shall therefore first draw on two stories one finds in the case-books of modern psychology. They concern some adventures of a little boy whom we may call Christopher. Both stories were recalled by Christopher himself after he had become an adult, and were recounted in roughly the following form.

The first episode occurs when Christopher was eight years old, early in the first morning following the end of his Christmas holiday. We find him lying slumbering in bed, sleeping late, as he had done on many of the mornings during the holiday. Suddenly he is abruptly and painfully awakened: his mother seizes his hair, yanks him out of bed, and spanks him. She had been calling him repeatedly to rise, to wash and dress, and prepare for school. But he had not heard; he had slept on; he was still on holiday. But not for long. Less than an hour later, on the way to school, trudging through the snow with his little sister, Mary, five years old, whom Christopher had to guide to and from school each day, he begins to cross-examine her about their mother. 'What do you feel about Mommy?' Christopher asks repeatedly. 'Don't you really hate her?' Sister protests her love of her mother; but Christopher is stubborn and persuasive – and he promises not to tell. Eventually, as they near school, Mary submits, and agrees that she really does hate their mother. That evening, after returning home from school, Christopher takes aside his mother to tell her: 'Mommy, Mary told me today that she hates you.' And then mother spanks Mary.

The second episode takes place about eighteen months later, in the summer, when Christopher was nine years old. His mother being devoutly religious, Christopher is sent regularly to church and taught religion at home as well. But he is a precocious lad and has already begun to doubt the stories of God and Jesus. We find him sitting on the porch of his family's house, in the warm summer evening, talking with his father. 'Daddy', he asks, 'was there really a Jesus? Did all those miracles really happen?' His father replies: 'Well, we don't really know; they may have – but perhaps not.' Christopher turns away almost immediately, goes inside to his mother, and reports accusingly: 'Mommy, Daddy says there wasn't any Jesus.' There followed an extraordinarily heated quarrel between Christopher's parents, one which his father, as was usual, lost.

We could hardly even begin this evening to explore the nuances latent in the report of these two episodes. But it is obvious what pattern is present in both these stories about a shockingly clever wicked little good boy who had not the slightest idea what he was doing, and yet at the same time in a sense may have known very well what he was doing.

In the first episode Christopher had felt himself wrongly punished – and quite possibly he was: mother perhaps ought to have been particularly indulgent at the end of the school holiday. But we do not know how things were with her: perhaps she had been having a deserved holiday too. Christopher, at any rate, was furious. His fury expressed itself most crudely, as hate for his mother – and perhaps for all things feminine: his sister, the school, his teachers, his having to care for his sister on the way to school. But Christopher also loved his mother;

and he knew from his teaching and from his religious and moral training that one ought only to love one's mother. He could not openly express his hostility towards his mother, and yet he could not bear *not* to have it expressed. So he virtually forced his little sister – only five years old and hardly aware of what had happened – to express, to *voice*, the evil sentiment. And then Christopher promptly saw to it that the crime was punished: he tattled on his sister, and saw her suffer the same punishment, spanking, that he had earlier endured.

The behavioural pattern is the same in the second episode. Christopher was unable or unwilling to express his forbidden doubts about religious teachings; he probably suspected that his father also harboured such doubts, for we are informed that his father did not go to church very often; and so, in a 'man to man' talk, he tricked his father into voicing the forbidden doubts. And once again Christopher saw to it that the crime was punished: his father was spanked verbally by his mother and stalked off in despair to the neighbourhood pub – perhaps thereby corroborating his wickedness in his son's eyes. In this extraordinary way Christopher's religious doubts were laid quietly, but oh so devilishly, to sleep, not to be yanked awake again for nearly a decade, at which time he was thrust into a severe neurosis.

If one is horrified by Christopher's behaviour, at the same time one need not hide a certain admiration for the skilful way in which he was able to manipulate his social environment. One of the chief reasons for this, of course, was its predictability, in particular the predictability of his mother. And when we take a closer look at his mother's predictability, we find that it consists largely in her rigidity, her unconsciousness, her lack of development – failures that were doubtless partly due to and partly reinforced by the dogmatic moral maxims which she virtually used as magic charms to deal with her own social environment. Christopher appears to have been able to predict, almost to the details, the sorts of actions she would take in response to the information which he fed her. She did not question his reports; she did not inquire how these issues – Mary's suddenly voiced hate for her or her husband's religious scepticism – had been raised. When her code appeared to have been violated she did not pause to make inquiries; she sought revenge. The life of his family appears to have revolved around Christopher in a curious way. Christopher, one might think, was a kind of vampire who cast a spell on the members of his family, sucking their lifeblood to nourish his existence. Christopher used the members of his family, one after the other, to commit the crimes he himself would like to have committed, and then called on his mother to bring down God's wrath on the criminals. But he could do this only because he knew that his mother would not *look* at the situation, but would *blindly* defend her moral magic. How the archetypes must have howled: for morality by magic is self-defeating, sustaining unconsciousness; putting nascent awareness to rest; spreading, not dispelling, man's confusion.

IV

Did Christopher do wrong? One may smile at the question; and yet, what expression is one supposed to wear on one's face when one discovers that there are two so-called 'schools of thought' about such questions which predominate in our ethics textbooks: one of them counselling us to examine motives; the other, consequences? Whatever the school-philosophers might say, I am inclined to doubt that we can give a very enlightening answer to our question by looking at Christopher's motives or intentions on the one hand, or by looking at the consequences of his behaviour on the other. Take the question of consequences first. One could of course say that any behaviour that led to Mary's being unjustly spanked was wrong. But to dismiss the issue so easily is rather flippant. Apart from the fact that it took the mother, as well as Christopher, to bring off the unjust spanking, one might well wonder whether that spanking might not have been one of the best things that ever happened to Mary? Perhaps it jarred her into erecting some defences against the 'loving brother' who may have guided her safely to school each day, but who did not hesitate monstrously to misuse her when it suited his purposes. We do not know.

We do know that Christopher himself later suffered from a serious neurosis. But to say that even this was necessarily an unfortunate consequence of his behaviour is to have made a host of assumptions. Hardly any psychiatrist, at least on the basis of the meagre evidence adduced here, would admit that Christopher's neurosis – even if we accept that that neurosis was unequivocally bad *for him* – was the direct effect of either or both of these two episodes. It may have been, or it may not; clearly, there are many children who have gone through experiences prima facie more damaging than these, and emerged relatively unscathed. Similar remarks might be made about any causal connection that might be traced between these actions of Christopher's and later unhappy relationships between Christopher's father and mother, or his mother and sister. It is evident that Christopher was already working within a highly charged and neurotic situation which was by no means his own creation.

One's perspective on this situation is not made much clearer by abandoning an attempt to evaluate in terms of consequences, an *Erfolgungsethik* or negative utilitarianism, and looking instead, in the manner of the traditional *Gesinnungsethiker*, to Christopher's 'motives' or 'intentions'. It is no news to those interested in philosophy that the notions of motivation and intention are filled with obscurity; but even if one overlooks this fact, one may raise the question whether, whatever they may mean, a satisfactory account of them must not presuppose a degree of self-awareness which we have no reason to suppose that Christopher possessed. In fact one might, if one did not look too closely, defend both Christopher's motives and his results in the second episode. In the moral universe then inhabited by Christopher, to doubt religious teaching was wrong, and to see that such doubts were punished was right. So his motivation – and the immediate result he achieved – could both be excused; some perhaps would even praise them. But of course to say this is not to look very deep.

So let us try to probe somewhat deeper. We have implied that a satisfactory account of motivation or intention – whether good or bad – must presuppose a degree of self-awareness which Christopher did not have. Christopher was of course a child. Is this what is after all meant by saying that children are innocent? One would not gather so from the literature about the 'lack of innocence' of children which has been produced during the past half-century. For in this, what has usually been stressed is their lack of innocence in a very primitive sense of the word: we have learned that children also inhabit the world of *sex*, that they are very aware sexually, and to that extent are not the innocent babes that some people once fancied them.

But perhaps our concept of innocence contains much richer connotations; and we mean, or people meant, when we or they speak or spoke of the innocence of children, that they *behave*, they do not *act*; that they literally do not know what they are doing. But to argue in this direction is to risk letting off everyone as innocent – or rendering us all children. After all, did Christopher's mother, who was no child, know what she was doing? How much self-awareness did she enjoy? How much self-awareness do most people enjoy? 'Father, forgive them, for they know not what they do,' we read in the gospels. I have already indicated my own rather pessimistic attitude towards such questions. Heinrich Zimmer was, I daresay, right when he wrote: 'Guilt and innocence are rarely obvious. They are unapparent, interwoven intimately with each other in a marvellously convoluted design.'[1]

Another example will help make this clearer, an example which I draw from an essay by Professor Donald MacKinnon.[2] Discussing various misuses to which the Christian doctrine of redemption through sacrifice may be put, MacKinnon writes:

> To sacrifice ourselves is, it is said, to realize the image of the crucified, whereas the self-sacrificing may simply be mutilating himself, purposively destroying the sweetness of existence in the name of illusion, in order to make himself a hero in his own eyes. . . . Those who are familiar with the problems of the care of old people will know very well what I call the phenomenon of the 'human sacrifice', the daughter in a large family who is described as 'devoted to her parents' (the language has a ritual quality), and who is therefore chosen to look after them in their decline. Not infrequently she is the

[1] Heinrich Zimmer, *The King and the Corpse* (New York, 1960), p. 224.
[2] D. M. MacKinnon, 'Moral Objections', in *Objections to Christian Belief* (London, 1963), esp. pp. 23 ff.

victim of various sorts of spiritual blackmail. Her patience
perhaps is exhausted by her mother's near senile can-
tankerousness and she is told 'you will be sorry one day, dear,
when I am dead and gone'; (and a discreet sob accompanies
the last words). She sees her life slipping from her and still
she is held in the vice-like grip, I will not say of dedication,
but of convention consecrated by the ecclesiastical image of
sacrifice. The ethic of sacrifice indeed provides a symbolism
under which all sorts of cruelties may be perpetrated, not so
much upon the weak as upon those who have been deceived
by a false image of goodness.

Just as in the former examples we asked whether Christopher
did wrong, we may in this instance ask whether the self-
sacrificing daughter was doing right. Here again we have a
particular example of innocence, guilt, exploitation, projection,
all working together to the destruction or at least impoverish-
ment of several human beings.

                              v

I have indicated, by these examples drawn from intimate
personal relationships, my prejudice that neither an ethic of
motive nor an ethic of consequence is much help in judging such
relationships and the behaviour that occurs within them. In
doing so I do not wish to suggest that the various sorts of
motivational and utilitarian accounts of moral judgement are
useless – let alone to suggest that they were authored with
malicious intent! Both are necessary; neither is sufficient; nor
are they sufficient when taken together.

   Were I to attempt to gather together some of my own intui-
tions about these matters, I should have to say something like
the following. We can neither act morally nor evaluate with
much competence the actions of other persons without an
extraordinarily deep knowledge of ourselves. The reason for
this is, as so many psychologists have stressed, that we are as
human beings very much at the mercy of our 'projections' –
that is, in the psychological sense, those interior states which

we impose on the external world in the course of interpreting it. I do not wish to labour the familiar or obvious, but an example would be of the shy man who, because of his own fears and hostilities and aggressive feelings towards other persons, projects these feelings onto certain of those other persons – even where the real attitudes of those persons do not merit any such projection – and assumes, or better, acts as if, these other persons harboured aggressive and hostile feelings towards him. When such psychological phenomena become systematised, as they do in occasional individuals, such conditions as paranoia may develop. But one need not adduce such unattractive states to elucidate the notion of projection : 'falling in love' is one of those rather more pleasant states of affairs where our projections may take possession of us.

So our interpretation of our social environment and its ills may be, and indeed usually is, severely distorted by our internal states. How does one achieve an internal psychological state, a relationship between consciousness and the unconscious, which does not precipitate a distorted view of the social environment? The question just raised is hardly one I can answer to anyone's satisfaction, including my own, this evening. For there are as many routes charted to this state of being as there are psychologists, not to mention religious leaders. But there are a few remarks one can make that are of special relevance to my topic. For one thing, as I have already indicated in speaking of Keynes and Moore, these internal quests might just as well be called religious. For another thing, they are not exactly pleasant: they may involve great stress and deep suffering. Freud himself, one of the great apostles of such self-awareness as may be achieved through psychoanalysis, occasionally wondered whether the whole process – and civilisation into the bargain – was worth the effort. One of the unpleasant things that is required if such quests are to be even moderately successful is a deep appreciation of the evil of which one is capable – whether this is expressed as one's 'sinfulness', as it might be within the Christian tradition, or as a recognition of one's knavery, to speak in terms that could be given an entirely pagan interpretation.

There is nothing novel about what has just been said. The

late C. G. Jung, for example, wrote as follows of the conquest of evil:

> The individual who wishes to have an answer to the problem of evil, as it is posed today, has need, first and foremost, of self-knowledge, that is, the utmost possible knowledge of his own wholeness. He must know relentlessly how much good he can do, and what crimes he is capable of, and must beware of regarding the one as real and the other as illusion. Both are elements within his nature, and both are bound to come to light in him, should he wish – as he ought – to live without self-deception or self-delusion.[1]

We have such advice not only from our psychologists, but also from our mythology and folklore. I wish that I could persuade you all to read Heinrich Zimmer's remarkable collection of stories, *The King and the Corpse*, from whose subtitle, 'Tales of the Soul's Conquest of Evil', I have borrowed the title of this lecture. In that book one reads of legendary figures like Conn-eda, an Irish prince, or, again, of the Hindu king after whom the collection is named: two heroes who are distinguished – and also imperilled – by their guilelessness and innocence, their trustfulness, their lack of knowledge or experience of evil, indeed, their lack of imagination for evil, which, paradoxically, put them at the mercy of the forces of evil. These figures, like many hero figures of legend and myth, must transform their inner selves by going through perilous trials in which they are initiated into evil – an initiation process which requires them to doff, or sacrifice, their earlier personalities, to acquire a penetrating knowledge of the dark as well as the light side of things, a more penetrating knowledge of both inner and outer 'social life' as it really is, to die to their old selves and to be 'born anew', and thereby to become fitter to perform their kingly tasks: 'to dispense *justice* as well as mercy'.[2]

The figures just mentioned are princely, heroic, strong, which helps to confirm that the conquest of evil is rarely undertaken at all successfully by those who are weak psychologically and intellectually but rather by those who are strong. The weak

[1] C. G. Jung, *Memories, Dreams, Reflections* (New York, 1961), p. 330.
[2] Heinrich Zimmer, *The King and the Corpse*, p. 42.

may well do things that are good; they rarely do good things. Nietzsche wrote in *Zarathustra*: 'There is nobody from whom I want beauty as much as from you who are powerful: let your kindness be your final self-conquest. Of all evil I deem you capable: therefore I want the good from you.'[1]

The deep pessimism of my talk will hardly have escaped you. Yet I am optimistic enough to think that such remarks about morality are still worth making.

[1] Friedrich Nietzsche, *Thus Spake Zarathustra*, in the chapter 'On Those Who Are Sublime'. See Walter Kaufmann's discussion in *The Owl and the Nightingale* (London, 1959).

7

GUILT, ETHICS AND RELIGION

Paul Ricoeur

AT the outset, I would like to thank the Royal Institute of Philosophy for inviting me to add my contribution to the general theme of the present session. Mr Vesey suggested that I speak on the notion of guilt from the twofold perspective of Ethics and of the Philosophy of Religion. I was very happy to accept his proposal, for it gave me the opportunity to gather together my own reflections on this difficult topic, which up to now have been somewhat scattered. My principal task will be to determine the distinction between ethical discourse and religious discourse on the question of guilt. These will be the two main divisions of my analysis.

But, before treating these two respective discourses with a view to distinguishing them and understanding their relationship, I suggest that first we come to an agreement about the meaning of the terms in question. Allow me, then, by way of preface, to develop a semantic analysis of the very term 'guilt'.

I. GUILT: SEMANTIC ANALYSIS

I propose, first, to consider this term, not in its psychological, psychiatric or psychoanalytic usage, but in the *texts* where its meaning has been constituted and fixed. These texts are those of penitential literature wherein the believing communities have expressed their avowal of evil; the language of these texts is a specific language which can be designated, in a very general way, as 'confession of sins', although no particular confessional connotation is attached to this expression, not even a specifically Jewish or Christian meaning. Some decades ago, Professor Pettazzoni of Rome wrote a collection of works covering the entire field of comparative religions. He called this precisely *Confession of Sins*. But it is not from the comparative point of view that I take up the problem. My point of departure is in a *phenomenology of confession* or avowal. Here I understand by phenomenology the description of meanings implied in experience in general, whether that experience be one of things, of values, of persons, etc. A phenomenology of confession is therefore a description of meanings and of signified intentions, present in a certain activity of language: the language of confession. Our task, in the framework of such a phenomenology, is to re-enact in ourselves the confession of evil, in order to uncover its aims. By sympathy and through imagination, the philosopher adopts the motivations and intentions of the confessing consciousness; he does not 'feel', he 'experiences' in a neutral manner, in the manner of an 'as if', that which has been lived in the confessing consciousness.

But with which expressions shall we start? Not with expressions of confessions that are the most developed, the most rationalised, for example, the concept or quasi-concept of 'original sin' which has often guided philosophical thought. On the contrary, philosophical reasoning should consult expressions of the confession of evil which are the least elaborated, the least articulated.

We should not be embarrassed by the fact that behind these rationalised expressions, behind these speculations, we encounter myths, that is, traditional narratives which tell of events which happened at the origin of time and which furnish the support of language to ritual actions. Today, for us, myths are no longer explanations of reality but, precisely because they have lost their explanatory pretension, they reveal an exploratory signification; they manifest a symbolic function, that is, a way of expressing indirectly the bond between man and what he considers sacred. Paradoxical as it may seem, myth thus demythologised in its contact with physics, cosmology and scientific history becomes a dimension of modern thought. In its turn, myth refers us to a level of expressions, more fundamental than any narration and any speculation. Thus, the narrative of the fall in the Bible draws its signification from an experience of sin rooted in the life of the community: it is the cultural activity and the prophetic call to justice and to 'mercy' which provide myth with its sub-structure of significations.

Therefore it is to this experience and to its language that we must have recourse; or rather, to this experience *in* its language. For it is the language of confession which elevates to the light of discourse an experience charged with emotion, fear, and anguish. Penitential literature manifests a linguistic inventiveness which marks the way for existential outbursts of the consciousness of fault.

Let us, therefore, interrogate this language.

The most remarkable characteristic of this language is that it does not involve expressions which are more primitive than the symbolic expressions to which myth refers. The language of confession is symbolic. Here I understand by symbol a language which designates a thing in an indirect way, by designating another thing which it directly indicates. It is in this way that I speak symbolically of elevated thoughts, low sentiments, clear ideas, the light of understanding, the kingdom of heaven, etc. Therefore, the work of repetition as applied to the expressions of evil is, in essence, the explicitation, the development of different levels of direct and indirect significations which are intermingled in the same symbol. The most archaic symbolism from which we can start is that of evil conceived as defilement or stain, that is, as a spot which contaminates from the outside. In more elaborated literatures, such as that of the Babylonians and especially of the Hebrews, sin is expressed in different symbolisms, such as to miss the target, to follow a tortuous path, to rebel, to have a stiff neck, to be unfaithful as in adultery, to be deaf, to be lost, to wander, to be empty and hollow, to be inconstant as dust.

This linguistic situation is astonishing; the consciousness of self, so intense in the sentiment of evil, does not, at first, have at its disposal an abstract language, but a very concrete language, on which a spontaneous work of interpretation is performed.

The second remarkable characteristic of this language is that it knows itself as symbolic and that, before any philosophy and theology, it is *en route* towards explicitation; as I have said elsewhere, the symbol 'invites' thought; the myth is on the way towards *logos*. This is true even of the archaic idea of defilement or stain: the idea of a quasi-material something which contaminates from the outside, which harms by means of invisible properties – this idea possesses a symbolic richness, a potential of symbolisation, which is attested to by the very survival of this symbol under more and more allegorical forms. We speak even today, in a non-medical sense, of contamination by the spirit of monetary profit, by racism, etc.; we have not completely abandoned the symbolism of the pure and the impure. And this, precisely because the quasi-material representation of stain is already symbolic of something else. From the beginning it has symbolic power. Stain has never literally signified a spot, impurity has never literally signified filth; it is located in the 'clear-obscure' of a quasi-physical infection and of a quasi-moral indignity. We see this clearly in rites of purification which are never just a simple washing; ablution and lustration are already partial and fictive actions which signify, on the level of body, a total action which addresses itself to the person considered as an undivided whole.

The symbolism of sin such as is found in Babylonian and Hebraic literature, in Greek tragedies or in Orphic writings, is certainly richer than that of stain, from which it is sharply distinguished. To the image of impure contact, it opposes that of a wounded relationship, between God and man, between man and man, between man and himself; but this relation, which will be thought of as a relation only by a philosopher, is symbolically signified by all the means of dramatisation offered in daily experience. So too the idea of sin is not reduced to the barren idea of the rupture of a relation; it adds to this the idea of a power which dominates man. Thus it maintains a certain affinity and continuity with the symbolism of stain. But this power is also the sign of the emptiness, of the vanity of man, represented by breath and by dust. So the symbol of sin is at one and the same time the symbol of something negative (rupture, estrangement, absence, vanity) and the symbol of something positive (power, possession, captivity, alienation). It is on this symbolic foundation, in this network of images and nascent interpretations that the word guilt should be resituated.

If we want to respect the proper intention of words, the expression guilt does not cover the whole semantic field of 'confession'. The idea of guilt represents the extreme form of interiorisation which we have seen sketched in the passage from stain to sin. Stain was still external contagion, sin already the rupture of a relation; but this rupture exists even if I do not know it; sin is a real condition, an objective situation; I would venture to say, an ontological dimension of existence.

Guilt, on the contrary, has a distinctly subjective accent: its symbolism is much more interior. It describes the consciousness of being overwhelmed by a burden which crushes. It indicates, further, the bite of a remorse which gnaws from within, in the completely interior brooding on fault. These two metaphors of burden and of biting express well the arrival at the level of existence. The most significant symbolism of guilt is that which is attached to the theme of tribunal; the tribunal is a public institution, but metaphorically transposed into the internal forum it becomes what we call the 'moral consciousness'. Thus guilt becomes a way of putting oneself before a sort of invisible tribunal which measures the offence, pronounces the condemnation, and inflicts the punishment; at the extreme point of interiorisation, moral consciousness is a look which watches, judges, and condemns; the sentiment of guilt is therefore the consciousness of being inculpated and incriminated by this interior tribunal. It is mingled with the anticipation of the punishment; in short the *coulpe*, in Latin *culpa*, is self-observation, self-accusation, and self-condemnation by a consciousness doubled back on itself.

This interiorisation of guilt gives rise to two series of results: on the one hand, the consciousness of guilt marks a definite progress in relation to what we have described as 'sin'; while sin is still a collective reality in which a whole community is implicated, guilt tends to individualise itself. (In Israel, the prophets of the exile are the artisans of this progress (Ezek. 31 : 34); this preaching is a liberating action; at a time when a collective return from exile, comparable to the ancient Exodus from Egypt, appeared impossible, a personal path of conversion opened itself to each one. In ancient Greece, it was the tragic poets who assured the passage from hereditary crime to the guilt of the individual hero, placed alone before his own destiny.) Moreover, in becoming individualised, guilt acquires degrees; to the egalitarian experience of sin is opposed the graduated experience of guilt: man is entirely and radically sinner, but more or less guilty. It is the progress of penal law itself, principally in Greece and Rome, which has an effect here on moral consciousness: the whole of penal law is actually an effort to limit and to gauge the penalty in function of the measure of the fault. The idea of a parallel scale of crimes and sins is interiorised, in its own turn, in favour of the metaphor of the tribunal; moral consciousness becomes itself a graduated consciousness of guilt.

This individualisation and this gradation of guilt surely indicate a progress in respect to the collective and unqualified character of sin. We cannot say as much for the other series of results: with guilt there arises indeed a sort of demand which can be called scrupulosity and whose ambiguous character is extremely interesting. A scrupulous consciousness is a delicate consciousness, a precise consciousness enamoured of increasing perfection; it is a consciousness anxious to observe all the commandments, to satisfy the law in all things, without making an exception of any sector of existence, without taking into account exterior obstacles, for example, the persecution of a prince, and which gives equal importance to little things as to great. But at the same time scrupulosity marks the entrance of moral consciousness into its own pathology; a scrupulous person encloses himself in the inextricable labyrinth of commandments; obligation takes on an enumerative and cumulative character, which contrasts with the simplicity and sobriety of the commandment to love God and man. The scrupulous consciousness never stops adding new commandments. This atomisation of the law into a multitude of commandments entails an endless 'juridisation' of action and a quasi-obsessional ritualisation of daily life. The scrupulous person never arrives at satisfying all the commandments, or even any one. At the same time even the notion of obedience is perverted; obedience to a commandment, because it is commanded, becomes more important than love of neighbour, and even love of God; this exactitude in observance is what we call legalism. With it we enter into the hell of guilt, such as St Paul described it: the law itself becomes a source of sin. In giving a knowledge of evil, it excites the desire of transgression, and incites the endless movement of condemnation and punishment. The commandment, says St Paul, 'has given life to sin', and thus 'hands me over to death' (Rom. 7). Law and sin give birth to one another mutually in a terrible vicious circle, which becomes a mortal circle.

Thus, guilt reveals the malediction of a life under the law. At the limit, when the confidence and tenderness, which are still expressed in the conjugal metaphors of Hosea, disappear, guilt leads to an accusation without accuser, a tribunal without judge, a verdict without author. Guilt has then become that irreversible misfortune described by Kafka: condemnation has become damnation.

A conclusion of this semantic analysis is that guilt does not cover the whole field of the human experience of evil; the study of these symbolic expressions has permitted us to distinguish in them a particular moment of this experience, the most ambiguous moment. On the one hand, guilt expresses the interiorisation of the experience of evil, and consequently the promotion of a morally responsible subject – but, on the other hand, it marks the beginning of a specific pathology, wherein scrupulosity marks the point of inversion.

Now the problem is posed: what do Ethics and the Philosophy of Religion make of this ambiguous experience of guilt and of the symbolic language in which it is expressed?

2. ETHICAL DIMENSION

In what sense is the problem of evil an ethical problem? In a twofold sense, it seems to me. Or rather, by reason of a double relationship, on the one hand with the question of freedom, and, on the other hand, with the question of obligation. Evil, freedom, obligation constitute a very complex network, which we shall try to unravel and to order in several stages of reflection. I shall begin and end with freedom, for it is the essential point.

In a first stage of reflection, I say: to affirm freedom is to take upon oneself the origin of evil. By this proposition, I affirm a link between evil and liberty, which is so close that the two terms imply one another mutually. Evil has the meaning of evil because it is the work of freedom. Freedom has the meaning of freedom because it is capable of evil: I both recognise and declare myself to be the author of evil. By that fact, I reject as an alibi the claim that evil exists after the manner of a substance or of a nature, that it has the same status as things which can be observed by an outside spectator. This claim is to be found not only in the metaphysical fantasies, such as those against which Augustine fought – Manicheism and all sorts of ontologies which conceive of evil as a being. This claim can take on a positive appearance, or even a scientific appearance, under the form of psychological or sociological determinism. To take upon oneself the origin of evil is to lay aside as a weakness the claim that evil is something, that it is an effect in a world of observable things, whether these things be physical, psychic or social realities. I say: it is I who have acted: *ego sum qui feci*. There is no evil-being; there is only the evil-done-by-me. To take evil upon oneself is an act of language comparable to the performative, in this sense, that it is a language which does something, that is to say, that it imputes the act to me.

I said that the relationship was reciprocal; indeed, if freedom qualified evil as a doing, evil is that which reveals freedom. By this I mean to say, evil is a privileged occasion for becoming aware of freedom. What does it actually mean to impute my own acts to myself? It is, first of all, to assume the consequences of these acts for the future; that is, he who has acted is also he who will admit the fault, who will repair the damages, who will bear the blame. In other words, I offer myself as the bearer of the sanction. I agree to enter into the dialectic of praise and blame. But in placing myself before the consequences of my act, I refer myself back to the moment prior to my act, and I designate myself as he who not only performed the act, but who could have done otherwise. This conviction of having

done something freely is not a matter of observation. It is once
again a performative: I declare myself, after the fact, as being
he who could have done otherwise; this 'after the fact' is the
backlash of taking upon oneself the consequences. He who
takes the consequences upon himself, declares himself free,
and discerns this freedom as already at work in the incriminated act. At that point I can say that I have committed the act.
This movement from in front of to behind the responsibility is
essential. It constitutes the identity of the moral subject through
past, present, and future. He who *will* bear the blame is the
same who *now* takes the act upon himself and he who *has*
acted. I posit the identity of him who accepts the future
responsibilities of his act, and he who has acted. And the two
dimensions, future and past, are linked in the present. The
future of sanction and the past of action committed are tied
together in the present of confession.

Such is the first stage of reflection in the experience of evil:
the reciprocal constitution of the signification of *free* and the
signification of *evil* is a specific performative: *confession*. The
second moment of reflection concerns the link between evil
and obligation. I do not at all want to discuss the meaning of
expressions such as 'You ought' nor their relation with the
predicates 'good' and 'evil'. This problem is well known to
English philosophy. My contribution to a reflection on evil will
be limited to this problem: let us take as our point of departure
the expression and the experience 'I could have done otherwise'. This is, as we have seen, an implication of the act by
which I impute to myself the responsibility for a past act.
But the awareness that one could have done otherwise is
closely linked to the awareness that one *should* have done otherwise. It is because I recognise my 'ought' that I recognise my
'could'. A being who is obligated is a being who presumes that
he can do what he should do. We are well aware of the usage
to which Kant put this affirmation: you must, therefore you
can. It is certainly not an argument, in the sense that I could
deduce the possibility from the obligation. I would rather say
that the 'ought' serves here as a detector: if I feel, or believe,
or know that I am obligated, it is because I am a being that can
act, not only under the impulsion or constraint of desire and

fear, but under the condition of a law which I represent to myself. In this sense Kant is right: to act according to the representation of a law is something other than to act according to laws. This power of acting according to the representation of a law is the will. But this discovery has long-range consequences: for in discovering the power to follow the law (or that which I consider as the law for myself) I discover also the *terrible* power of acting *against*. (Indeed, the experience of remorse which is the experience of the relation between freedom and obligation is a twofold experience; on the one hand, I recognise an obligation, and therefore a power corresponding to this obligation, but I admit to having acted against the law which continues to appear to me as obligatory. This is commonly called a transgression.) Freedom is the power to act according to the representation of a law *and* not to meet the obligation. ('Here is what I should have done, therefore what I could have done, and look at what I did.' The imputation of the past act is thus morally qualified by its relation to the 'ought' and 'can'.) By the same fact, a new determination of evil and a new determination of freedom appear together, in addition to the forms of reciprocity which are described above. The new determination of evil can be expressed in Kantian terms: it is the reversal of the relation between motive and law, interior to the maxim of my action. This definition is to be understood as follows: if I call a maxim the practical enunciation of what I propose to do, evil is nothing in itself; it has neither physical nor psychical reality; it is only an inverted relationship; it is a relation, not a thing, a relation inverted with regard to the order of preference and subordination indicated by obligation. In this way, we have achieved a 'de-realisation' of evil: not only does evil exist only in the act of taking it upon oneself, of assuming it, of claiming it, but what characterises it from a moral point of view is the order in which an agent disposes of his maxims; it is a preference which ought not to have been (an inverted relation within the maxim of action).

But a new determination of freedom appears at the same time. I spoke a moment ago of the *terrible* power of acting against. It is, indeed, in the confession of evil that I discover the power of subversion of the will. Let us call it the *arbitrary*, to

translate the German *Willkür*, which is at the same time free
choice, i.e. the power of contraries, that which we recognised
in the consciousness that one could have done otherwise, and
in the power not to follow an obligation which I simultaneously
recognise as just.

Have we exhausted the meaning of evil for Ethics? I do not
think so. In the 'Essay on Radical Evil' which begins *Religion
within the Limits of Reason Alone*, Kant poses the problem of a
common origin of all evil maxims; indeed, we have not gone
far in a reflection on evil, as long as we consider separately
one bad intention, and then another, and again another. 'We
must conclude', says Kant, 'from many, or even from a single
conscious evil action, *a priori* to an evil maxim as its foundation,
and from this maxim to a general foundation inherent in the
subject, of all morally bad maxims, a foundation which in its
own turn would be a maxim, so that finally we could qualify a
man as evil.'[1]

This movement towards greater depth which goes from evil
maxims to their evil foundation is the philosophical trans-
position of the movement of sins to sin (in the singular) of which
we spoke in section 1, on the level of symbolic expressions, and
in particular of myth. Among other things, the myth of Adam
signifies that all sins are referred to an unique root, which is,
in some way or other, anterior to each of the particular expressions of evil, yet the myth could be told because the confessing community raised itself to the level of a confession of
evil as involving all men. It is because the community con-
fesses a fundamental guilt that the myth can describe the
unique coming-to-be of evil as an event which happens only
once. The Kantian doctrine of radical evil is an attempt to
recapture philosophically the experience of this myth.

What qualifies this re-examination as philosophical? Essentially the treatment of radical evil as the foundation of multiple
evil maxims. It is therefore upon this notion of foundation
that we should bring to bear our critical effort.

Now, what do we mean by a foundation of evil maxims?
We might well call it an *a priori* condition in order to emphasise
that it is not a fact to be observed or a temporal origin to be

[1] *Religion within the Limits of Reason*, §§ 83–9.

retraced. It is not an empirical fact, but a first disposition of freedom that must be supposed so that the universal spectacle of human evil can be offered to experience. Neither is it a temporal origin, for this theory would lead back to a natural causality. Evil would cease to be evil, if it ceased to be 'a manner of being of freedom, which itself comes from freedom'. Therefore, evil does not have an origin in the sense of an antecedent cause. 'Every evil action, when pushed back to its rational origin, should be considered as if man had arrived at it directly from the state of innocence.'[1] (Everything is in this 'as if'. It is the philosophical equivalent of the myth of the fall; it is the rational myth of the coming-to-be of evil, of the instantaneous passage from innocence to sin; *as* Adam – rather than *in* Adam – we originate evil.)

But what is this unique coming-to-be which contains within itself all evil maxims? It must be admitted that we have no further concept for thinking of an evil will.

For this coming-to-be is not at all an act of my arbitrary will, which I could do or not do. For the enigma of this foundation is that reflection discovers, as a fact, that freedom has already chosen in an evil way. This evil is already there. It is in this sense that it is radical, that is anterior, as a non-temporal aspect of every evil intention, of every evil action.

But this failure of reflection is not in vain; it succeeds in giving a character, proper to a *philosophy of limit*, and in distinguishing itself from a philosophy of system, such as that of Hegel.

The limit is twofold: limit of my knowledge, limit of my power. On the one hand, *I do not know* the origin of my evil liberty; this non-knowledge of the origin is essential to the very act of confession of my radically evil freedom. The non-knowledge is a part of the performative of confession, or, in other words, of my self-recognition and self-appropriation. On the other hand, I discover the *non-power* of my freedom. (Curious non-power, for I declare that I am responsible for this non-power. This non-power is completely different from the claim of an outside contraint.) I claim that my freedom has already made itself not-free. This admission is the greatest

[1] Ibid., § 62.

paradox of ethics. It seems to contradict our point of departure. We began by saying: evil is what I could have not done; this remains true. But at the same time I claim: evil is this prior captivity, which makes it so that I must do evil. This contradiction is interior to my freedom, it marks the non-power of power, the non-freedom of freedom.

Is this a lesson in despair? Not at all: this admission is, on the contrary, the access to a point where everything can begin again. The return to the origin is a return to that place where freedom discovers itself, as something to be delivered – in brief to that place where it can *hope* to be delivered.

3. RELIGIOUS DIMENSION

I have just attempted with the aid of the Philosophy of Kant to characterise the problem of evil as an ethical problem. It is the twofold relation of evil to obligation and to freedom, which has seemed to me to characterise the problem of evil as an ethical problem.

Now, if I ask what is the specifically religious way of speaking about evil, I would not hesitate for a moment to answer: the language is that of Hope. This thesis requires an explanation. Leaving aside for a moment the question of evil to which I shall return later, I would like to justify the central role of hope in Christian theology. Hope has rarely been the central concept in theology. And yet we now know, since the work of Johannes Weiss and Albert Schweitzer, that the preaching of Jesus was concerned essentially with the Kingdom of God; the Kingdom is at hand; the Kingdom has drawn near to us; the Kingdom is in your midst. If the preaching of Jesus and of the primitive church thus proceeds from an eschatological perspective, we should rethink all of theology from this eschatological viewpoint. But this revision of theological concepts, taking its point of departure from the exegesis of the New Testament, centred on the preaching of the Kingdom-to-come, finds support in a parallel revision of the theology of the Old Testament. Thus Martin Buber contrasts the God of the promise – God of the desert and of the wandering – with the popular gods who manifest themselves in natural epiphanies, in the figure of the king or in the idols of the temple. The God who comes is a *name*, the god who shows himself is an *idol*. The God of the promise opens up a history, the god of epiphanies animates a nature. But the New Testament did not put an end to the theology of the Promise, for the Resurrection itself, which is at the centre of its message, is not only the fulfilment of the promise in an unique event, but the confirmation of the promise which becomes for all the hope of final victory over death.

What follows from this for freedom and for evil, which ethical consciousness has grasped in their unity? I shall begin by a discussion of freedom, for a reason which will become clear in a moment. It seems to me that religion is distinguished from ethics, in the fact that it requires that we think of freedom under the sign of hope.

In the language of the gospel, I would say: to consider freedom in the light of hope, is to re-situate my existence in the movement, which might be called, with Jürgen Moltmann, the 'future of the resurrection of Christ'. This 'kerygmatic' formula can be translated in several ways in contemporary language. First of all, with Kierkegaard, we could call freedom in the light of hope the 'passion for the *possible*'; this formula, in contrast to all wisdom of the present, to all submission to necessity, underscores the imprint of the promise on freedom. Freedom, entrusted to the 'God who comes', is open to the radically new; it is the creative imagination of the possible.

But, in a deeper dimension, freedom *in the light of hope* is a freedom which affirms itself, *in spite of* death, and in spite of all the signs of death; for, in a phrase of the Reformers, the Kingdom is hidden *sub contrario*, under its contrary, the cross. Freedom in the light of hope is freedom for the denial of death, freedom to decipher the signs of the Resurrection under the contrary appearance of death.

Likewise, the category of 'in spite of . . .' is the opposite or reverse side of a vital thrust, of a perspective of belief which finds its expression in the famous 'how much more' of St Paul. This category, more fundamental than the 'in spite of', expresses what might be called the logic of superabundance, which is the logic of hope. Here the words of St Paul to the Romans come to mind:

> But the free gift is not like the fault, for, if many died through one man's fault, *how much more* have the grace of God and the gift conferred by the grace of that one man, Jesus Christ, abounded for many. . . . If because of one man's fault, death reigned through that one man, *how much more* will those who receive the abundance of grace, the free gift of righteousness, reign in life through the one man, Jesus Christ. . . . Law came in to increase the fault; but where sin increased, grace abounded all the more. . . .' (Rom. 5: 15, 17, 20)

This logic of surplus and excess is to be uncovered in daily life, in work and in leisure, in politics and in universal history. The 'in spite of . . .' which keeps us in readiness for the denial is only the inverse, the shadow side, of this joyous 'how much more' by which freedom feels itself, knows itself, and wills itself to belong to this economy of superabundance.

This notion of an economy of superabundance permits us to return to the problem of evil. It is from this point of departure, and in it, that a religious or theological discourse on evil can be held. Ethics has said all it can about evil in calling it: (*i*) a work of freedom (*ii*) a subversion of the relation of the maxim to the law (*iii*) an unfathomable disposition of freedom which makes it unavailable to itself.

Religion uses another language about evil. And this language keeps itself entirely within the limits of the perimeter of the promise and under the sign of hope. First of all, this language places evil *before* God. 'Against you, against you alone have I sinned, I have done evil in your sight.' This invocation which transforms the moral confession into a confession of sin, appears, at first glance, to be an intensification in the consciousness of evil. But that is an illusion, the moralising illusion of Christianity. Situated before God, evil is installed again in the movement of the promise: the invocation is already the beginning of the restoration of a bond, the initiation of a new creation. The 'passion for the possible' has already taken possession of the confession of evil; repentance, essentially directed towards the

future, has already cut itself off from remorse which is a brooding reflection on the past.

Next, religious language profoundly changes the very content of the consciousness of evil. Evil in moral consciousness is
essentially transgression, that is, subversion of the law; it is
in this way that the majority of pious men continue to consider
sin. And yet, situated before God, evil is qualitatively changed;
it consists less in a transgression of a law than in a pretension
of man to be master of his life. The will to live according to
the law is, therefore, also an expression of evil – and even the
most deadly, because the most dissimulated: worse than injustice is one's own justice. Ethical consciousness does not
know this, but religious consciousness does. But this second
discovery can also be expressed in terms of promise and hope.

Indeed, the will is not constituted, as we have seemed to
believe in the context of the ethical analysis, merely by the
relation between the arbitrary and the law (in Kantian terms,
between the *Willkür* or arbitrary will and the *Wille* or determination by the law of reason). The will is more fundamentally
constituted by a desire of fulfilment or achievement. Kant
himself in the dialectical part of the *Critic of Practical Reason*
recognised this intended goal of totalisation. It is this precisely
which animates the *Dialectic of Practical Reason*, as the relation
to the law animates the *Analytic*. Now this tendency toward
totalisation, according to Kant, requires the reconciliation of
two moments which Rigorism has separated: 'virtue', that is,
obedience to pure duty, and 'happiness', that is, satisfaction
of desire. This reconciliation is the Kantian equivalent of hope.
This rebound of the philosophy of will entails a rebound of the
philosophy of evil. If the tendency toward totalisation is thus
the soul of the will, we have not yet reached the foundation of
the problem of evil so long as we have kept it within the limits
of a reflection of the relations of the arbitrary and the law.
The true evil, the evil of evil, shows itself in false syntheses, i.e.
in contemporary falsifications of the great undertakings of
totalisation of cultural experience, that is, in political and
ecclesiastical institutions. In this way, evil shows its true face –
the evil of evil is the lie of premature syntheses, of violent
totalisations.

Evil 'abounds' wherever man transcends himself in grandiose undertakings, wherein he sees the culmination of his existence in the higher works of culture, in politics and in religion. And so these great simulacra, the cult of race, the cult of the State, and all forms of false worship, are the very birth of idols, substituted for the 'Name', who should remain faceless.

But this greater deepening of our understanding of evil is, once again, a conquest of hope: it is because man is a goal of totality, a will of total fulfilment, that he plunges himself into totalitarianisms, which really constitute the pathology of hope. As the old proverb says, demons haunt only the courts of the gods. But, at the same time, we sense that evil itself is a part of the economy of superabundance. Paraphrasing St Paul, I dare to say: Wherever evil 'abounds', hope 'super-abounds'. We must therefore have the courage to incorporate evil into the epic of hope. In a way that we know not, evil itself co-operates, works toward the advancement of the Kingdom of God. This is the viewpoint of faith on evil. This view is not that of the moralist; the moralist contrasts the *predicate* evil with the predicate good; he condemns evil; he imputes it to freedom; and finally, he stops at the limit of the inscrutable; for we do not know how it is possible that freedom could be enslaved. Faith does not look in this direction; the origin of evil is not its problem; the end of evil is its problem. With the prophets, faith incorporates this end into the economy of the promise, with Jesus, into the preaching of the God who comes, with St Paul, into the law of superabundance. This is why the view of faith on events and on men is essentially benevolent. Faith justifies the man of the *Aufklärung* for whom, in the great romance of culture, evil is a factor in the education of the human race, rather than the puritan, who never succeeds in taking the step from condemnation to mercy, and who thus remains within the ethical dimension, and never enters into the perspective of the Kingdom which comes.

Such are the three 'discourses' which may be held about guilt: the semantic discourse is mainly a phenomenology of confession by means of an interpretation of symbolic expressions; the ethical discourse is an explanation of the relation between freedom, obligation and evil (it relies on the performatives through which I take on myself the origin of evil and constitute myself as a responsible will); the religious discourse is a re-interpretation of freedom and evil in the light of hope – in Christian terms, of hope in the universal resurrection from the dead.

If I consider these three discourses as a whole, they offer a kind of progression, which could be compared to the progression from the aesthetic stage to the ethical and the religious stage in Kierkegaard's philosophy. I should accept this comparison, if I did not find it disparaging and discouraging.

8

HEGEL AND THE RATIONALISATION OF MYSTICISM

Frederick C. Copleston

I

In the preface to his *Philosophy of Right* Hegel maintains that a philosophy is its own time apprehended in thought.[1] It is not the philosopher's business to create an imaginary world of his own. His task is to understand the present and actual as subsuming the past in itself, as the culmination (up to date) of a process of development.

Among the phenomena, the structure and development of which the philosopher can try to understand, is religion. And from one point of view at any rate religion can be regarded as a particular expression of the human spirit. Thus in the *Phenomenology of Spirit* and in the *Encyclopaedia of the Philosophical Sciences* religion forms the subject-matter of a particular section, while Hegel's lectures on the philosophy of religion form a series alongside other series, the lectures on the philosophy of history, on art and on the history of philosophy.

It would be a mistake, however, to conclude that the philosophy of religion is peripheral to Hegel's main line of thought. He tells us roundly that the subject-matter both of religion and philosophy is 'God and nothing but God and the self-unfolding of God'.[2] Moreover for Hegel the philosophy of religion is not simply reflection about religion from outside. Obviously,

[1] *Works* (Glockner, 1928), vii, p. 35. This edition will be referred to in footnote references as *W*.　　　　[2] *W*, xv, p. 37.

118

the development of religious beliefs and practices constitutes an historical phenomenon about which the philosopher can reflect, even if he does not accept any of the religions which he is considering. And Hegel certainly devotes a good deal of space to reflection about the historical development of religion. But he does so from the point of view of one who believes that Lutheran Christianity is the highest expression of religion, at any rate up to date. For Hegel the philosophy of religion is religion attaining the level of reflective self-awareness and self-understanding. This is why he thinks himself justified in maintaining that he is simply carrying further the programme of St Anselm and other mediaeval theologians, the programme of 'faith seeking understanding'. The instrument of understanding which Hegel employs is, of course, absolute idealism. And it is clearly arguable that what he regards as the process of understanding Christianity is really the process of transforming the Christian religion into idealist metaphysics. But this does not alter the fact that Hegel looks on himself as engaged in solving problems which arise out of a religion of which he is an adherent.

What is it that Hegel wishes to understand, to express in the language of philosophy? I select one basic problem, the relation between the world and God, between finite things and the infinite divine reality.

An obvious question is this. Why, or with what right, does Hegel assume in the first place that there is an infinite, a divine reality? It seems to me that there are two things to be borne in mind. In the first place Hegel enrolled in his youth in the Protestant theological faculty at Tübingen. It is indeed a notorious fact that his initial reaction not only to the theological lectures delivered at Tübingen but also to the Christian religion itself, as developed by the Apostles and their successors, was far from favourable. The point is, however, that Hegel came to philosophy from theology. This meant in effect that he assumed that Christian belief was in fact true, in some sense at any rate of the word 'true'; and that he then tried, by means of philosophical reflection, to exhibit what we may call the 'inner truth' in religious belief.[1] In the second place Hegel was

---

[1] With Leibniz we can already find a tendency to find an 'inner truth' in Christian beliefs. With Lessing, in his mature thought, this tendency is

convinced that from the philosophical point of view the finite is not intelligible except in the light of its relationship to an infinite whole, which is the ultimate reality. His philosophy is therefore concerned with exhibiting the nature of the ultimate reality rather than with trying to prove its existence.

The problem which I have selected for consideration can be expressed in this way. In the religious consciousness, as it manifests itself in both Judaism and Christianity, we find God objectified. God is set over against Nature and the finite subject. In other words, an opposition is asserted between God and the world, God and man. For Hegel, this opposition cannot be anything but repugnant to speculative philosophy. On the one hand God is declared to be infinite. On the other hand, if the alleged infinite is set over against the finite, so as to exclude it, how can it properly be described as infinite? Again, if the finite is set over against the infinite, is it not absolutised, with the result that the infinite becomes a superfluous hypothesis? In fine, pictorial theism, with its God 'out there' or 'up there', cannot satisfy the reflective mind.

Yet how can we overcome in thought the opposition between the finite and the infinite, between the world and God, between man and God? In Christianity there is indeed a synthesis, an overcoming of the estrangement of the finite subject from God. But this synthesis is lived rather than thought. The difficulty lies in thinking it, in constructing a genuinely philosophical theism. If on the one hand we use the term 'God' as a label for the Many in their given empirical existence, this is tantamount to embracing atheism. For the word 'God' would then refer simply to the class of finite things, the existence of which is not denied by the atheist. If on the other hand we declare the Many to be illusion, this is equivalent to embracing what Hegel describes as 'acosmism'.[1] In neither case can we be said to have solved the problem at issue. What we have done is to eliminate

---

much more marked. But whereas Lessing did not think of himself as a Christian, Hegel came to think of himself as a champion of Christianity, even if it is pretty obvious that in his developed system Christianity is transformed into exoteric Hegelianism, as McTaggart puts it.

[1] This is what Hegel understands by pantheism when he denies that he is a pantheist.

one of the factors (in the first case God, in the second case the world) which need to be brought together in a unity which at the same time preserves a distinction.

Hegel's problem, as actually raised and treated by him, has obviously to be seen in the light of the presuppositions involved in his adherence to the post-Kantian idealist movement. And, in my opinion, the spirit and demands of the romantic movement are also relevant factors. At the same time there is a real sense in which the problem to which I have been referring is a contemporary problem. We have only to think, for example, of the Bishop of Woolwich's famous book *Honest to God* and of its author's attack on pictorial theism, with its God 'out there'. There are, of course, contextual differences. For instance, one of Dr Robinson's themes is the apparent growing irrelevance of the concept of God when seen in the light of such factors as the growth of the scientific outlook and of depth psychology. But the differences can, I think, be exaggerated. It would be an obvious anachronism to attribute to Hegel a knowledge of depth psychology and of psychological explanations of the felt need for religion. But Hegel was by no means unaware of the way in which the God 'out there' can appear as a superfluous addition to the world. 'Science', he remarks, 'thus forms a universe of knowledge which has no need of God, lies outside religion and has, directly, nothing to do with it.'[1] In any case Dr Robinson's basic problem seems to me to be similar to that of Hegel. How are we to think of God if we are not to think of him as a super-person over against the world? In the language of Paul Tillich we can speak of both Hegel and the Bishop of Woolwich as trying to make the transition from 'God' to *God*.

II

In the notes which form the so-called *Fragment of a System* of 1800 Hegel expresses a serious doubt whether philosophy is capable of thinking, of conceptualising that is to say, the unity-in-difference between the divine spirit and the human spirit which is lived, but not clearly thought, on the level of Christian

[1] *W*, xv, p. 32.

love. Philosophy is a process of thinking; and thought posits an object over against itself, an object about which we think. Further, discursive thought, working with the categories of traditional logic, asserts antitheses, such as that between the infinite and the finite, which it is unable to overcome. 'Infinite' means 'not finite'; and there is an end of the matter. The same idea seems to be re-echoed in a recent book by the Bishop of Woolwich when he asserts that to express the overcoming of dualism (between Creator and creature) 'within the logic of non-contradiction is of course finally impossible'.[1] Hegel's conclusion is that 'philosophy therefore has to stop short of religion because it is a process of thinking'.[2]

Every student of Hegel is aware that the philosopher very soon looked to dialectical thinking to accomplish what was impossible for a 'static' logic which posited antitheses and then was unable to overcome them. It is not so obvious, however, that Hegel was concerned, in part, with thinking through, with raising to the level of pure conceptual thought, a relationship between the finite spirit and God which he regarded as having found expression in the paradoxical utterances of religious mystics. I am not indeed prepared to follow Richard Kroner in describing Hegel as a 'Christian mystic, seeking adequate speculative expression'.[3] For it seems to me extravagant to speak of Hegel himself as a mystic, whether Christian or otherwise. But when Professor W. T. Stace maintains that Hegel endeavoured to turn the mystical idea of identity-in-distinction into a logical concept,[4] and when Mr G. R. G. Mure writes of Hegel's 'strenuous and uncompromising effort, which has no serious parallel, to rationalize and to bring to light the mystic union of God and man proclaimed by men such as Meister Eckhart and Jacob Böhme, to reveal it as a union through distinction for which the whole world is evidence',[5] they are saying, I think, what is quite true. Hegel was doubtless hostile to the taking of short cuts in philosophy by substituting appeals to intuition or to mystical insights in place of the

---

[1] *Exploration into God* (London, 1967), p. 141.
[2] *Hegel's Early Theological Writings* (Chicago, 1948), p. 313.
[3] Ibid., p. 8.   [4] In *Mysticism and Philosophy* (London, 1961).
[5] *The Philosophy of Hegel* (London, 1965), p. 103.

patient effort to understand and to express the truth in a systematic way. Moreover, his sarcastic references in the preface to the *Phenomenology* to Schelling's insistence on approaching the Absolute by the 'negative way' are well known. But it by no means follows that Hegel did not regard mystical writers as having given expression, even if in paradoxical form, to valid insights which the philosopher should try to conceptualise, exhibiting their universal significance.[1] In point of fact he quotes Meister Eckhart to the effect that 'the eye with which God sees me is the eye with which I see him; my eye and his eye are one. . . . If God were not, I should not be; if I were not, he would not be either'.[2] Hegel further remarks that the older theologians among whom he numbers Eckhart had, as he puts it, a better grasp of 'this depth'[3] than their modern successors. So I do not think that it is at all far-fetched to represent Hegel as trying to give philosophical expression to a mystical insight.

III

Now perhaps I have given the impression that in my opinion Hegel regards the sphere of religion as concerned only with feeling and with emotive language. This impression would, however, be erroneous. In his phenomenological analysis of the religious consciousness Hegel does indeed allow for the basic importance of immediacy, of feeling, the feeling of dependence for example. But he is very far from equating religion with feeling. In his view thought and knowledge are essential to the development of the religious consciousness. He tells us, for example, that 'knowledge is an essential element of the Christian religion itself';[4] and he insists on the truth of the Christian dogmas. It is indeed true that for Hegel the mode of thinking characteristic of the religious consciousness is pictorial thought. And inasmuch as philosophy, in his view, converts pictorial

---

[1] For example, if a religious mystic writes simply of an exceptional state of union between the soul and God, Hegel would see in what the mystic says a general metaphysical truth about the relation between the finite and the infinite.

[2] *W*, xv, p. 228.   [3] Ibid.   [4] *W*, xv, p. 35.

thought into pure conceptual thought, we can say that for Hegel philosophy demythologises the content of religious belief. At the same time it must be added that he regards this process of demythologisation as starting within the religious sphere; in, that is to say, the course of the historical development of the religious consciousness and its self-expression. In other words, even though Hegel asserts a distinction between the modes of conception characteristic of the religious consciousness and of speculative philosophy, he also asserts a continuity. This is why he feels entitled to make the claim, to which I have already referred, that he is continuing the task of theologians such as St Anselm, and why he thinks himself justified in making such statements as that philosophy 'only unfolds itself when it unfolds religion, and when it unfolds itself it unfolds religion'.[1]

This point, namely that there is continuity as well as distinction between the modes of conception characteristic of the religious consciousness and of speculative philosophy, has, I think, a certain importance for the understanding of Hegel. We are told, for example, that if we ask 'what is God?' or 'what does the term *God* signify?', we are trying to grasp the nature of God in thought, and that 'the nature of God as grasped in thought'[2] is what is called in philosophy the Absolute. Hegel thus translates talk about God into talk about the Absolute or transforms the concept of God into that of the Absolute. And we may thus draw the conclusion that according to Hegel the religious consciousness projects the ultimate reality into the celestial sphere in the form of a personal transcendent being out there, over against the world and the human spirit, whereas philosophy rejects this externalisation of God and conceives the ultimate reality as the all-comprehensive Life, the self-actualising Absolute. Though, however, there is certainly some truth in this account of the matter, the account is defective or inadequate. For it neglects the fact that, according to Hegel, the truth of the fundamental unity between the finite spirit and the divine spirit finds expression in the Christian religion in such doctrines as those of the historic Incarnation, the indwelling of the Holy Spirit in the Church, the Eucharist and the communion of saints. In other words, what philosophy

[1] Ibid., p. 37.   [2] *W*, xv, p. 42.

does is not to supply a truth of which religion has no inkling but rather to present the truth as following from the nature of the Absolute instead of presenting it in the form of contingent propositions, depending for their truth on historic events which might or might not have occurred.

To put the matter in another way, at the time of the Enlightenment it was generally agreed, both by opponents and defenders of Christianity, that the Christian religion stood or fell according as it was able or unable to make good certain historic claims. Hegel, however, is trying to show that Christian beliefs are true independently of these historic claims. This means, of course, that Christianity is presented, to use McTaggart's phrase, as exoteric Hegelianism, while absolute idealism is presented as esoteric Christianity. And the natural conclusion is that the fall of absolute idealism would entail the fall of Christianity. For absolute idealism, according to Hegel, is Christianity, in its cognitive aspect at any rate, when in possession of full self-understanding. This is indeed an idea which most Christian theologians would hardly receive with enthusiasm. And understandably so. But the point which I am trying to make here is simply that Hegel does not separate the concept of truth from religious statements and attach it only to philosophical statements. Religious statements can be true. And when the philosopher expresses their truth in a different form, it is the same truth which he is presenting. That is to say, in Hegel's opinion the truth remains the same.

Now if we consider the sort of statements to which Hegel refers in the writings of mystics such as Eckhart, it is clear that they assert a unity between God and man, between the finite spirit and the divine spirit. At the same time it is clear that they do not assert the reducibility of the concept of God to the concept of man. Whatever may seem to be the literal meaning of some of Eckhart's utterances, the general line of his thought makes it quite clear that he had no intention of asserting that 'God' and 'man' are convertible terms. It is also clear, I think, that mystics such as Eckhart did not assume that a realisation of the unity between man and God is something given from the start. Rather is it something to which the human spirit can attain, though it does not necessarily do so. In other words, there is a unity-in-distinction which the human mind can grasp or apprehend, though it does not always or necessarily do so.

These, it seems to me, are some of the ideas to which Hegel thinks that he has given expression in terms of absolute idealism. In the first place the Hegelian Absolute is clearly not reducible without residue to the human mind. For it is the One which, though not temporally prior to the Many, manifests itself or expresses itself in the world. In Hegel's opinion, the national State, considered as an organic whole enduring in time, is irreducible to any given set of citizens, to those, for example, who are living here and now. In an analogous manner the Absolute is irreducible to any given set of finite things, including finite minds. The Absolute or God is, in St Paul's words, he in whom 'we live and move and have our being'.[1]

In the second place, just as the national State does not exist apart from its citizens but in and through them, though at the same time it is more than the sum of them, so does the Absolute exist in and through the Many, imminent in them while comprising them within its own life.

In the third place, though the Absolute must be defined as self-thinking thought (for this is what it is in essence, as Aristotle saw), it must also be conceived as a dynamic process of self-actualisation. When Hegel asserts that 'of the Absolute it must be said that it is essentially [a] result, that only at the end is it what it is in very truth',[2] and that the Absolute is 'the essence which completes (or actualizes) itself through its own development',[3] I think that he means precisely what he says. That is to say, the Absolute comes to know itself in actuality in and through the human mind as its vehicle. But when Hegel says that 'God knows himself in the finite spirit',[4] it is not any and every sort of knowledge to which he is referring. He is referring above all to the knowledge of God in religion and philosophy. It is this knowledge which from another point of view is God's knowledge of himself. 'Finite consciousness knows God only in so far as God knows himself in it.'[5] That

---

[1] Acts 17: 28.   [2] *W*, ii, p. 24.
[3] Ibid.   [4] *W*, xvi, p. 192.   [5] Ibid., p. 191.

is to say, at the level at which the finite spirit becomes the vehicle of the divine self-knowledge it rises above its particularity and becomes in actuality a moment in the divine life. The divine self-knowledge is not reducible to any individual's knowledge of God; but the individual's knowledge of God is a moment in the process of the Absolute's return to itself in self-reflection.

Awareness of the identity-in-distinction which obtains between the human spirit and the infinite spirit is not something given from the start. Just as we cannot come to know the true nature of the universal in general except by first objectifying it as a reality apart from particulars (as in the traditional interpretation of Platonism), so the human mind cannot come to know the true nature of God except by first objectifying him as a personal transcendent being 'out there', over against the world and man. This is a dialectically necessary stage in the process by which the universal spirit comes to see itself, in and through the human mind, as the one reality, the Alpha and Omega. As we have noted, Hegel believes that the true view of God is expressed in the Christian dogmas in the form appropriate to the religious consciousness. What philosophy does is to exhibit the unity between the human spirit and God, not as a privilege gratuitously bestowed upon some men but rather as a truth which follows from the nature of reality itself. It exhibits spirit, manifesting itself in the religious and philosophical development of mankind, as 'the living process by which the implicit unity of divine and human nature becomes actual and attains concrete existence'.[1]

IV

From what I have been saying it should be clear that I accept neither the right-wing interpretation of Hegel, according to which God in himself is to be conceived as enjoying self-knowledge independently of all creation, nor the interpretation which pretty well identifies the position of Hegel with that of Feuerbach. As for the right-wing interpretation, I am, of

[1] *W*, xvi, p. 210.

course, aware that in his very favourable review in the *Jahrbuch für wissenschaftliche Kritik*[1] of K. F. Göschel's book of aphorisms Hegel refers with approval to Göschel's statement that God in himself is self-knowledge in itself, while as knowing himself in creatures God is self-knowledge outside himself. But though I may be wrong, I do not think that Hegel really commits himself to saying more than that the divine essence must be defined as self-thinking thought. As for the identification of Hegel's position with that of Feuerbach, Hegel is not concerned, as Feuerbach was, with transforming theology into anthropology, with reducing God to man. He is concerned with bringing God and man together by employing the concept of identity-in-distinction. This was, I think, seen by Kierkegaard. The Danish thinker's picture of Hegel as producing a *tertium quid*, a fantastic metaphysical abstraction, absolute thought, in which both God and man disappear, may be a caricature, but it at any rate expresses Kierkegaard's recognition of the fact that Hegel does not aim at a reduction without residue either of God to man or of man to God.

Hegel might perhaps be described as a panentheist by intention. Needless to say, he is not concerned with overcoming theism in the sense of imaginative representations of God as an old man on a throne beyond the clouds. The theism to which he tries to give consistent philosophical expression already recognises God as infinite spirit. And what Hegel endeavours to accomplish is to think the relation between the infinite and the finite in such a way as to allow the infinite to fill, as it were, all reality while at the same time a distinction is preserved. If we take pantheism as representing the concept of identity and theism that of distinction, Hegel's aim is to show how the two concepts, which appear antithetical, can be reconciled at a higher level. All things are 'in God', moments in the divine life; but God, as the One, is not simply reducible to 'all things', to the Many. To give, however, a clear statement of this idea is no easy task. And it is arguable that the result of Hegel's reflections is so ambiguous that it is questionable whether it can be properly described as theism of any kind, unless the meaning of the term is extended well beyond what seems to be

[1] *W*, pp. 276–313.

permitted by ordinary usage. This is why I suggest that Hegel might be best described as a panentheist 'by intention'.

V

The ambiguity of the results of Hegel's philosophising is a point which merits a little amplification. As we have noted, he regards the philosopher as concerned primarily with the problems which arise out of his contemporary world. And in the sphere of religion he mentions this problem. 'There was a time when all knowledge was knowledge of God.'[1] That is to say, there was a time when knowledge of God himself was considered the highest form of knowledge and when knowledge of the world was thought to be in some sense knowledge of God, that is, of God's handiwork. In the modern world, however, scientific knowledge of finite things has increased to such an extent that the sphere of the knowledge of God has been progressively contracted. Indeed, 'it is a matter of no concern to our age that it knows nothing of God. On the contrary, the belief that this knowledge is not even possible passes for the highest degree of insight'.[2] Hegel, however, believing that the real is the rational and the rational the real, that God is the supreme reality and hence the supremely rational (or, rather absolute reason itself), and that the rational must be penetrable by reason, insists that the essence of God can be known by the human reason. In fact it is not altogether unreasonable to say that the task which Hegel proposes to the philosopher is that of attaining by philosophical reflection to what the mediaeval theologians called the beatific vision of God and which they reserved for heaven. This idea, however, would be clearly absurd if God were represented as a transcendent reality of such a kind that we know of him, as Aquinas put it, what he is not rather than what he is. Given therefore Hegel's conviction of the power and scope of the human mind, he has, so to speak, to bring God down from his state of transcendence and at the same time to elevate man. And this means in effect two things. First, what traditional Christian doctrine represents as

[1] *W*, xv, p. 52. [2] *W*, xv, p. 53.

the free creation of a world by a transcendent creator must be represented, from the philosophical point of view, as a divine self-exteriorisation which is essential to the divine life. Secondly, man's knowledge of God and God's knowledge of himself must be depicted as two aspects of one reality. Hence Hegel can say that 'without the world God is not God'.[1] That is to say, the essence of the Absolute as self-thinking thought is not actualised in concrete reality except in the sphere of spirit which requires the sphere of Nature as its necessary presupposition. And in the sphere of spirit man's knowledge of God is God's knowledge of himself.

Now Hegel himself did not think of this doctrine as equivalent to the elimination of God. Individual human beings perish, but the One remains. The individual's knowledge of God, considered precisely as knowledge possessed by this individual, is transitory; but the development of the religious consciousness in general continues. The universal mind lives in and through particular minds; but while particulars are transitory, the universal abides. At the same time there is no great difficulty in seeing the force of the contention that Hegel's theory is well on its way to becoming a recommendation to look on the world in a special way, namely as one organic and developing whole which, with the emergence of man and the subsequent growth of scientific knowledge, can be represented as coming to know itself in and through the human mind.

In other words, a plausible case can be made for representing Hegel's philosophy of religion as a stage in a process in which the concept of God is progressively eliminated. Hegel, it may be said, undertakes a demythologisation of Christian doctrine. But the result of his own philosophising is a cloud of metaphysical mystification which is subsequently dissipated by naturalism and positivism. Hegel saw the problems arising out of traditional theism. But he was unable to solve them, not because he lacked ability, but because they are insoluble. If therefore religion is to be preserved, it has to be separated from talk about God. Or, if the word 'God' is retained, it must be given a meaning which involves no reference to an alleged transcendent being of any kind. We can thus see in the con-

[1] *W*, xv, p. 210.

temporary Death-of-God theology the spiritual heir of Hegelianism, even if Hegel himself would not have been prepared to recognise it as such.

VI

If this point of view is adopted, it follows that the statements about God which were made by men such as Meister Eckhart and which evidently impressed Hegel were not about God at all, about God, that is to say, as an existent reality. Suppose, however, that we believe that the claim of religious mystics to have enjoyed knowledge by acquaintance of a reality which is identifiable neither with Nature nor with the finite spirit and which is in some sense the only 'true' reality cannot be simply dismissed. Or suppose that we believe that God is inescapable in the sense that a One reveals itself as the attracting goal of the human spirit's movement towards an ultimate unity or as the hidden ground of the demands which impose themselves upon us in the recognition of ideal values in relation to the successive situations which call for action in the world. If we have beliefs of this kind, we could, I suppose, pursue a policy of Wittgensteinian silence and refrain from trying to state their content. But if we choose to speak, we shall need the word 'God' or some equivalent term.

Once, however, we begin to speak, we encounter the sort of problems which Hegel encountered, such as the problem of stating the relation between the world and God. As this relation is presumably unique, we might designate it by the symbol x. But though the construction of a purely artificial language might conceivably be of some use in academic discussion, provided that we could state some rules for the manipulation of the selected symbols, it would be useless for general communication and for exhibiting the relevance of our beliefs to human life and society. Hence in practice we are inevitably thrown back on ordinary language. And this means in effect that we have to use counterbalancing analogies and 'projections', by means of which we try to grasp and state that which cannot be adequately grasped and stated. To anyone who believes that all that can be said can be said clearly, this is not a satisfactory state of affairs. But it is an essential characteristic of this particular language-game, talk about God. And if we try to eliminate it by translating talk about God into the language of the absolute idealism of Hegel or into that of logical positivism, we shall soon find ourselves talking about something else, about the world when looked at in a special way, or about man, no longer about God. In fine, Hegel attempted, in my opinion, to do what cannot be done, namely to make plain to view what can only be simply apprehended through the use of analogies and symbols.

A final point. The analogies and projections which we use tend to get a grip on the mind, holding it captive and leading it to imagine that it understands more than it does. The mystical writers, however, such as St John of the Cross, remind us of the inadequacy of our conceptual representations of God, of the shortcomings of our language in this region of thought. To employ once again a phrase of Paul Tillich, it is the religious mystics who most strikingly exemplify the movement of the human spirit from 'God' to *God*. But this, I think, is a feature of mysticism of which Hegel failed to appreciate the significance.

9

OLD WINE IN NEW BOTTLES?
TILLICH AND SPINOZA

Cornelius de Deugd

I SHALL begin by making a brief comparison between Spinoza
and Tillich and then, in the second half of my paper, ask a few
questions, and discuss some details, with regard to the nature
of the type of thinking they exhibit which, in the broadest
sense of the word, is metaphysical. My interest is not purely
historical, although I believe that historical comparisons can
throw light on what very many of our contemporaries have in
mind. In fact, this is in part my justification for this paper, and
it is perhaps as well, at the outset, to make clear the point of
view from which I propose to look into the matter.

When I last visited the Royal Institute of Philosophy, I heard
Professor Robinson speak on 'The Logic of Religious Language'.
I have a feeling that I have less confidence in the logic of
religious language than he has, having at the same time less
confidence than he has in the possibilities of linguistic analysis
to display that logic. Rather, it is my impression that, instead
of getting anywhere with the discussion of religious language
and metaphysics, things become more problematic all the time,
and I ought not to pretend that I think otherwise. In fact, I
do not claim to know precisely what I am talking about when I
use such terms as 'substance', 'being', 'God', etc. But I have
two reasons for using them. First, I want to do everything in
my power to understand what people mean when they use
these terms; as the logical aspect is the most *fragwürdig* I try
to understand, also, with the help of other than strictly logical
means, with the aid of mental powers like imagination and

empathy, in order to grasp to some extent – to get at least a glimpse of – what they can mean by them. In the second place there is what can perhaps be called a kind of anthropological interest on my part. These are, or can be, things which are of great and existential interest to millions of my fellow-men, either in a philosophical or in a religious sense. It is, of course, possible to cut short the philosophical discussion by applying some form of the verification principle, but that is likely to end all other forms of communication also, and for reasons of 'human interest' I want to keep the discussion going with all the means at our disposal.

After this lengthy preamble, I propose to discuss three major features of Tillich's system. First, a conspicuous methodological presupposition, that of the autonomy of reason; second, the basic tenet of his system, which is his conception of God; and, third, the most obvious ethical, that is practical, consequence of his thinking, that of man's self-affirmation in the 'courage to be'. All three will prove to be closely related to Spinoza's philosophy.

As to the first of these three the discussion can be very brief, partly because this point is fairly well-known, I believe, and in addition it is something which is so evident particularly in comparison with Spinoza. Tillich, making a distinction between an ontological and a technical concept of reason, endorses the principle of the autonomy of reason and adheres to this position consistently in all his writings and especially in the three-volume *Systematic Theology*. To give an impression of the force with which this idea is put to the fore I need quote only one sentence from the extensive discussion of 'Reason and Revelation' in vol. i of the *Systematic Theology*: 'The denial of reason in the classical sense is anti-human because it is anti-divine.'[1]

For those who know Spinoza the rationalist no elaboration is needed to show the similarity with respect to this important methodological aspect. It is better to save our time for the next point, that of Tillich's conception of God, which merits a far more extensive discussion.

[1] *Systematic Theology* (Chicago, 1951), i, p. 72. The full discussion of this feature of his thought is to be found on pp. 71–105.

Tillich's conception of God is not the one which, for centuries, has traditionally prevailed in theistic Christianity. That is to say, it is not the conception of a person of superhuman potentialities who, though a spirit (cf. John 4: 24) and thus thought of as immaterial, is yet somehow located in space by saying that he is 'above' or 'in heaven'. God is considered the highest being but, as this expression implies, *a* being nonetheless, a being alongside other beings. Tillich has left far behind him both this idea and the accompanying terminology. In speaking of this conception he employs the term 'supranaturalism'. And when in the newest theological developments it is said that 'God is dead' it is primarily this idea of the supranaturalist God which is declared to be dead. Tillich's influence on this point is a profound one indeed.

However, the question to be asked here is what is going on in Tillich's world when viewed from a strictly philosophical point of view. Seeing it thus, it is very interesting to note that, although Tillich's conception of God is expressed in what he himself calls a philosophical system, one is nevertheless constantly reminded of the tradition of philosophical metaphysics.

Tillich speaks of 'being itself' or 'the power of being', and this concept he equates with 'God'. God is being-itself; he is 'ultimate reality'; this is the basic thesis of his thought. This conviction is generally known, I believe, particularly in Britain where Bishop Robinson in *Honest to God* has capitalised heavily upon it, developing, in a most interesting way, the theological possibilities of these ideas. Hearing expressions like 'being-itself', or 'the ground of being', one may be inclined to think of fully traditional philosophical points of view, such as, for instance, pantheism. Tillich himself would dismiss any such interpretation. I now quote a few lines from the *Systematic Theology*: 'Being-itself infinitely transcends every finite being. There is no proportion or gradation between the finite and the infinite. There is an absolute break, an infinite "jump". On the other hand, everything finite participates in being-itself and in its infinity. Otherwise it would not have the power of being.'[1]

On the basis of pronouncements like these Tillich is apt not only to dismiss traditional religious ideas, but also to claim a

---

[1] *Systematic Theology*, i, p. 237.

large measure of originality with respect to the age-old epistemological problems that surround the possibility of knowing a
supreme being.

The words I have just quoted speak of God as being-itself and
of the being of finite things. To be understood properly this
passage has to be read in the light of Tillich's method of
correlation, but that is a methodological aspect upon which I
cannot touch in the present context. It is worth noting that
despite the 'break' between the finite and the infinite all things
finite participate in being-itself. And because of this participation they 'have' the power of being.

This idea, which to many has come as a great surprise, to
say the least, we should attempt to understand against the
background of Tillich's equating God with being-itself, and
his subsequently arguing that, 'therefore', God *has* being, *is*
being, but is not *a* being alongside or above other beings. If
he were, Tillich argues, he would be subjected 'to the categories of finitude'.[1] Now if God is thought of as the ground of
being and the all-pervading, all-encompassing power of being it
follows of necessity that finite things are dependent upon this
ground of being to the extent of receiving their power of being
from it. All finitude, in other words, lives, moves and has its
being in this ontological God.

This, in a few words, is Tillich's position over against the
traditional theistic notions which he, as said before, designates
as 'supranaturalism'. And in returning to this term, supranaturalism, the problem in hand has been placed in the light
of the history of ideas. Tillich himself, speaking more or less
in historical terms, has endeavoured to distinguish three different ways of interpreting the meaning of the term 'God'.[2]

The first is the one for which Tillich uses the term supranaturalism; it is, as said before, the conception of God as a
being, separated from all other beings, existing alongside and
above them, from which position he has created the universe
and still governs it according to his plans. 'The protest of
atheism against such a highest person is correct', Tillich says.[3]
The main argument against it, he thinks, is that it transforms

---

[1] Ibid., p. 235.   [2] *Systematic Theology*, ii, pp. 6–10.
[3] *Systematic Theology*, i, p. 245.

the infinity of God into a finiteness which is merely an extension of the categories of finitude.

The second way of interpreting the meaning of the term 'God' is the way one finds in the naturalist tradition. Naturalism, according to Tillich, identifies God with the universe, with its essence or with special powers within it.[1] God is the name for the power and meaning of reality. Tillich is sufficiently careful to point out that this does not mean that God is identified with the totality of things. Expressed in popular language: God is not 'everything', as is sometimes said, for instance, in superficially defining pantheism. Tillich not only affirms the correctness of the atheist protest against supranaturalism, he also considers the naturalist arguments against it to be valid. But he does not, at least he says he does not, endorse the naturalist point of view. His objection against it is that it denies 'the infinite distance between the whole of finite things and their infinite ground, with the consequence that the term "God" becomes interchangeable with the term "universe" and therefore is semantically superfluous'.[2]

Having this criticism of the naturalist position as his point of departure, Tillich comes to his own (that is, the third) way of understanding the term 'God'.

As you will remember, I began by describing a few of the chief characteristics of his view, pointing to the central thesis of it, which is the idea that God is being-itself. Here the picture can be completed by discussing the fact that Tillich tries to formulate his ideas in such a way as to arrive at a position which not only replaces the supranaturalism of traditional theism (and deism for that matter) but which also goes beyond naturalism. At this point, as we shall see, Spinoza comes in and his appearance is first of all related to the question whether Tillich succeeds in going beyond the naturalist tradition. For that is the moot point.

To describe his own way of approaching the meaning of the term 'God' Tillich speaks of 'ecstatic' or 'self-transcending' naturalism. The adjectives 'self-transcending' and 'ecstatic' suggest that this naturalism is to be differentiated from the

---

[1] *Systematic Theology*, ii, p. 6.
[2] Ibid., p. 7.

naturalism which Tillich rejects. I now quote verbatim from a passage which has puzzled me a great deal.

> The term 'self-transcendent' has two elements: 'transcending' and 'self'. God as the ground of being infinitely transcends that of which he is the ground. He stands *against* the world, in so far as the world stands against him, and stands *for* the world thereby causing it to stand for him. This mutual freedom from each other and for each other is the only meaningful sense in which the 'supra' in 'supranaturalism' can be used. Only in this sense can we speak of transcendent with respect to the relation of God and the world. To call God transcendent in this sense does not mean that one must establish a 'superworld' of divine objects. It does mean that, within itself, the finite world points beyond itself. In other words, it is self-transcendent.[1]

As I said, this is to me a puzzling statement. Now I do not apply the so-called verification principle, neither in the old logical positivist sense, nor in any more modern, modified form. I refrain from applying such principles not because I think *a priori* that they are useless but because application means cutting short the discussion with far too many of our contemporaries who think and believe like Tillich, and, as I said before, I like to keep the discussion going as long as possible. All I am trying to do is to understand something of what Tillich could possibly mean and in doing so I am even willing to accept the possibility of something like a power or a ground of being, a creative principle, a principle perhaps comparable to 'growth' or 'sustenance', or whatever it can be called, that underlies, or sustains, or encompasses all existing things and somehow makes it possible for them to 'have' existence. Employing thus an expression like 'the power of being' I can at least think of something, 'perceive' something; I can, somehow, have an 'idea' of what we are talking about. Knowledge may be partial or imperfect, it can still be useful, even if it is only in a tentative sense. Evidently, this 'perception' or 'idea' by itself does not testify to the truth or the reality of being-itself or the power of being, yet the fact that as an 'idea'

[1] Ibid., p. 7.

it is there clearly demonstrates that there is still some form of communication possible – and on that basis we can proceed to ask how the self-transcendence brings about a different form of naturalism.

Earlier we have heard Tillich's criticism of the traditional naturalist position; 'it denies', he says, 'the infinite distance between the whole of finite things and their infinite ground' and he emphatically teaches that there is such an infinite distance. One here recognises a main theme of twentieth-century religious and philosophical thought: it is to be found in Kierkegaard's 'infinite qualitative difference between man and God'; it returns in Heidegger's anxiety that *das Sein* would be mistaken for a special and highest *Seiendes*; it is even more pronounced in Karl Barth, and of this recurrent pattern we here find the Tillichian variety. However, when Tillich says, as he does in the *Systematic Theology*,[1] that God as being-itself is the 'creative ground' of all finite things, that he is not 'above' them but that 'he is nearer to them than they are to themselves' – when he speaks thus, speaking, we should not forget, in ontological terms, he is saying something that is radically opposed to the concept of transcendence, as much as it is opposed to the idea of an infinite distance between the whole of finite things and their infinite ground. These two descriptions cannot possibly be reconciled rationally.

Is it simply a paradox, in the face of which one loses one's capacity for somehow 'perceiving at least something', which I just mentioned and which enables one to continue on the level of useful communication? Perhaps it *is* a paradoxical statement such as those we know so well from European thinking in the wake of Kierkegaard.

But in all likelihood it is something more, or, if you like, something else. In a study of Tillich published in 1961 I arrived at the conclusion that his thinking, though not the thought of a mystic in the traditional sense of the word, is at bottom determined by very strong mystical tendencies.[2] In this context, it seems, one encounters one more example of this mystical undercurrent. Here it is of major importance, for it determines a

[1] Ibid., p. 7.
[2] *Paul Tillich's filosofische Theologie* (Utrecht, 1961), p. 52.

conviction (namely that of self-transcendent naturalism) which, in Tillich's own words, underlies the whole of his system.[1]

Tillich's conception of being-itself is in fact accompanied by the idea of immanence as much as by the idea of transcendence and one cannot help noticing that, when approaching him without prejudice and with empathy and imagination one can go along with Tillich quite far, but that one cannot go with him all the way. For his pronouncements on the ground of all being, etc., seem to be an attempt at formulating an experience of immanency, but one which is, in this context, exceeded – if exceeded is the word I want – by the idea of transcendence.

He seems to be giving expression to the mystical experience of the mutual immanence of the divine and the human, which we know from the history of mysticism, and for which, in this case, the idea of 'the ultimate concern' has paved the way. It creates no surprise that Tillich makes use of the notion of 'ecstasy', speaking, as he does, of self-transcending or *ecstatic* naturalism. The idea of transcendence, which Tillich applies 'in addition', can hardly have any meaning in this context, I think, for the immanence with which he starts out (and without which his use of the terms 'being itself', 'the power of being', etc., is inconceivable) excludes the 'subsequent' transcendence. The idea of one reality which is implied in the mutual immanence, emerging from Tillich's descriptions, is incompatible with the concept of transcendence, and actually Tillich does not deny that he deals with one reality but he says that it 'is experienced' – and our attention should be drawn to the word 'experienced' – 'in different dimensions'. This becomes apparent particularly when one asks the question: to what does the finite world point when pointing beyond itself? Tillich's answer is: 'The finitude of the finite points to the infinitude of the infinite. It goes beyond itself in order to return to itself in a new dimension. This is what self-transcendence means'.[2]

What is possible on the level of the mystical experience of the individual who recognises a principle like the creative

---

[1] *Systematic Theology*, ii, p. 8.
[2] Ibid., p. 8.

ground of being, I can scarcely be expected to say, but I do think it can be said that the attempt to incorporate in this way such an experience into a system of thought recognising fully the autonomy of reason, a system, moreover, which hinges on a continuous correlation with philosophy – that such an attempt seems destined to fail.

Returning to what was quoted earlier about naturalism denying, in Tillich's view, the distance between the whole of finite things and their infinite ground, it might be suggested that it is difficult to see how he himself can maintain such a distance, and that at this point one can discern a strong re-semblance to Spinoza's thought. In fact Spinoza's substance, the most fundamental concept of his philosophy, seems to come dangerously close to Tillich's being-itself. Evidently there are some differences but the similarities are so striking that they deserve more attention than I can give them in this paper. They throw light both on Tillich's thought and on the intricate difficulties of metaphysical thinking in general. The most remarkable thing is, I think, that going through Tillich's own works one can find a sufficient number of pronouncements on Spinoza to buttress such an interpretation. It is therefore possible to have him state these similarities himself, although he refrains from doing what I am doing now, namely, piecing them together and trying to see the final outcome.

Tillich himself thus points out that, as he phrases it, Spinoza's 'universal substance ... is based on an immediate experience of something ultimate in value and being of which one can be-come intuitively aware'.[1] These are almost literally the words which he employs, as we have seen, in regard to being-itself and, generally speaking, it is obvious after what has been quoted from Tillich, that Spinoza's concept of 'substance', or God, as 'ultimate being', that is, as self-caused, self-sustaining, un-conditionally independent being, is in almost every respect reminiscent of Tillich's descriptions of being-itself. This will be even more apparent when I discuss Spinoza's doctrines of *conatus* and self-preservation.

In *The Courage to Be*, an important work if one wants to grasp Tillich's conception of God, he says that 'substance' is

[1] *Systematic Theology*, i, p. 9.

Spinoza's name 'for the ultimate power of being'.[1] The similarity could hardly be articulated in a more straightforward
manner! Furthermore, that Tillich here realises that the
application of the adjective 'static' to Spinoza's definition of
substance is incorrect is not only obvious from the context,
it can also be learned from the *Systematic Theology*. Tillich
there states that the phrase *deus sive natura*, Spinoza's famous
equation, 'does not say that God is identical with nature but
that he is identical with the *natura naturans*, the creative nature,
the creative ground of all natural objects'.[2] And this description
we should compare, finally, with what he says in *The Theology
of Paul Tillich*; he there explains that 'ground of being means
the creative source of everything that has being',[3] and reading
these words one sees how closely related is Spinoza's most
fundamental notion to the most fundamental notion in Tillich's
system.

Now does this mean that Tillich is simply to be called a
naturalist in the traditional sense that the notion of a transcendent being is wholly absent from his thought, and so on? I
hesitate to say 'yes' but I propose to return to this problem
later when I shall ask a few questions about the nature of this
type of thinking.

Having spoken of Tillich's autonomy of reason as a methodological presupposition, and of his conception of God as the
basic tenet of his system, I now come to the third and last
point, that of man's self-affirmation as the most obvious
practical outcome of his thinking.

This time it is possible to begin with Tillich and Spinoza
simultaneously by referring to what Tillich says about Spinoza
in *The Courage to Be*. This book is generally recognised as one
of the most significant of his works; it has made him widely
known, even outside ecclesiastical circles, and the idea it deals
with is a direct consequence of the basic features of his system.

Tillich has at the back of his mind Spinoza's doctrine of

[1] *The Courage to Be* (New Haven, 1952), p. 180.
[2] *Systematic Theology*, ii, p. 6.
[3] 'Reply to Interpretation and Criticism', in Charles W. Kegley and
Robert W. Bretall (eds.), *The Theology of Paul Tillich*, 4th ed. (New York,
1959), p. 341.

conatus, endeavour, the striving towards something. In the *Ethics* (iii, Prop. 7) Spinoza speaks of 'the effort by which each thing endeavours to persevere in its own being' and he calls this 'nothing but the actual essence of the thing itself'. This *conatus*, as Tillich himself summarises the second definition of Book ii of the *Ethics*, 'makes a thing what it is, so that if it disappears the thing itself disappears'. 'Striving toward self-preservation or self-affirmation', Tillich continues, 'makes a thing be what it is.' This striving, which is the essence of a thing, is as such also its power, so that Tillich finds here the identification of essence, self-affirmation, and, using a terminology which is not Spinoza's, the power of being.

Tillich advances this in his historical review of the development of the ideas about courage, in the course of which he also discusses Plato, the Stoics, Nietzsche, etc. But Spinoza is in fact much more to him than one historical figure among others. Spinoza's doctrine of *conatus* may be somewhere in the background, his self-preservation, interpreted by Tillich as self-affirmation, comes unmistakably clearly into the foreground. This happens, first, when Tillich, in the context just quoted from, points to the way Spinoza connects these ideas with man's courage and, second, when he later on, in the final part of his book, develops his own idea of the 'courage to be'.

At the former place he says that Spinoza's self-affirmation 'is participation in the divine self-affirmation' (p. 22), quoting from Book iv of the *Ethics* (4, Dem.), where Spinoza says: 'The power by which individual things and consequently man preserve their being is the actual power of God or Nature'. At the latter place, towards the end of *The Courage to Be*, after having devoted four chapters to an analysis of the human situation of anxiety, guilt and courage, Tillich elaborates his own theme, namely that the power of being is the source of the courage to be (pp. 156 ff.). He there distinguishes between the courage to be based on a mystical union with the ground of being (which he ascribes to Spinoza) and the courage to be based on the personal encounter with the ground of being or God. The latter of the two is his own version of this ontological courage in the face of the vicissitudes of the *condition humaine*.

But this distinction is of little practical significance seen in the light of his own contention (p. 160) that mysticism is an element of every form of the relation to the ground of being. In one respect the two are even identical, he says elsewhere, namely with respect to being grasped by the power of being (p. 173). In other words, one sees that the distinction between Spinoza's alleged mystical union and Tillich's personal encounter is but of relative, not of absolute importance; furthermore, one notices again the mystical undercurrent in Tillich's thought coming to the surface, and, finally, one discerns between the two philosophers the same striking similarity we had occasion to observe earlier.

What has been said thus far seems to enable us to infer that Tillich's system exhibits at least a threefold relationship with Spinoza's philosophy: first of all, in a most conspicuous epistemological presupposition; second, in its basic, its most fundamental feature; and, finally, in its most important ethical, that is practical, consequences.

It seems justified to inquire whether any other conclusions could be drawn, any other questions be raised, or whether there would be anything else one could learn from this state of affairs. I think there are, but what I can do at present is not much more than raise these questions. They pertain to the problem of the nature of this type of metaphysical thinking and to the possibilities of philosophy generally.

Is it nothing but a coincidence that a twentieth-century thinker, influenced by modern art and literature, Existentialism, psychoanalysis and other strictly contemporary phenomena, goes back to a seventeenth-century metaphysician *tout court* for no less than three indispensable elements of his system? Does it point to the poverty and the deficiencies of metaphysical thinking? Does it mean that metaphysics, to put it simply, has exhausted its supply of notions, that nothing new can be drummed up any more and that a return to metaphysics in the traditional sense or, as in Tillich's case, the introduction of metaphysical conceptions into a semi-philosophical system, amounts to little more than making the same old rounds again? Or is it a matter of two people following similar lines of thought because of similarity in the structure of the two personalities, supplying at least one proof for Fichte's well-known *dictum* that one's choice of a philosophy depends on what kind of a person one is?

There are, however, questions and problems of yet another nature.

We remember that Tillich, expounding his ideas on being-itself, was wholly immersed in ideas of immanency but nevertheless tried to hold on to some form of transcendence. He did admit, finally, that he was dealing with one reality, but stated that it is *experienced* in two dimensions. It seemed impossible to accept as legitimate these convictions in a system like this. Yet I hesitated to call Tillich a naturalist like Spinoza, though he and Spinoza differ hardly at all as far as their expressed doctrine is concerned.

The reasons for this hesitation may seem at first sight strange in this context for they are entirely subjective and personal. I knew Professor Tillich while I was a student in the graduate school at Harvard for two years, in seminars, lectures and person-to-person discussions, and I became convinced that for him there really was more to this idea of being-itself than the immanency of the one reality he speaks of. I am convinced that he experienced it as both immanent and transcendent, and that this awareness of the transcendence made him feel linked with the time-honoured tradition of Christian thinking and doctrinal standards.

But, you are likely to ask, is this a reason for ascribing to Tillich's philosophical theology the notion of transcendence? And my answer is no; no, it is not, but it raises a problem of general philosophical interest, the implications of which surpass by far the relation between Tillich and Spinoza.

As we all know there 'are' things which we can talk about but to which there does not correspond anything real. Expressed somewhat technically: one fails to find their objective reference; expressed popularly: one can name things that do not exist. Fairies and ghosts do not exist but we do have names for them. (Some would say the same of God.) On the other hand, there are things which we seem to be unable to communicate by linguistic means. And this does not seem to be necessarily a matter of subjectivity, as I hope we shall see. This aspect seems

to have received far less attention than the first one, the one of
the ghosts and fairies. I propose to consider Tillich's case from
this angle, and to see where it leads us.

Doing so one can say that Tillich has become a victim of
language, but not in the sense we all know so well and which is
Wittgenstein's target in his famous remark: 'Philosophy is a
battle against the bewitchment of our intelligence by means of
language'. Tillich is a victim in the sense of *not being able* to
make intelligible what he had in mind. This phenomenon is
quite interesting and I believe it is far more wide-spread than
we as a rule are aware of. The most elementary forms of it have
found their way into daily speech. Repeatedly we say, or hear
people saying, things like: 'so to speak', or 'I don't know how to
put it', 'as it were', 'you know what I mean', and so on, or re-
peating the same ideas two, three or even more times, every time
introducing the sentence with 'I mean', or 'what I mean'. Except
when this is just a habit of speech there is, somehow, a feeling
of disconnection or incompetence. We all know this situation;
one has something 'in mind', as we say, but one is unable to
express it in a satisfactory way and occasionally one feels one
cannot express it at all.[1] There is a content which apparently
resists being moulded into a form; one does not succeed in
form-ulating it, or, one formulates something that is not con-
gruent with the formless idea one had in mind. This 'content',
which resists its appropriate form, must be at least something of
the nature of a concept, however barely glimpsed at. And
especially when we feel that we have formulated something we
did not intend to formulate, we realise how elusive our concepts
can be. In this connection one might wonder whether Warnock
is correct when he says that 'words are not distinguishable
from the concepts they express or involve'[2] or whether this
statement does not stand in need of at least some modification.
He is aware of the fact that our concepts can be 'more complex
than our linguistic forms'[3] but what I am driving at is more
than just that; what is at stake here is the unity of form and
content which is indispensable if we are to have normal

---

[1] Cf. C. F. P. Stutterheim, *Problemen der Literatuurwetenschap* (Antwerpen–
Amsterdam, 1953), pp. 238–9.

[2] *English Philosophy since 1900* (London, 1963), p. 161.   [3] Ibid., p. 109.

linguistic communication at all. I use the word 'normal' because there are also forms of linguistic communication where
form and content are not united, for instance in the language
of symbolist poetry as I shall have occasion to discuss briefly
hereafter.

Considering these difficulties to be at least comparable to
those encountered in Tillich's case, it seems pertinent in this
connection to ask: what or who is failing here? When something cannot be expressed, or cannot be expressed adequately,
in language, could that be a reason to infer that it does not
exist and that clinging to it is a matter of self-deception? What
is the decisive criterion? Must we blame language for it, or
reason, or the allegedly inscrutable workings of man's consciousness? Is it perhaps a matter of some kind of mental short-
circuit somewhere between experience or concepts on the one
hand and words on the other hand?

Is it impossible that Tillich had the experience, and at least
some kind of a conception, of a transcendent *and* immanent
power of being simply because he could not make me 'see' the
reality of it in comprehensible language? But even if we consider it to be possible and yet decide that we have to dismiss
the things Tillich talks of because they seem incommunicable
by means of language, are we not, in that case, making language the only important and unconditionally decisive factor,
even to such an extent that we should instantly stop laughing
at Foster's Old Lady who exclaimed: 'How can I tell what I
think till I see what I say?' However this may be, where are
the limits of Tillich's language and where are the limits of his
world? Also, Wittgenstein's words that everything that can be
said can be said clearly seem to imply the possibility of things
that cannot be said. But does that mean that in those cases there
are concepts for which there are no corresponding words? Or
must we ask, rather, whether there are things for which we do
not even have concepts and, consequently, no words, no
linguistic forms? And what is the epistemological status of things
that cannot be said? Can we do anything with such 'things'?

Of course, having arrived at this point, one could say that
Tillich's case is one of subjective, personal experience (perhaps not communicable at all) which ought to be relegated to

the realm of psychology rather than being made the subject of philosophical discussion. I myself have gone to the length of interpreting Tillich's thesis as engendered by what is at bottom a mystical experience.

In mentioning 'subjectivity', 'mysticism' and such-like topics in relation to language we have touched upon a subject which certainly is not new. All of you know, I suppose, that Wittgenstein in his *Tractatus* is of the opinion that mystical experiences do occur but that they cannot be expressed by linguistic means. On the other hand there is Professor Mascall's study, *Words and Images* (1957), in which the author appeals precisely to mystical experiences in order to refute the thesis of the logical positivists that religious language has no significance in a cognitive sense.

Those who have dismissed an appeal to mystical experiences have usually done so because such experiences are attainable by some but not by all people. But this seems to be an argument that few people could take seriously. One can with equal justification point to those who do experience them instead of to those who do not. In this connection it may be observed that mystical elements similar to those found in Tillich appear in many varieties of religious experience as much as in widely divergent types of philosophy, in both East and West; that, furthermore, as far as Tillich's system is concerned there are many followers who think and feel like him and that *Honest to God* by Dr Robinson, based entirely on Tillich's conception of God, has been very influential and has sold nearly a million copies, something unheard of in the modern history of printing serious philosophical and theological works. Now apart from the anthropological interest, of which I spoke at the beginning and which in the face of such facts should, I think, be properly aroused, one is justified in asking whether or not some form of objectivity comes in when great numbers of people testify to the existence of certain experiences, conceptions, etc., even though they are as yet puzzling from an epistemological and linguistic angle.

However, this aspect must not detain us here; we should continue asking questions about 'mental content' and its expression in linguistic forms, questions which seem to be of importance in relation to men like Tillich and Spinoza and to the *raison d'être* of metaphysics in general.

Having seen Tillich not being able to express something which, somehow, he seems to have known, and having seen, afterwards, the difficulties of formulating formless contents also when not related to metaphysical subjects, we are now somewhat better situated to look at an interesting possibility in the use of language, namely that of a conveyance of ideas by means of words, while these words, in fact, express something else. I am referring here to the language of symbolist poets. In their writings, it seems to me, the relationship between concepts and words becomes highly problematical, the more so, perhaps, because they *can have assertional sense*, can contain knowledge, although this is of course not always necessarily the case. This language does not appear very frequently, but then, the aim here is only to call attention to the phenomenon as a linguistic possibility, not only because of the opportunity it affords for implicit or explicit comparison with Tillich's case, but also because I am not certain that a comparable mechanism is not at work in other linguistic utterances.

Poetry in the symbolist tradition once had its representatives all over the continent and Great Britain; in our days also it is still written and it is likely that it will be written throughout the centuries, for it has a very particular charm, especially for readers of more or less intellectualist tastes. What, in fact, is the distinguishing characteristic of this type of writing?

Reading a symbolist poem we find a form and a content, united as is normal. There is a meaning conveyed as in all traditional, non-experimental poetry. This meaning is expressed, so to speak, immediately. As an example one could think of *Les Pas* by Valéry, in which the poet tells of his beloved who wakes him with a kiss. With a view strictly, and only, to the content and apart from aesthetic values and intentions, one can say that this language imparts this knowledge about the poet's life. But then the symbolist element comes in. These lines can and must be read as having yet another meaning, another content or subject matter. One then reads as it were another poem, from line to line a 'different story'. It is a tale about the way in which the muse visits him, the poet, and wakes him up

M   T.O.G.

from the sleep of non-activity to the life of creative action. Read thus – and it has been written to be read in this way – one reads what the French call the *sens superposés*, the superimposed meaning, or, occasionally, meanings (for there may be two or more).

Here we see that words *are* 'distinguishable from the concepts they express or involve', in other words, concepts can be expressed by means of words that in fact express other concepts.

In recapitulating we can perhaps see somewhat more clearly both the possibilities and the difficulties which are involved. In Tillich's case there were concepts which he could put into words but not in such a way as to make them become intelligible. In the case of those disunities we found exemplified in daily speech, there are concepts for which one cannot find words, or cannot find the right words. And, finally, with the use of symbolist devices, there is the case of one set of words and, corresponding with that set, two sets of concepts.

It would be possible to enter upon an additional discussion of certain uses of language which display similar possibilities and cognate problems, as well as new aspects, e.g. the use of allegorical language, but that would of course carry us too far.

If you now ask me what I have done, I am prepared to admit that I have done very little. On the basis of a comparison of two metaphysical thinkers, one from the seventeenth and one from the twentieth century, a comparison displaying a remarkable degree of similarity, I have asked a few questions, first, about the possible consequences of that similarity and, second, about one specific aspect (of a psycho-linguistic nature) of one of the two systems, having a choice from dozens of such aspects from both systems. All this has resulted in only one certainty, namely that if one is unwilling to dismiss, at the very outset, all religious and metaphysical talk, one can hardly continue to talk at all, for the problems and difficulties just seem to multiply.

If, after all this, the situation with respect to metaphysical thinking has become a little more problematical than it was to you before – then, though having done little, I shall have achieved what I had hoped to achieve.

I have little hope that with the means philosophy at present employs in isolation, phenomenological, positivistic, analytical means, and so on, we shall arrive at a more satisfactory state of affairs. I believe it can easily be seen that we are not much further than in Spinoza's time and that we have centuries of old wine and hardly any new bottles.

But I do have hope; I have hope that one day we shall witness the growth of a general, comprehensive Philosophy of Language, a philosophy which shall consider language not only from the angle of logic and meaning as linguistic philosophy does, but which shall approach it from every corner into which language reaches; a philosophy in which shall be asked what anthropology, sociology, literary criticism, general linguistics, psychology, literary theory, etc. have to say about language and its uses. Naturally, this can only be a collective venture for it could not be done by one person or one 'school'. There can be little doubt that much material as has been gathered in recent years in various quarters (often considered as mutually excluding each other) will prove to be useful later when the time comes for what I like to think of as the synthetical effort of all those who hold the careful scrutiny of language to be of essential value to philosophy.

10

THE GOD OF RELIGION AND THE GOD OF PHILOSOPHY

Charles Hartshorne

I n several great religions God is thought of as an agent or active individual exalted in principle above other agents, the supreme creative and controlling power. But, however exalted, the deity is still, in spite of what Tillich and others say, an individual being, somehow analogous to a human person. Indeed, man is said to be created in the divine image. Without this analogy religion loses an essential trait. Not only in faiths derived from Judaism, but also in Zoroastrianism, and even in much Hinduism and some Buddhism, the analogy plays a central role.

In India, however, and even in the West, the view was often taken that, although supreme personality is admissible as an object of worship, one must distinguish between the supreme person and the supreme reality. Ishvara, or the divine person, is on this view neither simply real nor simply unreal; rather, he shares the twilight status of the world of common sense, that of being almost real, Maya. Compared to mere dreams or hallucinations, Ishvara or Saguna Brahman, Brahman qualified by personality, is real; compared to Nirguna Brahman, unqualified Brahman, the highest, most genuine reality, Ishvara is unreal. In England, Bradley held some such view.

In religions of semitic origin, and in Zoroastrianism, the idea that anything could be more real or worthy of respect than God is blasphemous. This is my view: I hold that though God must be personal he must also be such that nothing could be superior to him. Some Hindu sects agree with this. But the orthodox Hindus or Advaita Vedantists were right, in my opinion, on one point. If the highest reality is what many philosophers have meant by 'the absolute', or what Aristotle and the scholastics called 'the unmoved mover', then the personal deity is not the highest reality. There can be no analogy between persons and something wholly absolute, self-sufficient, infinite, or immutable. Medieval philosophers, and Immanuel Kant as belated medievalist, were, I hold, as wrong in asserting this form of the theological analogy as the Vedantists were in asserting a superior to God. The God of religion, though not inferior to the absolute, is also not identical with it. Hume's Cleanthes was almost free from this error, but Kant, in his so-called Ideal of Pure Reason, reinstated it. And it is still with us, though now at last very much on the defensive.

The root mistake is the failure to realise that expressions like 'the absolute' or 'the unmoved mover' have clear and consistent meanings only when used to refer to something extremely abstract. The multiplication table is almost absolute enough, immutable enough. What could change it? God is indeed absolute but not *the* absolute, as though this were his whole character. Since he is more than an abstraction, his absoluteness is only one side of his nature. It is just as necessary that a supreme form of relativity should also belong to him. Indeed, his overall character is this supreme relativity. As the concrete is more than the abstract and includes it, so the relative is more than and includes the non-relative. Only something extremely abstract can be independent of relations to concrete things. To lack relations to the concrete is to lack concreteness. Concrete things have relations to other concrete things and to the abstract as well. Sheer independence is negative, a lack of something, not only verbally but really. The proof is seen in knowledge, which relates the knower to the things known. We are independent of and do not know remote contemporaries out in space; did we know them our dependence upon them, their influence upon us, would already have begun.

As Fechner saw long ago, what exalts God is not his immutable and self-sufficient perfection, but his perfect capacity to surpass himself as well as all others by taking each phase of creation into his own life. Before developing this idea further, let us consider more explicitly the personal character of God.

In spite of the vast difference between the two sides of the analogy, God was spoken of – at least in religious practice even if not theory – as a conscious agent knowingly interacting with inferior agents, ruling over them, though – in the best religious forms – not as a nervous tyrant unwilling that they should decide anything for themselves, but rather as a wise and generous ruler or parent who wishes them, within proper limits, to make their own decisions. The interpretation of such analogies was of course problematic, but that *some* good interpretation was possible forms part of the very meaning of the religious term 'God'. God was to be loved as a person is loved and he was said himself to be the supremely loving individual. He was not to be loved merely as a mathematician loves a beautiful piece of reasoning, or as a philosopher may love his system of ideas, rather, as one loves a father, ruler, or friend of exalted qualities. And how was God himself said to love? Not by unintentionally causing benefits to the creatures, as the rain or sun – or perhaps Plato's Form of Good – may do, but with conscious appreciation or concern for their happiness, in other words, love in the proper social sense.

It was also said that God has made or created all things. But here the meaning is somewhat less obvious. For while human life exhibits cases of love between individuals, or of an individual ruling over others, in what sense does it exhibit cases of an individual creating others? A potter makes a pot; but this analogy is not helpful. A pot is only in a weak sense an individual. It is not a dynamic agent, acting individually, as its own molecules presumably are, and as we are. Moreover, not the mind of the potter but only his hands or tools directly influence the clay; God is without hands, and apparently must as pure spirit act on physical things. This objection holds also against the analogy of begetting or procreation. And if it be said that God creates the very stuff or matter which he shapes, then indeed what glimmering of analogy is left to give human meaning to the theological statement? After all, human terms must acquire their meanings through human experiences.

Once an infant is born, there is a good sense in which parents, and also nurses, teachers, friends, even enemies, could be said to create much of the experience, thought, and character of the growing child. For they impart or suggest to it modes of response which tend to form its very substance or nature. And a ruler creates elements of civil order in the lives of the ruled which become important factors in their natures. But in these analogies, too, the creative influence works through the bodies of the parents, teachers, or rulers. So we still have no basis for the idea of God as pure spirit getting results in the world.

There is at least one further analogy – not the potter's hands shaping the clay, but the potter's mind, his thought and intention, putting his hands through the required behaviour. How is this possible? The hands are his, but this of itself explains nothing, and is the problem over again. What is the mysterious relation between human purpose and the bodily members which enable the latter to express the former? If we knew *that*, we might have some basis for an analogical idea of the creative power of deity.

The mind-body analogy, in spite of its relevance, has not ordinarily occurred in religious language. The reasons for this avoidance are not hard to guess. It was highly important to discourage thinking about God as simply a more powerful human being or animal, with a superior but still localised body – hence, one might suppose, dependent upon an external environment, subject to birth and death, illness and insanity, threats and bribery. To exclude these features, one must form the idea of a body which is not less than the entire universe, and this is no object to which ordinary persons, or as yet even modern astronomers, have ready access. The universe cannot be seen or touched, as animals are seen and touched; one cannot stand outside it to observe or feel its boundaries or limits. On the whole it is little wonder that God was not, in naïve religious circles, thought of as a besouled organism. Still, Plato did use this analogy, and Ramanuja used it later in India. But these men were exceptions. Even now it is a difficult analogy to interpret. Yet it is, I think, indispensable, for only in the mind-body relation do we have an instance of mind dealing directly with physical – by which I here mean visible, tangible – reality. All other experiences of influence between mind and physical things – apart from abnormal and controversial cases of table-lifting and the like – are indirect, and operate through the mind-body relation.

Another important but not obvious analogy for the religious idea of God is seen if we consider the question of immortality. God was unhesitatingly viewed as secure against death or destruction. In many religions human beings were also held to be immortal. The ancient Jews, however, and some of the Greeks, were able to see themselves as strictly mortal, renouncing immortality as a unique privilege of deity. How was this possible? If death is sheer destruction of an individual, and all human individuals face this destruction, what in the long run do they accomplish by their endeavours? What meaning or lasting value have human lives? Modern sceptics are wont to reply by referring to 'social immortality', or the contributions our lives may make to posterity. And certainly the ancient Jews thought a good deal about the future of their people or nation. But is social immortality a sufficient counterbalance to death? What we contribute to posterity seems a highly variable and capricious affair, and it is not obvious that the whole permanent value of our having lived can be satisfactorily measured in this way. In addition there is no possible proof that the human species is literally immortal. Species last longer than individuals, but that seems to be all we know or ever could know on this subject.

There is another way of giving meaning to human lives without assuming that the individual or the species will survive forever, at least as this survival is commonly conceived. Social immortality means influencing and contributing value to the experiences of those living after we are dead. But God will be living after we are dead and after the dying out of no matter what species of animal. God, we are told, is all-knowing; also he loves us. This surely means that he will continue to know and cherish us no matter how long we have been dead. If we will have value in the memories of friends and admirers who survive us, much more can we have value in the consciousness of God, who endures forever, and who alone can fully appreciate all that we have been, felt, or thought. A few poets have expressed what this can mean religiously, but on the whole it has been a neglected implication of the religious idea. As with the body-mind analogy, its relevance is not measured by the amount of attention it has received. It is the only counterbalance to death which involves no assumptions besides the mere belief in God. By contrast, human immortality, as commonly construed, attributes to man an absoluteness or infinity of individual duration in the future, an infinity which, in this dimension, even God could not surpass. (One cannot endure longer than forever.) Man, to all appearances finite in time as in space, ventures to claim at least a prospective infinity for himself. This infinity he must, as believer, attribute to God; but should he appropriate it for himself as well? Where does one stop in posing as rival to deity?

For these reasons, I deeply honour that ancient people who, almost alone in the world, could accept their status as neither divine nor immortal. But, implicitly at least, they were assured of a kind of immortality from this alone, that God would everlastingly know and love them just as they were in their earthly careers. For there cannot be a counterpart to forgetting in God. Thus it is logically impossible to believe in God and not accede a kind of immortality to the creatures. To be sure, all creatures whatever, not just man, would likewise be everlasting as objects of divine awareness. Yet with this difference, that man alone has the privilege of consciously believing in his everlastingness. He can in the present enjoy his coming immortality-for-God, as well as be destined to it.

Thus we may conclude that not only is God, analogically speaking, creator, ruler, friend, and soul of the cosmos; he is also the ultimate posterity, the final locus of social immortality. But this implication of belief was seldom made adequately clear.

Closely related to the neglect of the role of God as the ultimate posterity is the onesided view generally taken of the interaction between God and creatures. God does things to and for us, this was agreed; do we do anything to or for God? This was often denied. Man is the weak or needful party calling to God for help; could God obtain benefits from mere man? In primitive stages of religion, to be sure, sacrifices were offered to the gods, as though they could with profit to themselves receive gifts from their worshippers. Also, even in more advanced stages, there is talk about 'serving' God. And if service is not doing something beneficial to the one served, what does the word mean? Still, there was a haunting notion that really the creatures serve only themselves and each other in 'doing God's will', since their actions can confer no benefits upon the deity. But this, if taken literally and absolutely, destroys the religious idea of God.

There may be philosophical ideas according to which there is but a one-way street between worshippers and worshipped, only God being giver and only creatures receivers of value, but this is not the religious idea. Buber, in *I and Thou*, was brilliantly right on this point, and so were Berdyaev and various other writers of our time. But the majority of theologians and theistic philosophers through the centuries have taken the onesided view. My point is, they have taken it not as worshippers but as theorists, and highly prejudiced theorists, trying to interpret worship.

Religion is concerned with interaction between creator and creatures, not with mere action by the one upon the others. Examine any basic aspect of religious practice. It will exhibit divine-human reciprocity as essential. Apart from such reciprocity, all the analogies spoken of earlier in this talk collapse, whether it be the ruler analogy, the father analogy, the friend analogy, the mind-body analogy. Cast all these aside, and you may use the word God, but you are not talking religious language. And no good ruler, parent, friend, but is genuinely interested in the ruled, the child, the friend, to the extent of taking pleasure in their welfare, and grieving over their misfortunes. Taking pleasure in something is deriving benefit from it, if I know the use of such words. 'Grieving over' may seem to imply the opposite, but this would be an exaggeration. Sorrowful love is a better, more satisfying, experience than mere indifference. The mind-body analogy yields the same result, perhaps even more obviously: the cells of our bodies benefit us by their good health; and though we derive less value from them when they sicken, always we derive value.

Ramanuja defines a body for a given soul or mind as that group of things over which the soul constantly rules or has control. By this definition the supreme Lord or God is, he argued, the soul of the cosmic organism. But Ramanuja seems to forget, or even to deny, that if the soul influences the bodily parts, the parts influence the soul. This oversight or onesidedness is all too characteristic of philosophers in the various religious traditions.

The onesided view of the creator-creature interaction has grave penalties. If, relative to God, we are helpless to contribute value, if God acts upon us, not we upon him, then what about our acting upon other creatures? This is the old problem of 'secondary causes'. God is supreme cause, and – it was often suggested – this means that he determines everything unilaterally by his unlimited power. But if God determines everything, we, it seems, determine nothing. Malebranche and others who held that God alone caused physical changes in the world were only carrying out more consistently a onesidedness inherent in religion for centuries.

Linguistic analysis, the favourite tool of contemporary philosophy, has an important clarification to effect here. If God determines all events, decides whatever is decided, then what human meaning do words like 'determine' or 'decide' retain? Do we learn how to use these words by observing the decisions or doings of God, or of men? What can it mean to speak of God doing or deciding unless it first of all means something to speak of men in this way? And if the meaning is derived from the human paradigm, how can we also use the word to attribute a sheer monopoly of acting or decision-making to deity?

In the Book of Job, that great prephilosophical discussion of divine power, Job is finally told that he does not understand the conventional talk about God creating or controlling the world. A common interpretation of the book is that Job is so humbled by the display of divine might that he no longer dares to press the question of divine justice. This seems subtly to miss the point. Job learns not simply how great is divine power, but how radically different from ours and therefore how difficult for human beings to understand. He learns that he has been presumptuous, not in daring, weak as he is, to challenge divine majesty, but rather in daring, limited in experience as he is, to suppose that he knows what one means in saying, God 'does' such and such. The mistake is not with respect to divine purpose or justice; indeed the voice from the whirlwind says nothing about justice and almost nothing about purpose. The mystery is not in the relation of divine deeds to divine righteousness, but simply in the nature and identity of the deeds themselves.

In modern terms, Job comes to realise that the supposed concept of 'omnipotence', or 'creation', at least as then entertained, was too unclear or mysterious to entitle men to make deductions from it. How strange to see Anthony Flew and others today proceeding as though the idea of God stands or falls with that of omnipotence, and as though this latter idea were so clear that we can safely use it to infer that if a man is ill, God has deliberately inflicted this illness upon him, or at least has deliberately neglected to protect him from it! The man is ill, but then God is not the only, even though the supreme, agent in reality. If he were the only agent, we could not use the word agency with its commonsense meaning. And to suppose that the supreme agent decides all things and ordinary agents simply reiterate items in the supreme decision is to play fast and loose with the notion of decision-making. If I really decide X, then God does not decide X, and if I do not really decide anything, then how is the word 'decide' in my vocabulary? This is my version of linguistic analysis with respect to the alleged problem of evil. It is a linguistically improper problem.

Illness may be caused by all sorts of agents other than God, including bacteria. Moreover, since divine attributes are the supreme forms of universal properties, such as power or agency, every creature must have power in some form, however humble. Decision-making, which is the essence of power, cannot in its broadest meaning be confined to God, nor even to God and man, no, not even to God and the animals. Rather it pervades reality generally. If it be said that the supreme agent could have prevented the lesser agents from harming the man, the answer is, how far could the creatures be reduced to mere puppets, and still exist as creatures? (Remember that the molecules in a puppet are not puppets. A puppet is a statistical outline only, not an active individual.) I wonder if Flew is much wiser in this matter than Job?

I have spoken as though there were but a single religious idea of God. With some qualification, I believe this to be the case.

One must of course have the high religions in mind, and neglect fanciful polytheistic notions of demons and quasidivine figures. Once that is done, I find a rather definite, coherent, and universal idea as the religious meaning of the word 'God', or Ishvara in Sanskrit, or Allah in Arabic, or the Holy One of Israel, blessed be he! It is partly the philosophers who have multiplied conceptions of God. This is not altogether surprising if it be true that the idea is religious in its intuitive origin, and the effort of philosophy has been to find logical forms or patterns appropriate to express the intuitive idea. In the process of fitting religious intuition into these logical patterns, mistakes could easily be made. There are always various ways to miss the truth. Once made, mistakes are not easily corrected, for religion has a conservative tendency, and when theologians adopted a philosophical account of their religion, and they generally did so, the philosophical tenets, mistakes and all, often became a part of some sacred tradition. This happened in Europe, it happened in Asia. Philosophy and religion are still struggling with the results.

The logical patterns just spoken of were expressed in such terms as first cause, unmoved mover, infinity, absoluteness, necessity, perfection, creation *ex nihilo*. For religion God is indeed 'the creator', and philosophers (hastily, I think) took this to mean that he is cause, and only cause, in any relation in which he is involved. He is universal cause, cause of *all* things, and this might *seem* to imply that he was in no sense effect of anything. Again, a Biblical text uses the term 'perfect' of God, and other texts say that he does not change. Philosophers took this to mean that God was immutable and perfect in the unqualified sense found, for example, in Plato's *Republic*, or in Aristotle's metaphysics, according to which God was eternally in actual possession of all that was worth having, and hence could in no way acquire additional value, whether from the creatures or otherwise, so that any change would for him be useless or meaningless. Thus we have, as it seems, a complete harmony between Greek philosophy and sacred scripture. What an illusion! When, in the New Testament, Jesus called upon his followers to be perfect as their heavenly father is perfect, was he talking about being like an unmoved mover, or about being cause and in no way effect? How can anyone believe that being a follower of Jesus is like being an imitator of Aristotle's divine Aristocrat, who is serenely indifferent to the world's turmoil? Spinoza put it bluntly. The finding of philosophical, by which he meant essentially Greek, doctrines in the Bible was a mistake from the start. These are incompatible ways of thinking. I am far from a Spinozist, but on this point I think Spinoza was like a man awake in a world of dreamers.

If the traditional Greek concept of immutable perfection, or of the absolute, fails to express the religious idea, how else can philosophers translate this idea into technical terms? Or *can* it be translated at all into logically disciplined language? Perhaps we must, with Tillich, develop a theory of the 'symbolic' rather than literal meaning of religious talk. In its own interest, however, if not in that of religion, philosophy should not lightly renounce the hope of speaking logically and literally even about God. What *can* be spoken of rationally ought to be so spoken of, at least by some persons, and by whom if not philosophers? Moreover, the history of ideas suggests that somehow the religious idea is the central human conception. Only after every reasonable possibility of arriving at a philosophical theism has been explored will it be in order to give up the attempt. Has every such possibility been explored? Perhaps, but not in the standard histories and textbooks. In these, the Greek dogma that God is simply the religious term for the philosophical absolute, the immutably perfect, is almost the sole approach seriously considered, with a few glances at the extreme contrary of a merely finite or relative deity, a notion which is at least as obviously incapable of defining what the high religions are concerned with.

What I propose is the following. The standard terms of religious philosophising – absolute, infinite, immutable, eternal, self-sufficient, necessary, universal cause – do apply to the God of religion, but they apply less simply and exclusively than has been supposed. God is *somehow* absolute, infinite, immutable, and supreme cause; but in such fashion that he can *also* be relative, finite, mutable, and supreme effect. God comes under both sides of the basic contraries. On both sides he is different in principle from other individuals. He is cause in a radically unique or 'eminent' sense; he is also effect in an equally unique sense; he is infinite as no one else is, but also finite as no one else is. I call this the 'principle of dual transcendence'. I could fill volumes, indeed I have filled volumes, on this topic (though the phrase, 'dual transcendence', first occurred to me recently). I cannot tell you here and now my entire thought on the matter. I can, however, give a few glimpses of the relevant system of ideas.

Most Western philosophers and theologians have rejected Aristotle's conception of a God unaware of the world, knowing only his own knowing of his own knowing – of what? So let us grant that God knows the world. It follows, I submit, that his knowledge is finite as well as infinite. The existing world is not the only possible one. God then knows which among possible universes is the existing one; he knows the merely possible universes too, but only *as* possible. (For to say that he knows them as existing would be to attribute error to him, not knowledge.) Thus divine knowledge of actuality is necessarily limited to just those possibilities which are in fact actualised. God could know the actualisation of other possibilities were there such actualisation, but since there is not, he does not. This implies finitude in the divine knowledge.

Divine knowledge is also infinite in a definite and unique sense. Consider the totality of possible world states. This is 'infinite' if the word means anything. Not only does God know this infinite totality, but he could and would know the realisation of any of the possibilities were it to be realised. Thus his *potential* knowledge is absolutely infinite in the strictest sense conceivable. Nothing could be which he could not and would not know. With the creatures, not only is their actual knowledge limited, but even their potential knowledge is narrowly circumscribed. For example, no human being could have direct knowledge of a world state in which human life would be impossible. Nor could any of us ever have vivid and distinct knowledge of what it feels like to be an elephant. But God can know these things.

I said above that on both sides of the contraries, such as infinite and finite, God is equally unique. How, you may wonder, is the divine knowledge of actuality unique if, like ours, it is finite? I answer: our knowledge of actuality is not merely finite, it is fallible and fragmentary, a partial, uncertain consciousness which is in all basic respects capable of being surpassed by others cleverer or more fortunate than we. God's knowledge of actuality, though finite, is complete, not fragmentary. It covers the whole of actuality with certainty and ideal clarity.

Consider another pair of contraries, cause and effect, or condition and conditioned, or influencing and being influenced. We creatures influence *some* other creatures, but not all others. Which of us has influenced persons who died before he was even conceived? Or contemporaries remote from himself in space? The uniqueness of the divine influence is, at least, its universality; all things whatsoever undergo this influence. But what about an equally universal capacity for being influenced? None of us can receive influences from contemporaries in remote parts of space, any more than he can exert influences upon them. Indeed our limitation in the one way is the exact counterpart of our limitation in the other. Only loose thinking and ignorance could have made it possible to speak of 'the relative', or the dependent, as one kind of thing, and the independent or absolute as another kind of thing. Actually, a man is as literally independent as he is dependent, though not with respect to the same things. Consider, then, a capacity to receive influence as universal in scope as the divine capacity to exert influence. Only God, I maintain, could possess either capacity. Perhaps you now see the point of the principle of dual transcendence. I seriously believe that it, and not the traditional notion, expresses in technical language what religion has meant by God.

Please do not suppose that I claim sheer originality for this principle. No one else has so baptised it, or has analysed the relevant issues so extensively; but the gist of the idea is found in several philosophers and theologians, a dozen or more altogether. Whitehead is the most famous of these, but I got a first hint of the idea from my Harvard teacher, W. E. Hocking, and later also from reading the German psychologist Fechner, who, though learned historians seem not to know this, was about the most original and penetrating natural theologian of the last century. There were also Pfleiderer in Germany, Jules Lequier in France, and, in our century, W. P. Montague in the United States, and others, including Martin Buber, in at least five countries.

Let us now take another look at the idea of God as creator. God is pictured as saying, 'Let there be light.' What do the words, 'Let there be light' stand for if not for a decision in the divine life? This decision, according to most religious thought, is free, and free not only in the sense urged by strict determinists, who confuse mere voluntariness with creative freedom. In spite of Spinoza, God's decisions are not subjects for causal derivation, unless in a weaker or different sense than classical determinism supposes. Moreover, if what I have been saying about the human origin of human ideas is correct, there must be something analogous to divine creativity in human decisions. We too must have, in our humbler way, capacity to do what no presupposed causes (including God as cause) fully determine or require. In short, classical determinism is theologically unacceptable for linguistic reasons. It is also at best controversial even in physics. The basic principle of causality should not, for a theist, be the equivalence of cause and effect; rather there must be more in an effect than in its causal antecedents. The stream rises above its source. Causation is creation, the enriching of reality, its self-transcendence. Causality as the prefiguring of the effect in its conditions is a secondary and approximate aspect only.

God's decisions, being freely creative or contingent, must be additions to his necessary or eternal reality. In short, the first phase of God's creativity is an enhancement of his own being, implying a kind of divine change. Karl Barth, for one, has admitted this. Divine creation is divine self-creation. Ikhnaton said long ago that his God 'fashions himself'. A pre-Spanish Mexican poet said, 'The creator of all is creator of himself.' But, so far as I can see, no other view makes sense. For consider the human basis of the idea of creation. We say, a man *makes* a decision, or makes a resolve to do so and so, or 'makes up' his mind. What is the character of the adult man but a sort of composite of his past decisions? As Lequier saw with such brilliant clarity (long before Whitehead or Sartre), we human beings, in considerable measure, are self-created. In his words: 'Thou hast created me creator of myself.' But Lequier saw more. God knows what we freely decide, and therefore, we decide something in God, namely some aspect of the content of his knowledge. We perpetually create content not only in ourselves but in God also. In addition we contribute creatively to the experiences our fellow creatures have of us. So all creation is self-creation which becomes an element in the self-creation of other subjects.

Since deity is the supreme explanatory factor, and since eminent creativity is a divine attribute, realities other than God must have their appropriate, noneminent forms of creativity. Creaturely properties can only be derivative, humbler forms of the divine attributes. This is an old idea, especially stressed by some of the Renaissance predecessors of Leibniz and by Leibniz himself; but not adequately worked out by them. Granted that only God has unsurpassable freedom, and only man has human freedom, nevertheless dogs must have doggish freedom; yes, and atoms atomic freedom. The physicists seem to admit the possibility; should not philosophy of religion affirm its reality? According to this doctrine, it is illegitimate to reason from observed evils to a divine intention that the evils should occur. God is the cosmic ruler, but no ruler makes all of the subjects' decisions. Indeed no ruler literally makes any concrete decisions of subjects. He only sets limits within which the ruled make their own decisions. God is not more desirous of a monopoly of power than human beings. Rather he radically surpasses them in generous willingness to delegate decision-making to others.

I have said nothing about reasons for believing in God. This is a subject for another occasion. But if philosophers have mistaken the meaning of the religious idea of God as badly as I hold that they have mistaken it, is it likely that they have succeeded any better in their efforts to judge the truth of the idea? I think this is a task which must be taken up afresh.

Our contentions may be summarised as follows. The God of religion is personal, the philosophical absolute is impersonal; the two are not identical. There is no such thing as the absolute, the infinite, the unmoved mover, save as a mere abstraction, but there is an absolute, infinite, unmoved aspect of the personal God of religion, whose exaltation above all other individuals is expressed by the principle of 'dual transcendence', being dependent and independent, finite and infinite, changeable and unchangeable, individual and universal, each in a uniquely excellent way. Since the relative side is concrete and the abstract is real only in the concrete, the transcendent relativity of God is his overall property. Like all genuine persons, he reacts to others, engages with them as eminent partner in the process of shared self-creation which is the highest meaning of freedom and love.

11

THE ELUSIVE SELF AND THE
I-THOU RELATION

H. D. Lewis

THE elusive self! Let me first indicate how I understand these
terms. For those who posit, as I do, a self that is more than its
passing states, and which may not be reduced at all to observable phenomena, the problem arises at once of how such a self
is to be described and identified. It cannot be identified in terms
of any pattern of experience or of any relation to a physically
identifiable body. How then can it be known at all? It is
known, I maintain, solely in the way each one, in the first
instance, knows himself to be the unique being he is. No one, at
this level, is in any doubt as to who he is – he is himself. He
knows himself as no other. This does not mean that he may not,
in other ways, fail to know who he is. He may fail to know much
about his own nature or dispositions; he may, through loss of
memory, be unaware of some of the more important things in
his own history, the sort of things by which he is outwardly
identified – where he was born, where he lives and works, and
so forth. But in a more basic sense he still knows that this
happened to the unique being he finds himself to be. He cannot
say anything to identify himself in this sense, he just knows what
he knows. The mistake of many who defend a substantival
view of the self is to take up the challenge of those who demand
some description of such a self; for the moment they do so, as
we all know, they are in the hands of their critics. On the other
hand, it would be a mistake to suppose that the self which is
thus uniquely known to itself can be known or be thought to
exist apart from its having certain experiences. It knows itself

168

in having its experiences and the peculiar belongingness which characterises these. It just could not *be* otherwise, although the particular nature of the experiences could be quite different. The self is not 'a thing apart' but it is all the same more than its experiences and uniquely known in each case by each person.

I shall not pursue this theme further now, for to do so would be pointless without making that the main theme of my lecture. I wish only to indicate in the briefest outline what are the main things I wish to take for granted in my lecture and to make it clear that I am not speaking of the self as essentially elusive in some merely linguistic sense or in the sense of being hidden from us, or needing layer upon layer to be removed to uncover it. There are hidden deeps in our nature in that sense. But I am concerned now with a much more fundamental issue, and I maintain that what has bedevilled much of the discussion of the nature of persons, both on the side of those who favour some kind of reductionism and on that of those who defend a pure self, has been the failure to appreciate properly how each person knows himself to be himself in a way that eludes capture in any kind of description or normal identification. I am what I am and simply could be no other, however different my history and physical attributes may have been. The aim of the present lecture is to bring out the bearing of this notion on some further problems and especially on some forms of existentialist thought and, in particular, on what is important about the idea, now very familiar in some contexts, of an 'I-Thou relation'.

When we understand how the self is inwardly known to itself, not as an entity apart and capable of being characterised on its own account, but as a unique being identified for itself in having any experience, then we are able to see the point and importance of much that is said about persons in existentialist thought. This strain in contemporary culture has many forms; it is often hard to distinguish these and sort out the influences which they reflect. Existentialist writers have presumed much on the sympathy and understanding of their readers and have not always been sufficiently at pains to explain the unusual terms they use or to remove misunderstanding. Their work is sometimes notoriously obscure, and it is hard on occasion to avoid the conclusion that the difficulty of the subject and the complexities which invite unusual language and methods are being exploited by writers who should have taken much greater pains to sort out their own ideas and find more effective means of expressing them. But when every allowance has been made for these vexatious features of existentialist thought, one cannot but conclude that it draws attention to aspects of our situation and experience which we are much apt to overlook, in particular because they are so difficult to handle intellectually with the precision and clarity which those who are engaged in the pursuit of truth set as their aims and standard. Nowhere is this more apparent than in a short but remarkable work which has already become an established classic, namely Martin Buber's *I and Thou*. It is not by any means from this source alone that recent existentialist thought has drawn its strength, it has been fed by many other streams; and in some of its forms it owes a good deal less to Martin Buber than to other eminent writers. But there can be little doubt of the influence of Buber or of the extent to which his ideas have been formative in a great deal of recent philosophy and religious literature. His thought is not obscured by elaborate terminology and it affords a splendid example of the insights to be found in this kind of philosophy and also of the ease with which these may be misrepresented or distorted even by those who initially acquired them.

I propose now to look at some of the things Martin Buber has to say and bring out the bearing of it on the views outlined above. I confine myself almost wholly to Buber and resist the temptation, for the course of the present lecture, of deviating into discussion of some of the illuminating things we find in kindred writers. For the most part I shall also keep to *I and Thou*.

Buber begins with his famous account of 'primary words'. These are 'I-Thou' and 'I-It'. These 'do not signify things, but they intimate relations'. This seems formally obvious, and one can easily see also why it is added that the two terms of these 'primary words' cannot be said in separation. If 'Thou' is said the 'I' is said along with it. At the ordinary level this would mean that we cannot think of others as persons without being aware of being persons ourselves. Likewise, if we say 'It' we must also say 'I'. We cannot think of the world or of things without being conscious of ourselves in contrast to them. But Buber also adds: 'There is no I taken in itself, but only the I of the primary word I-Thou and the I of the primary word I-It'. This seems also understandable, but it is a little ambiguous and we are at the start of the difficulties many have felt in their study of Buber. It will be evident now in what sense I myself would agree that 'There is no I taken in itself'. There is no self as an entity apart, but only the self that is involved in having some experience. What this involves further in the way of an objective reality need not be considered. Neither is there need here to go into the question of solipsism. For these are not the matters with which Buber is now concerned. He certainly seems to be saying, however, the sort of thing I have been maintaining about the impossibility of prising the self off from any kind of experience and considering it as a thing apart. The trouble is that this is not all that he seems to mean, nor is it clear that it is the main thing he wants to say. But what else then does he mean? We get a further indication of his meaning when he adds: 'The existence of I and the speaking of I are one and the same thing'. This is a strange remark, and on the face of it, it is clearly not true. I do not exist just when I speak, least of all just when I involve myself in what I say. But clearly we have to probe deeper than this for Buber's meaning. I think he means, in part at least, that the self cannot exist without being aware of itself, and affirming itself, in the adoption of some posture towards the world. It thus takes its 'stand in the word', and this seems to mean that the 'I' is actually constituted by the adoption of an appropriate attitude. It has no reality at all in itself.

The latter seems to me to be Buber's main theme, although he is not as explicit about it in the case of I-It as in that of I-Thou. In that case he is going much further than I do in his presentation of the view that the self cannot be described or characterised. I have certainly no intention of denying that the self is real in itself. I simply hold that it is *sui generis* and known by each person in being himself and having the experience without which he would not exist. I believe Buber has this in mind too, or at least that this is what gives plausibility to much that he says and has made it attractive to others. But this insight tends to be overlaid or distorted by a different, and in my view quite mistaken, notion that the self simply exists in certain relations. The mistake does not hinder Buber from bringing out important consequences of the general view that the self cannot be laid hold upon as a thing or entity apart. But he could have done better justice to his insights if he had not been so disposed to think of the self entirely in terms of its 'twofold attitude',[1] as he puts it, or if he had paused before saying at the start that 'primary words do not signify things, but they intimate relations'.[2]

It is certainly the relation that counts for Buber when a man is alleged to 'say Thou'. Here 'the speaker has no *thing*, he has indeed nothing. But he takes his stand in relation'.[3] This is in fact the central affirmation of the book. And it appears that it has to be understood in a twofold way. When a person says 'Thou' he is not only not a thing himself but he is not involved with things. It is the relation alone that matters and the constitutive qualities of things drop out of the picture. Those matter only when we say 'I-It'. As he puts it:

> Man travels over the surface of things and experiences them. He extracts knowledge about their constitution from them: he wins an experience from them. He experiences what belongs to the things.
>
> But the world is not presented to man by experiences alone. These present him only with a world composed of It and He and She and It again.[4]

This is no different if we speak of inner rather than outer experiences. We are still learning what things are like. 'If we add "secret" to "open" experiences, nothing in the situation is changed.'[4] 'Inner things or outer things, what are they but things and things.'[4] If we set up 'a closed compartment in things', we have still only 'It, always It'.

There is obviously an important point here, although not everyone would put it in the same terms. The distinction between inner and outer is indeed important, and I have been much concerned elsewhere with the need to recognise the

[1] Martin Buber, *I and Thou*, p. 1.   [2] Ibid., p. 1.
[3] Ibid., p. 4.   [4] Ibid., p. 5.

private or 'inner' character of mental processes. But I have also urged that the elusiveness of mental processes, in the sense that we cannot say what it is for them to be mental and not external or observable phenomena, is matched by the elusiveness of the individual person which is not found by his having this or that course of experience or history but rather in something plain to himself which beggars all description. This has at least much in common with Buber's view. For he is also anxious to avoid a characterisation of what is ultimate and of most distinctiveness in the lives of persons in terms of the course of their lives or their experiences and aptitudes. But Buber himself achieves this end largely by treating the Thou, to keep to his own term, entirely in terms of the relation in which it 'takes its stand'.

He might have avoided this consequence, and some of the further disasters that follow from it, had he passed a little less lightly over the distinction between 'inner' and 'outer' things in his proper opposition of both to the ultimate reality of individual persons. For he might have found, in the elusiveness of inner things, a clue to an elusiveness of the true being of persons that would not have involved their reduction to the tenuousness of relations or divorced them from the reality of the experiences in which they are essentially involved and which belong pre-eminently to them. This latter error is as serious as the first.

But, in the case of the I-Thou relation, it is not merely the Thou which is thought of entirely in terms of the relation in which it takes its stand; the same situation holds in reverse for some Thou which is being addressed. Not even where entities in the world of nature are concerned should they be thought of, in their I-Thou relation, as things to be characterised or situated in the ordinary sense. Here also 'relation is mutual',[1] and there seems to be nothing but relation.

Buber is of course fully aware that we do not subsist entirely in this rarefied role of standing in 'mutual relation'. That only holds when we 'say Thou'. But there is also commerce with the world in its qualified and quantified form as object-reality. We learn about the world in this way, we manipulate it, we 'win' experience from it. In this way I can take in the details of a

[1] Ibid., p. 8.

tree when I look at it. I observe its colour, shape, situation and so forth. I 'perceive it as movement; flowing veins on clinging, pressing pith, suck of the roots, breathing of the leaves, ceaseless commerce with earth and air – and the obscure growth itself'.[1] 'I can classify it in a species and study it as a type in its structure and mode of life.'[1] But 'in all this the tree remains my object, occupies space and time, and has its nature and constitution'.[1] It remains a thing, an It.

But while Buber allows that, in our ordinary commerce with the world, whether in the form of natural objects or of persons, we have to treat it as an It and take proper account of the characteristics of things as they confront us, yet, in the I-Thou relation, we have to think of even natural entities, including inanimate objects, in terms of the relation in which they take their stand. On no side does there seem to be anything other than relation.

We must be careful, however, not to misrepresent Buber here. He does not maintain that, once the I-Thou relation is established, we can simply disregard the characterisation of things and persons. In his own example of the tree, he expressly declares:

'To effect this' [that is 'to be bound up in relation to' the tree] 'it is not necessary for me to give up any of the ways in which I consider the tree. There is nothing from which I would have to turn my eyes away in order to see, and no knowledge that I would have to forget.'[1] 'The tree is no impression, no play of my imagination, no value depending on my mood, but it is bodied over against me and has to do with me, as I with it – only in a different way.'[2]

On the other hand it is not any form of animism that is being commended to us here. It is not that there is something akin to the life of persons belonging to the tree in addition to its natural properties. Buber is quite explicit about this. He puts the question himself: 'The tree will have a consciousness, then, similar to our own?' and he replies, 'Of that I have no experience', 'I encounter no soul or dryad of the tree, but the tree itself'.[2]

It seems clear then what are some of the things we are not to

[1] Ibid., p. 7.   [2] Ibid., p. 8.

suppose. But this makes the position all the more mysterious. For although we do not set aside the properties of things in the I-Thou relation, we somehow supersede them, they become 'united' in the 'mutual relation'. As the position is summed up:[1]

- What, then, do we experience of Thou?
- Just nothing. For we do not experience it.
- What, then, do we know of Thou?
- Just everything. For we know nothing isolated about it any more.

Knowledge which is 'everything' and involves no 'isolation' or particularising is not knowledge in any ordinary sense, and we are expressly told that 'No system of ideas, no foreknowledge, and no fancy intervene between *I* and *Thou*'.[1] There is simply 'meeting' and 'All real living is meeting'.[1]

This is undoubtedly baffling, and it is not surprising that many are disposed to give up altogether at this point and treat utterances like the ones just noticed as of no account or at best a 'philosophical prose poem' which does not provide any helpful philosophical enlightenment. The irritation is increased when admirers of Buber echo his thoughts in distorted forms of their own, sometimes with little heed to what Buber himself may have meant. I believe however that Buber is saying something of the utmost importance at the point where his thoughts are most bewildering.

I believe that one of the things he has in mind, at the point where he speaks of 'meeting' or being in relation with natural objects, is that particular things, including here persons as well as other entities in the world of nature, can be significant in a profound and instructive way in virtue of their distinctiveness and particularity. How this comes about can not be easily explained, for an account of what is significant about things in the present sense can not be obtained by just reviewing their properties. It is a work of artistic illumination which makes things articulate in their particularity. One of the reasons why Plato, himself a supreme artist who felt profoundly the lure of art, was apt to dismiss the artist as of no account was his pre-occupation with form and universal truth. This is a tale that has

[1] Ibid., p. 11.

often been told and I have myself attempted a variation on it in my essay 'On Poetic Truth'.[1] All art, I have there maintained, is concerned with the particular, and even universal ideas have to be invested with some kind of particularity by their context to be proper features in a work of art.

This is a theme which calls for elaboration on its own account. I shall not attempt that here, but simply draw attention to what many, myself among them, have maintained about the way the artist makes some particular object or event alive to us in its distinctness; he provides a confrontation or a means for things to make some peculiar impact upon us. We thus see natural objects as we do not normally see them, they become alive to us and have an interest well beyond our ordinary use and placing of them. They are a source of wonderment and fascination because of some newness with which the artist invests them, by unexpected associations perhaps, by exaggeration or distortion of some of their features, by presentation in an unusual setting of sounds or other harmonies. The world is made to speak to us, to become strange, alarming, delightful and so on in a variety of ways and by endless devices. This is the insight of the artist and the mode of illumination which he provides.

This is also what Buber appears to have in mind, in great measure, in what he says about confrontation and meeting. Nor are there many more suggestive sources for the study of this view of art, and of the world being made peculiarly articulate for us, than Buber's *I and Thou*. A poet speaks here about what poetry means to him. This, then, is one way of understanding what Buber is saying in this book. But if this were all, notwithstanding its importance and his grasp of it, he would be introducing needless encumbrances and complexities into his presentation of it. And the truth is that, while Buber was conveying his extreme sensitivity to these illuminations which involve the particular in its starkness and finality, he was also at one and the same time feeling after certain other matters of equal, and perhaps greater importance. Nor was it clear at all to Buber himself, alas, just how these different insights shaded into one another, and how they stand apart. This is why we have to work so hard to be sure what he wants to say.

[1] In *Morals and Revelation* (London, 1951).

A further thought which is obviously very much in Buber's mind in this context, though much overlaid by others, is that anything we may encounter, animate and inanimate alike, leads out eventually to God or the infinite. God is involved in the being of anything, and there are moments of illumination when this is seen sharply in our contemplation of particular things. This has been impressively put by Professor E. L. Mascall when he refers to 'the common experience of people making their first retreat, that after the first day or so natural objects seem to acquire a peculiar character of transparency and vitality, so that they appear as only very thinly veiling the creative activity of God'.[1] In this way there may be a meeting with things which is also a meeting with God; and it is evident that Buber has this very much in mind. He writes:

> Every particular Thou is a glimpse through to the eternal Thou; by means of every particular Thou the primary word addresses the eternal Thou. Through this mediation of the Thou of all beings fulfilment, and non-fulfilment, of relations comes to them: the inborn Thou is realized in each relation and consummated in none. It is consummated only in the direct relation with the Thou that by its nature cannot become It.[2]

It may be that Buber does not understand 'the glimpse through to the eternal Thou' in quite the same way as Mascall and others when they find natural objects thinly veiling the activity of God. But if so, then I think that is due largely to his own failure or reluctance to sort out his various insights effectively. One of the ways in which his work rings the bell with many people is, I much suspect, just this involvement of the eternal in every particular, and the moments of illumination when this becomes plain.

This sort of illumination has much in common with the way particular things may become articulate in art and kindred ways. But the two sorts of insights must not be confused or conflated. The artist is not bound to be, even implicitly, a religious visionary. He may just hit on the means to make what is normally present to us have its proper impact, and he need

---

[1] *He Who Is* (London, 1943), p. 80.   [2] *I and Thou*, p. 75.

not in any way be a minor artist if that is all he does. On the other hand the artistic insight may readily become a religious one, and as there are further ways in which, in divine disclosure, the eternal involves itself in particular things and events, the blending of art and religion may be exceptionally close and fruitful, as may well be seen in the history of both. It is not surprising therefore that what Buber has to say has been found impressive by different people in very different ways.

The religious aspect of the I-Thou relation is not, in my understanding, the whole of it for Buber. But it is for him essential, and for that reason it tends to eclipse what may be said about other features of it on their own account. On its religious side, it is understandable that the I-Thou relation should be apt to be taken entirely in the sense of taking one's stand in the relation. For where God, as eternal or transcendent being, is concerned, there is nothing specific that we learn about Him in the immediate sense of His presence in all things. We simply know that He has to be as the ultimate mysterious ground of the being of all else – He is just 'He who Is'. To that extent we just stand in relation to Him and He to us. This is not a relation to nothing, or some bare relation without terms, whatever that could be. God is real, supremely so, and we are real. But in the immediate awareness we have of God, as involved in the being of everything else, we do not learn anything expressly about the essence of God, we do not understand what it is to be God, as we have at least some partial understanding of any finite entity we postulate to explain natural phenomena in the ordinary way. God is not known as an object among objects, or some term in the finite relations of things. He remains to that extent an unfathomable mystery. This point has been very much stressed of late, and I shall not dwell upon it. But it can be understood how, in the light of this reflection, it becomes plausible to say that, in our initial awareness of God which is regulative for all further awareness of Him, we do not experience Him in the ordinary way but stand in relation to Him.

I am not maintaining that this is the best way, or even a satisfactory way, of putting the matter. For the insight we have into there having to be God is itself an experience, and it is an experience in which we apprehend what is of the utmost consequence in all other experience. It is not without content, but has the richest content of all. At the same time what we apprehend is grasped, not in the delineation of its properties, but in the inevitability of its being and the perfection therein involved. It is to that extent some standing in a relation.

If, however, Buber had not allowed this idea to be so dominant over his other ideas and draw the latter into itself, he might well have been put in the way of presenting his religious thought in a way that would have allowed a much more fruitful development. For the sense that he has of the impact which objects may make upon us, and the way they could thus become alive and articulate, could have opened up a way of thinking of encounter and meeting which did not have to be conceived so finely and cautiously as to empty it of all but the standing in relation. It would not be devoid of content, though its content would not be the world as we normally experience it; it would not be sharply opposed, in all respects, to experience as such.

This would have two results. It would have taken the sting out of much of the usual criticisms of the theology of encounter. For the latter need not then have taken the course it has so often taken, namely that of by-passing all problems of our particular knowledge of God, on the score that, in true religion, it is not 'knowledge about' God that we have but encounter. It has often been urged, by myself among many others, that there can be no mere encounter. This seems certainly true in our ordinary dealings with each other. How can I encounter anyone unless I know something about him? In like manner religious life, at least all but the most incipient, has some filling or content obtained from some experience of God or divine disclosure. Religion is not just the sense of the being of God. It contains more precise beliefs about what God is like, how He deals with us and how we experience Him, what He requires of us and so forth. Some account must be given of this and the way it is warranted. We cannot just cry 'Encounter', and dodge the issue. Many have been tempted to do so, and they have taken their cue from Buber. But if they had learnt the lesson of other insights that Buber has, they might have been much less disposed to do so.

In the second place, there would have been not only an appreciation of the limitation of the idea of meeting as such or of bare encounter, a way would have been opened up of indicating how, in peculiar relationships like those of religion, this takes place. For the way things become alive and articulate to us in their impact upon us, as the artist in particular mediates it, provides a peculiarly fruitful approach to problems of the way God, who cannot be known as He is in Himself, may be found by us through some impact He indirectly makes upon us through the events of our lives and history. There is in Buber much which, if only it were enabled to be more explicit on its own account, is most suggestive for the student of the philosophical problem of revelation.

There is also the bearing of Buber's teaching on the place which is given to the idea of respect for persons in a social or ethical context. This is an important principle, although it is hard to see the precise implication of it for practice. The distinction that is sometimes drawn between treating people as persons and treating them as things or as a means is certainly not absolute. We never strictly treat a person as 'a thing', if this means wholly disregarding the fact that he is a person. Into our respect for persons there surely enters the thought of what they are like. There is also something more of which I shall give an indication in a moment. But this something more is not to be detached from what Buber has in mind when he talks of the way we experience persons; and if he had paid more heed to the content of our normal exchanges and the way we evaluate them, he could have made his more original and germinative thought about the subject a good deal more fruitful in its application to practice.

This brings us back to what seems to me central in Buber's position. I believe that what has impressed him most, although he does not sort it out and present it as explicitly as he might, is the fact that we just cannot characterise or identify the self by some distinctive feature in the respect in which it is uniquely known and identified for itself. There is nothing to be said about the self at this level, we do not learn about it, and for that reason we see why it is not quite appropriate to say that we experience it. We can, as is quite obvious, have experience of one another in another way. We can learn what other persons feel and think, what has been their history and so forth. But the basic sense in which it is the history of this particular person, the way his experiences belong to him, this, in the last analysis, we cannot know. Each must know it for himself in his own case. He knows himself as a distinct and ultimate being in a way that is not dependent on what he happens to think and feel, and so on, and what has occurred to him. We never expressly share the consciousness each one has of himself in this way, we only ascribe it, without further justification, on the assumption that what we do ascribe, on the basis of our observations and so forth, in the way of experience must carry with it, in the case of another person, the same recognition of an irreducible distinctness as we find in our own case.

There is thus a sense in which other persons are essentially mysterious to us. This is not the mystery of transcendent being, as in the case of God, although we do come closer here to the irreducible mystery of transcendence than anywhere else in our limited existence. It is not that we have no notion at all what it must be to be the other person. We presume that he has a mind, or thoughts and feelings, not unlike our own. For him to be thinking about philosophy is substantially the same as for me to do so, he suffers and he enjoys things as I do. But what it is for all this to happen to *him*, that I cannot explicitly know at all. I can only presume that he knows it as I know who I am. The other is in some sense essentially mysterious.

It is hardly necessary to add that the present sense in which each is some kind of world of his own has nothing directly to do with the fact that there is a great deal which we are not in fact able to learn about one another. There are depths in our hearts and thoughts which others may find it particularly difficult to probe, and there are many things we deliberately keep away from others. There are many disguises we wear, and it needs the trained observer or the novelist to get behind them. There is much which, in some measure at least, we hide from ourselves. But this is contingent, there is no reason in principle why all may not be laid bare, at the present level, to ourselves or to others, however unlikely in fact. This is altogether different from the inherent or irreducible mystery of the other, in the

sense that only the other person properly knows what it is for
him to be himself.

There are, however, moments when we become peculiarly
conscious of the fact that the other person is distinctively other
and strange in the sense indicated. These are moments of
exceptional intimacy, sometimes sweet and sometimes disturbing and alarming. We are truly closer to the other just because
he also stands in our presence as a stranger. We must not
presume too much, although now we are truly face to face, we
are in the presence of a being who is as irreducibly and finally
himself, one might almost say a world of his own, as we are.
This adds great depth and enrichment to our mutual awareness,
whether our relation be friendly or hostile, and it has the utmost
significance for major problems of human existence, as I hope
to show in a further study.

In the meantime it must suffice here to show how plausible
it is to speak of the moments of encounter, in the sense indicated,
as a case of taking one's stand in relation, not having experience
of or learning about another. It is a confrontation, although
this does not mean that we abstract from experience or what is
'learnt about'. The distinctive thing is the sense of the other as
other, although in further ways the encounter draws its
significance from the specific content of our experience.

A weakness in Buber's own position is that he tends to think
of the moment of standing in relation in too great a detachment
from the varied content of all the experience we have of one
another. It is not that he denies such experience; he acknow-
ledges, on the contrary, that we have it and need it to continue
the round of our lives. But he is apt also to treat it as altogether inferior, almost an encumbrance, and not very
different in merit or importance from the knowledge of natural
objects we require in order to manipulate them. I-It is thus
on an altogether different plane, even in the case of persons,
from the I-Thou, and the ideal must be always to pass beyond
the world of I-It, although for regrettable practical reasons we
cannot disregard it, to the more rarefied and truly significant
world of I-Thou.

This is indeed a very grave mistake. It takes away all that
gives point and direction to our aspirations and our dealings

with each other. It renders negligible the judgement, the discernment, the sympathy, the forbearance, which we should cultivate in seeking to know one another and supply one another's needs, the need for fellowship above all. The art of mutual understanding is a supreme one in the right conduct of human life, but we are not likely to succeed in it if we withdraw from the world in which we feel and think this or that to a world which is altogether above such disparities and above the battle they present.

Indeed, if this withdrawal is too complete, it may even defeat the aim of recognising the other in his ultimate distinctness as other. It may lead to a conflation in which no one properly takes his stand in relation to the other, a merging such as we find in some forms of mysticism. This is not because the distinctness is made what it is by the particular events of our lives and experience. The corrective is not found by just stressing those, and if we thought this we should miss the point of what is most suggestive and profound in Buber's own insight. It is simply that the very insight into the finality of our distinctness, as each one apprehends it in his own case, is put in jeopardy if it is viewed in the sort of void which is created by thinking of persons entirely in terms of the confrontation of one by the other in the finality of his otherness – the obverse of the error which we find in idealist philosophy.

This error is bound up with another. We have already seen that Buber's conception of the I-Thou relation is much affected by his sense of the eternal Thou and the way this is involved in any other relation to a Thou. That affords one reason for the proneness of Buber to think of us, in what is distinctive and of worth in our lives, as merely standing in a relation. For in one sense, as we saw, this is very nearly how we must conceive of ourselves in relation to transcendent being, although this, as was also stressed, is far from being the whole story. But, in like manner, the preoccupation with persons in the sense in which they stand starkly opposed as other, to the neglect of the peculiarities of their natures and history, has repercussions on the way Buber thinks of God and our relation to Him. For the way he conceives of the I-Thou relation at the finite level, and the rarefied notion of it solely in terms of standing in relation, tends to determine for him also the character of the relation we have with the eternal Thou. This becomes also tenuous in all respects and the way is prepared thus again for the sort of mysticism in which all distinctness is lost.

There are undoubtedly strains of this kind of mysticism in Buber, and it is by no means easy to determine how far he has travelled in that direction. But to the extent that he does so we have one of those curious paradoxes we find in the history of thought by which a slight distortion of some position brings about an affirmation of almost the opposite of it – as when extreme individualism in political thought culminates in the doctrine of the general will. For what is of the utmost importance in Buber's thought is just the recognition of the irreducible way in which I confront a Thou. Of this he writes with great sensitivity and it is for this that we are indebted to him. But, if I am right, the clue to what is central and most impressive in Buber's teaching, and the way to avoid the pitfalls along the course he is taking, is to have due appreciation of the elusiveness of the self, in its ultimacy and distinctness, whereby it is more than its experiences or its aptitudes and character, but more in a way which cannot in turn be described or characterised any more than it could be thought to subsist in isolation from its experiences and the propensities which condition them. This is the self which each one knows himself to be and which he ascribes to another, as known to him, in the moments of confrontation which give the greatest depth and significance to our commerce together in this world – and beyond it.

12

THE PERSON GOD IS

Peter A. Bertocci

I. WHAT IS THE QUESTION OF GOD?

Since my childhood I have given up several conceptions of
God. Each time there was quite a wrench, for, in my own
limited way, I had been walking with my 'living' God. In my
philosophical and theological studies, I have been impressed by
the fact that one deep-souled thinker found the living God of
another 'dead'. And then I realised that a God is 'living' or
'dead' insofar as 'He' answers questions that are vital to the
given believer.

Every believer in God, I am suggesting, lives by some 'model'
of God that helps him to live with the practical and theoretical
problems he faces from day to day as an actor and a thinker, or,
if you will, as a thinker-actor. And he keeps that 'model' of God
frequently long after he has begun to realise that it conflicts
with the vital evidence as he sees it. He will go on living by it
until another view makes more sense to him as a thinker-actor.
Sometimes he changes his thought and action with a wrench;
sometimes he finds that gradually one view of God died as
another came alive. Note, this does not mean that God, granted
he exists, died; it means that a given view of God is first
challenged by another and then rejected because the other
now seems more illuminating. This change of views is no
different from what happens every day in our thinking about the
world. We are changing our ideas about the moon (and the
possibility of life on it) to accord with better evidence.

But the same line of reasoning may be used with regard to the very existence of God. A person may find that any conception of God simply is incoherent with the problems that arise out of his thinking-acting life. Then not only does *a* conception of God die, but the conception that any God at all exists dies. For, it is now held, belief in any God simply does not fit the evidence at hand.

Of course, this matter of what it means to fit the evidence, that is, what our standard of truth requires, is the crucial question. But we shall in this essay assume what has already been implied, that belief in God and belief in a specific kind of God, is a person's thinking-acting response to a conception of God that seems to him more coherent, and that fits in better than any other conception with the evidence.

Any of us who has tried to keep alive to the history of even one great theological-philosophical tradition without losing our sensitivity to the intellectual, religious, and social developments of our own day realises that a philosophical and theological *aggiornamento* must always be part of our task. Yet – and even here our criterion of truth begins to exert itself – *aggiornamento* must mean bringing the present into challenging relation to the past. The assumption that the 'past' must be brought up to date is as questionable as the assumption that the 'past' can learn nothing from 'the present'. Perhaps, as I think reflection will show, we can, *as thinkers*, forget the labels 'new' and 'old' and ask which idea, hypothesis, which view of God, best illumines the evidence at hand from every source.

If this be granted, then any real dialogue about the nature and existence of God must presuppose a willingness on the part of participants to realise that they cannot hold a fixed view of 'what God must be like' regardless of what the evidence indicates. Great minds, alas, have said: 'There is no God', when all that their argument showed is that a certain view of God is untenable in the light of what they regarded as relevant considerations.

Spinoza, for example, argued (in part) that the Cartesian view of God as Creator was really not God. Why? Because a God who is a Creator is one who presumably would have somehow existed 'in want' until he did create the world and man.

This, of course is nonsense, but only if the model of God guiding Spinoza is the real God! Again, Tillich argued that God cannot be one being alongside, or among, other beings, for this would not really be God, but some sort of great, yet finite Being. Yet one who knows what Tillich means by truth, and how he believes we come to know it, will see that his view of un-conditioned Being is related to the evidence he considers crucial. He may be correct, with Spinoza, but I cannot help wondering why a particular model of God is asserted to be the only being worthy of being called *God*? Obviously, each of us will believe, and should believe that the conception of God which fits the evidence is the true conception of God, but we cannot pre-suppose what the true God is and then fit the evidence to our view.

To come at last to my purpose here. I know that many have insisted that if God is not a Person he is dead. I see no good reason for such an adamant stand. But because I find it almost fashionable not to know *what considerations led thinkers* to believe that God is a Person, I should like to indicate what it means to say that God is a certain kind of Person. Obviously I cannot speak for all personalistic theists, or for a perspective called classical theism, but only for *a* way of expressing the meaning of God in relation to man and Nature.

2. IF NO PERSON-GOD, THEN NO UNITY AND UNIFORMITY OF NATURE

First, then, what is the essence of the view of person that serves as a guiding model? Any *person* is the kind of being who is a knowing-willing-caring unity in continuity. Let us limit our-selves first to the notion of a person as a unity-in-continuity. The inescapable model is myself as a person. I don't know how it happens, but I cannot escape the fact that I am self-identical as I change. It is as simple and difficult as that! I, as a person, am not a fusion of, or collection of, parts; I am an initial unity which, though changing, nevertheless retains self-identity. Without self-identity there can be no knowing of change. But more, if there were nothing persisting in change we should say not that a being changes, but that one being had been substituted for another (as one actor substitutes for another). This is not all there is to being a person, but it is essential.

Thus, using this model, to say that God is a Person is to assert a Being who, however related to all other beings, is not a unity *of* them; he is self-identical. The question that arises, from some who seem to know already what God's nature *must* be, is whether God can, being God, change in any respect. This view of a God who is unchanging Alpha and Omega may be correct. But we need to remind ourselves that to call God *person* is to insist only that God is Unity-Continuity and is unchanging in the unity of his essential being. As a Person he does not change, even if the particular content or quality of his being changes (as when he 'rejoices' when the prodigal son returns).

But why claim that such a being exists at all? What does the Person-God as Unity-Continuity enable us to understand?

Human thought and action are grounded in the regularity and order in the events of the world. To speak of a *universe* is to presuppose beings and events united in such a way that what occurs at one place is connected in an understandable way with what takes place elsewhere. We may not now know how or why one part of the universe is related to the other, but we think and act as if it is not unknowable *in principle*. Order and regularity of some sort constitute 'the way of things'.

Now, such inter-related unity and continuity among the beings and events in the world are illuminated, says the personalistic *theist*, by supposing that there is a Unity-Continuity that creates and sustains all there is, in such a way that basic order, regularity, and connectivity is possible among all the parts.

There are personalistic *pantheists* or monists who would want to assure such ordered connectivity by maintaining that all the beings or events in the world are parts, modes, or centres, of one Absolute Person. Either personalist, theistic or monistic, takes one fundamental stand: no cosmic Unity-Continuant, then no ultimate Ground for the trust we all have in the order of things. (Unless further notice is given, I shall use the word 'personalist' to mean personalistic theist – for whom God is transcendent of, yet immanent in, Nature.) Both pantheistic and theistic personalists argue that we can *reasonably* trust our ventures into the presently unknown only if we can reasonably believe that the unknown is basically continuous with the character of what we do know. And this leads us to the second characteristic of Person, knowing.

3. THE PERSON GOD IS: COSMIC KNOWER

Important as the emphasis on Unity-Continuity is, it is the insistence that Unity-Continuity is most coherent only as it is a knowing Person which gives the personalistic view its name. The personalist holds that the self-sufficient, cosmic Unity-Continuity is, like the finite person, a Knower, a Mind or Spirit.

The storm that has raged around this concept has been caused by the 'model' that controlled the use of the word 'person'. The pre-Socratic Xenophanes wryly exclaimed: The Ethiopians 'make their gods black-haired and flat-nosed, and the Thracians make theirs red-haired and blue-eyed'. What adolescent mind has not sooner or later smartly commented that, after all, men made God after their own image – as if this ended the matter once and for all! Yet, if the world is a universe, and if some Unity-Continuity can be postulated, our thought cannot rest without trying to conceive of what its nature 'must' be in order to fit what we know. And the fundamental fact is that we, as persons, not only ask the questions, but also believe that our human logical questions when supported by human observations will not lead us astray in this universe. Can this universal unity be unlike ours *in principle*?

It is not unsuggestive that Xenophanes, who found no reason for holding that God had blue eyes, did nevertheless say that the nature of Ultimate Being was Thought! That God-intoxicated philosopher, Spinoza, de-anthropomorphised God by saying that the One Substance was no more like a finite person than the celestial constellation, 'the Dog', was like a barking dog. But the same Spinoza insisted that, of the infinite number of attributes of Substance, *thought* as well as extension defines the essence of Substance. While Paul Tillich cannot define Unconditioned Being as person, he says: 'The God who is *a* person is transcended by the God who is the Personal-Itself, the ground and abyss of every person'.[1]

Any personalistic theist must be sympathetic with every attempt to keep before the believer the realisation that no concept of the cosmic Unity will comprehend it completely, that all man's concepts will leak, if for no other reason than that man's knowledge is incomplete. He can also understand why it makes sense to say that no part of the universe, including the human, can, without qualification, describe the cosmic Unity. Yet he urges that it must remain a matter of live debate whether there is any 'model' other than Mind, even as we know it in ourselves, that will be more helpful to us in defining the *kind* of unity, continuity, and order that will account for the fact that our minds, existing in this world, have been able to fathom its nature progressively.

After all, the basic drift of scientific and philosophical theorising presupposes that what lies beyond man can be understood by the human mind. This is not to say that man will understand all, but it does mean that the schemes of Nature, however far-flung, are not intrinsically and in principle beyond disciplined human knowing. Indeed, when a person doubts concretely that a particular conclusion in science and philosophy is true, is he not using other considerations, which he believes to be true descriptions of the world, to support his doubting? In the last analysis, we do not believe that the segment of the world we do seem to know will be basically rejected by the rest of the universe we do not now know. The maps we now have will need revision, the models will be fashioned by the very minds that learn from their mistakes and yet press on in the faith that the next map, the next model, will be more illuminating for thought and action.

It is this kind of consideration that leads the personalist to find, expressed in the order of the world, a Mind that in its basic structure is not foreign to his own. If *our* map-making, encouraged and discouraged by the terrain about us, if *our* models suggested by what we know and remodelled in the light of what we encounter, do get us on with the total business of

[1] *Biblical Religion and the Search for the Ultimate Reality* (Chicago, 1952), p. 38.

understanding and living in both the microscopic and macro-scopic realms, can it be that the total universe as we envision it and interact with it, is alien to our being as persons? To change the figure, if the key 'in our natures' can open the lock of the world to any extent, why is it far-fetched to suppose that the key and the lock do not bespeak a common locksmith? It is easy to scoff at what I believe to be a *legitimate* anthropo-morphism. Yet is not the scoffer boasting of his luck if he continues to urge that the way to know what is real is to think logically, observe thoroughly, hypothesise in the light of evidence at hand, and act on hypotheses with concerted further thought and action?

Whenever a personalist, then, hears someone say 'but the universe is beyond anything the human mind can know', his rejoinder is insistent. 'This is logically possible. But do you claim your mind can know *that*? If it can, and if your mind can *know* that, aren't you asserting that somehow your mind has the secret to its own impotence? It is one thing to assert that we don't know all: it is another to say that what we know in our-selves and in the world provides no good ground for supposing that out progress is helping us to identify the nature of a cosmic Mind.'

Here the retort may readily be made: But do you mean that the word 'know' is to be used for God in the same sense as it is used for man? The answer: Whatever the particular knowing processes in God are remains open for further discussion. A responsible philosophical theology must be as clear as it can be about the nature of this knowing. It will not evade such questions as: Is God's knowing intellectual in the sense in which our logic is syllogistic, or is it non-discursive and intuitive?

We might at least bear in mind, in passing, that God does not 'speak' either in English or German, use words – but neither do animals or the deaf and dumb express their level of awareness in such ways. More relevant is the suggestion that we seek analogies within the whole range of human *awareness*, inclusive of aesthetic, moral, and religious awareness. But the minimum intellective awareness is knowing similarity and differences in itself and everywhere else. In short, the essential personalistic contention is that, whatever the 'infinity' of a cosmic Unity entails, we endanger the Unity if we deny that it is self-conscious and knows the difference between himself and his world, including persons.

Again, there is a basic problem here. When we stress the immensity of the universe, the unlimited majesty of God, the unconditioned nature of his Being, or what have you, do we mean that no link, no common bond, exists between man and God? Do we mean to say that what is logical to us would be non-logical or illogical to that Being? The personalist, while he must speculate about the nature of the difference between man and God, insists on the essential continuity between the best in his own experience and in the universe, including God. Why court mystery here when we decry impalpable mystery elsewhere? In the name of modesty and humility we can urge that no human symbols are adequate, but if we take this seriously we belie the amount of success our symbolising has had, and we tend to foster more scepticism than we intended. At the same time we have disqualified a particular view of God's nature by what are ultimately loaded views of God's ultimacy and perfection.

Again, what does it add to say that God is what we can know *and more*? For if the word 'more' means 'more of the same', it can be granted. But if the 'more' means difference in kind, we simply cannot know what *that* 'more' means even though we seem wise and modest in saying so. What would happen to the construction of computers if we said, for example, that, though the actual process be different, what goes on in the structure of a computer has *no* counterpart in the structure of man, even though, for example, the computer can solve problems it would take ages for man to solve? What would happen to our attempts to understand what goes on in lower animals and in plants if we let our realisation that there is 'more than we know in ourselves' stifle reasonable analogy?

Obviously, much needs to be added. It is not incidental, however, to remark that what tends to control thinking here is the model of the finite person we have in mind when we say: God is a Person. If I thought that the person is identical with his brain and body, I would not use the word 'person' for God. In our day there are many who, unwittingly or wittingly, think of a person as some sort of body. But do these same persons think that a person is a male or a female, or are they assigning 'person' to a being, who, however his body is related to him, is *not identical* with that body? Ambiguity courts disaster at these points.

Once more, if, as many in our day hold, the person is a social-biological phenomenon, then the denial that God is a person is understandable. For God's nature, if it is to fit our cosmological evidence, is not the product of learning in some environment (and I say this even though I myself hold that God in some respects does change in response to changes initiated by our persons).[1] For the personalist, however, the word 'person' identifies an agent capable of self-consciousness and of action in the light of rational and moral-aesthetic-religious ideals.

To summarise: in hypothesising that the cosmic Unity is a Person we are carrying on the same kind of process, of moving from the unknown on the basis of what is known, that activates careful reflection in the other concrete areas of human investigation. If by careful observation, guided as far as possible by scientific method, we discover that our thought-forms do engage us with the world beyond in such a way that one discovery leads to another, on what grounds, consistent with experiential procedures, can we argue that the Being manifest in our world is totally different from our mind-form?

To say that Being or Unity is more than we are is, after all,

[1] Indeed, while much of this paper reflects the influence of F. R. Tennant, it is the influence of Edgar S. Brightman, Alfred N. Whitehead, H. Bergson, and Charles Hartshorne that has led me to conceive of change in God in ways similar to Hartshorne's view (as expressed in his essay, p. 158, and elsewhere). At present my main hesitancy stems from the way in which the person is related to God in Whitehead, Bergson, and Hartshorne, for as I now see it the independence of the person is not adequately protected. For example, while the case for personal immortality must be argued, of course, I cannot accept the suggestion that there is wishful thinking and a false sense of values in the desire for personal immortality. On the contrary, if to be a person is to be a person-in-and-for-oneself I fail to see why, in a universe that presumably conserves and increases value, it is an increase in value to preserve a memory, even in God (in Hartshorne's sense), while personhood ceases to be. Yet, I expect that the nature of creation (see below) and of personal continuity is the bone of contention.

to say something very innocuous theoretically. This dictum applies not only to God but to everything we know. But, as I suggest, in the actual course of argument, this 'more' in God is used to disqualify attempts, built on reasoning however inadequate, to say what seems reasonable granted given evidence at least. In every area, the theoretical problem is always one of defining what the nature of 'the more' is. But do we dare move without the reasonably established faith that the more is not unlike what we already know? In a word, the faith of the personalist at this point is, minimally, an extension of the faith that guides all theoretical activity.

4. THE PERSON GOD IS: LOVING AGENT

We have argued that if God is conceived as a Person, as a unified Knower, then we can the better understand why our thought-forms have succeeded in knowing the interconnected order of Nature. To think of God as a cosmic Person is not to indulge a human whim, but to ground more adequately all of our theoretical ventures, including the scientific. But is God good? Let us ask the same question we asked before. What problem would be solved by this conception?

In answer, we turn again to human experience and ask what the lasting basis of human goodness is. Many factors contribute to human existence and to the growth of quality in human experience. But if the personalist were to be limited to any other one factor, beyond knowing, which makes for *quality* in every area of *human experience in this world*, he would select *loving*. Thinking-loving gives support to thinking-acting; they are the creative matrix in which every other human good is strengthened. Without the other each falters. Accordingly, the personalist argues, thinking-loving is the clue to the best the universe makes possible, as far as we know.

To elaborate: When a person dedicates himself to the growth of other persons in full awareness of their mutual potential for growth, we say that he loves. And he loves unto forgiveness when he does all in his power to enable even those who have purposely abused his love to join the fellowship and community of love. And separation, as Ian Ramsey says, is 'hell'.[1] In a word, in human experience there is no greater good than to be a responsive-responsible member in a community dedicated to mutual growth. This good we call love. Any being whose purposes include the growth of persons-in-community, and who does all in his power to realise this purpose, is loving. The Person God, says the personalist, is good; he is a loving agent. The grounds for this contention may be further elaborated in two steps.

First, is it not experientially sound to say that to the extent to which love is realised in an individual personality, in a family, and in a community, every other value that human beings find worthwhile is enhanced? For the ideal of love-unto-forgiveness (I do not mean sentimentality) is not a dream. It is an actual description of how persons, in relation to other persons, can fulfil themselves in the world as they know it, within themselves, and beyond themselves. Persons are desperate when they feel alienated both from the best in themselves and the best in others. They are more likely to improve and grow if they feel the forgiveness that, looking beyond the harm they have done, draws them into a community of mutual concern. These are requirements for growth in self-fulfilment in community.

Man does not make up these requirements any more than he makes up the laws governing the growth of bodies or the changes in molecules. He finds them – not as he finds the stars or the law of gravitation, however. He finds them in the midst of his very attempt to know what he can best be-in-act. A loving man is a knowing-willing man developing dimensions of his own being and of other beings, dimensions that come into being *as* he loves. His *knowing in loving is a more comprehensive knowledge* which tells him about himself and his fellowmen even as they both *realise* their potential and fulfil each other with a minimum of fruitless conflict.

To put this in a different way: What the personalist is calling to our attention is that men and Nature do not stand in an indifferent relation to each other; they are not juxtaposed. Men are facts about the total world that includes biological and physical beings; but they are also facts for each other in that

[1] See pp. 211, 221.

larger world. For them to understand themselves is for them to become aware of their physical and social environment, in such a way as to keep all of these in a responsive-creative relation to each other. Thus, when a man discovers that mutual respect for another's freedom is the best condition for their mutual personal growth, *he is discovering a fact that the total world, including himself, makes possible*. When he goes on to realise that such freedom – guided by knowledge of self, of others, of Nature – is supported and kept from self-destruction only as it is disciplined by loving, he is also discovering what his life-in-the-world can be.

This first step in the psycho-logic of love encourages a personalist to argue that the same universe which makes it possible for man to know, and to live by that knowledge, is the very universe which makes it impossible for man to perfect that knowledge unless he meets the conditions of love. He must learn to respect both 'the structure and potential of things' for their own sake and the structure and potential of other persons for their own sakes. As long as a man lives in this world, he, given his nature, will not be able to fulfil himself simply for himself; he will not be able to treat either the world or others as if they were meant *only* for him. He will grow without fruitless conflict only as he grows *within* and *for* a community in which persons both respect each other, and co-operate with each other in responsive-responsible growth. It is this fact about the world that best defines what it is and can be in relation to man. Thus, when the personalist says that God is a unity-in-continuity of knowing-willing-caring, he is asserting that the essential constitution of the world and the essential constitution of man are such that the highest good of man is realised in that kind of community in which persons respect and care for each other's growth.

A second step in the personalist's reasoning articulates the first by calling attention to what is involved in the human search for truth. As a matter of actual dynamics within the individual personality and within the community, knowledge grows not merely because the world is knowable. Knowledge grows apace only as it is put to use, and only as it is motivated by respect for other persons and by mutuality in the total venture of knowing. For, in their own way, the community of scholars, the growth of knowledge, the zest for the venture, grow apace as scholars know that their mistaken and misguided efforts will be sympathetically understood, that their errors will be rejected but their efforts encouraged. Thus, in the venture of acquiring and sharing knowledge, without which human existence is inconceivable, love is not an addendum which investigators may disregard.

This point is so simple that its very simplicity allows many to underestimate its importance, and to be parasitic upon what makes for community in the knowledge-venture. Again, the search for knowledge is encouraged by love for more than knowledge; it is sustained by mutual concern for the growth of persons as investigators who find and express themselves in sharing of insights.

Furthermore, truth-seekers in any one community must be free to respond to the lure of truth. But they will feel threatened in their efforts if they believe that the larger community upon which they depend will be intolerant especially when their discoveries challenge the *status quo*, or that the community will judge them only by their failures. Truth-seekers themselves, of course, must be willing to suffer, especially before the intellectual conscience of man. But their courage to seek will be inspired if they can live in the assurance that they will not suffer vindictive punishment.

To summarise: Man, the lover-knower *in* the world, is the lover-knower not threatened by that world but nurtured, challenged, and supported by it as he grows within it. Love has no meaning without such challenge and support, whatever else it involves. Why not then hold that love is the broader principle involved in world-being as we know it? For man's justifiable hope for himself in his world is rooted in his daily discovery that, in disciplining himself by the norms of truth and love, he is part of 'the drift' of things. In knowing-loving he enters into a fuller relationship with a universe that responds to him in his growth as inspired by truth and love. Why not then conceive of the Unity-Continuity of the cosmic-Knower as a loving Person? This is the way to say that man's own joy in self-discovery and in mutual growth is no cosmic surprise, for it is

P   T.O.G.

grounded in a Universe that responds to man's creative effort as knower and carer.

It should now be clear that a personal God is not one that human beings somehow add to their experience or their world. Personalists do not argue *that* there is a God and then add labels to that Being. They argue that, in the very attempt to discover what they are and can best become in their world, persons find a Person at work with them *in* and *through* their world. For the personalist, the God 'up there' does not exist because he never did, as far as they know. He is always at work in the world and in relation to persons. But this takes us directly to the reasons for saying that God is the Creator of man and the world.

5. THE PERSON GOD IS: COSMIC CREATOR

The finite person, it has been argued, is dependent for his very being and sustenance on God. But finite as the person is, he is free to choose and to create within limits. In the context suggested above, each man, given basic cognitive and conative capacities, is free to choose, within the limits of these capacities, the knowledge ventures and the quality of caring he believes to be best. For this moral development man is himself so responsible that he is a creator.

Such a view of freedom is a minimal requirement for a personalistic view of the person; it is not argued here. But the consequences of this view are crucial for the personalist's thought about man's relation to God. As we have seen, a person is indeed related to his total environment, including God. But a person does not overlap with anything else in the world or with God. His being is his unity-in-continuity of knowing-willing-caring. God in turn, as a person, does not overlap with, or include, any other person.

This whole idea is not easy to conceive, let alone imagine. But it should be clear at the outset that it is the personalist's concern to protect the individuality of the person-man, and of the Person-God, that leads him to propose his doctrine of creation. Unless the context of the doctrine of creation is understood, this doctrine, mysterious enough at best, will be cast aside disdainfully as 'impossible'.

There are two other ways of conceiving God's relation to man and the world other than holding that God creates them 'out of nothing' (*creatio ex nihilo*).

According to the first, which follows suggestions Plato made in the *Timaeus*, God may be likened to a sculptor who creates not 'out of nothing' but out of the material or 'stuff' at hand. This stuff is in itself relatively inchoate, and by itself would never take on any structure or order. While more than one specific order can be introduced into such inchoate being, no pervasive structure is to be found in its formless nature. Yet, because it is an eternal something rather than 'nothing', it will 'respond' to some forms of order better than to others. It may be of some help to think of clay or marble, which will conform to more than one 'idea'; yet clay cannot become exactly what a block of marble can become.

Great philosophers have grappled with the problem of introducing any specific structure – regularity, order, form – into inchoate being which is something (not nothing) and yet in itself almost without any form. They have preferred to postulate some such formless matrix, or 'womb of all becoming', rather than postulate what seemed preposterous – creation '*ex nihilo*', which they translated literally *out of nothing*. Better to suppose that God is somehow co-eternal with such 'material for becoming'; better to hold that God did not create such being and that it could not create him. Better to hold that God and 'matter' are two eternal Principles, two Kinds of Being, both needing each other if anything is to be developed in what is.

Such alternatives all sound so much more picturable and conceivable than 'creation out of nothing' until we ask some other questions. Plato, for example, had to take one more step. For if God is the Sculptor, and the Material (the Receptacle) is that which takes on form, whence the Forms, whence the Ideas or Ideals, that guide the Sculptor in his creative work? There is reason to suppose that Plato believed that they too constituted a realm of their own, co-eternal with 'matter' and God. They are not dependent upon God or upon 'matter' for their existence – in part because as Ideals they are to give form to both God and 'matter'. Hence Plato conceived of God as a cosmic Lover of Forms (Ideas or Ideals) that he did not create. Neither the forms nor the inchoate Being, then, are dependent upon each other. There results a co-eternal trinity of beings in Plato's system at this point. And none of these beings, by definition, is related to the other.

Nevertheless, says Plato, this imperfect, but relatively orderly world can be explained by thinking of God as this cosmic Artist or Demi-urge, who with his eye fixed on the co-eternal Ideals, 'persuades' the co-eternal, inchoate being to take on as much form and order as possible. For Plato, the complex orderly world which man sees about him, and man's own capacity to know and interact with both the world and God, testify to the 'creative' goodness of one member of the co-eternal 'trinity'. Other thinkers decreased the difficulty to be mentioned by moving the Ideals into the mind of God, conceiving of them as the eternal Ideals guiding his will. For them God is still co-eternal with Matter of some sort, and cosmic Trinity gives way to Duality. We need not stop to elaborate on this view, for our concern is to understand why either a co-eternal Two or Three gave way to *creatio ex nihilo*.

It might be urged that any such one-of-two, or one-of-three, view of God was unacceptable to early Christians because it is unbiblical to make God finite. But this only skirts the real difficulty, which is the following. If there are two or three ultimate, co-eternal Beings, is it not completely incomprehensible that they should be so complementary? Why should they find that they can interact in a way that does make this kind of orderly world possible? The mystery of mysteries, opaque to our human intelligence because it contravenes what we always assume in our known realms, stuns us. For, when beings are at all related to each other, we assume that, despite their differences, they are not separated by chasms as impassable as these co-eternally different kinds of being must be by definition. Our minds demand that Creator, Ideas, and Stuff (or Creator and Stuff) have something in common if they are to interact at all. Indeed, the world as we know it, despite its dissonances and evils, is sufficiently good and sufficiently orderly to suggest that a better marriage actually took place than the one to be expected if both beings are completely independent of each other.

Once more, then, creation 'out of nothing' may be mysterious. But on what grounds may we expect two eternally different principles to be able to interact in such a way as to produce the kind of orderly world we observe? If it offends religious sensitivity, on the one hand, to conceive of God as limited by some co-eternal independent principle, then the theoretical reason cries out, on the other hand, against explaining the kind of orderly world we have by postulating two or three co-eternal, different beings (if we take their independence seriously).

The personalist has no easy task in defending *creatio ex nihilo*. It is only when we become aware of difficulties in *absolute* monism and in *absolute* dualism or pluralism that we see why this difficult alternative became palatable to him. Accordingly, the personalist holds that God, the cosmic Person, *created* the world *ex nihilo*. But this 'out of nothing' is the personalist's way of emphasising his rejection of any co-eternal, independent factor with which God has to deal. It is not simply that God is rendered finite if there is an independent non-created matter'; it is that we cannot account for the world's being an orderly world at all! Difficult as *creatio ex nihilo* is, it is not so utterly indefensible once one fully understands what is at stake.

The personalist, accordingly, goes on to explain that God's knowledge of all the possibilities and compossibilities guided him in his care to create the orderly world in which persons are sustained. But, more important, the doctrine of *creatio ex nihilo* is also the personalist's way of saying that God is not identical with the world and with persons. Further still, God is not one 'alongside' all the created beings, for they depend ultimately upon his will for whatever independence they have. Without his continuous creation and involvement in accordance with his own being and purpose there would be no 'universe'. The personalist in this doctrine, therefore, seeks to explain the order of the world in a way that preserves differences without endangering the autonomy and perfection of God.

Nevertheless, argue the critics of personalism, the cost of this doctrine is too high. They still find the notion of creation mysterious. The theist would agree that the doctrine is mysterious. But he urges that at worst this doctrine, *if* it is exemplified nowhere *in* our experience, nevertheless is not contradictory of anything we do find. Furthermore, every metaphysics and theology has some ultimate that is mysterious in that we cannot point to instances of it in the world. But the personalist does advance one other consideration to take the edge off this criticism.

Finally *creatio ex nihilo* does not actually mean that God took 'nothing' and made something out of it. The theist would agree that 'from nothing' nothing can come. Neither God nor man can do what is not even thinkable, make nothing become something! But creation out of nothing does not mean that God 'took nothing and made something out of it'. 'Out of' nothing, nothing comes, to be sure. But the personalist does not start with 'nothing'. He starts with God and says that this Person (far from being nothing himself) is the Creator-Ground of all.

In a word, to say that God creates is to say that beings now exist *that did not exist before*. Finite beings are not made 'out of God' or 'out of some co-eternal being'. They are made, produced, created. There is nothing contradictory in saying that a Creator brings into being what was non-existent without the act of creation; to create means just that!

6. THE PERSON GOD IS: CREATOR OF CO-CREATORS

Yet before the personalistic theist can persist in this difficult theory of creation, he must explain why he does not find another great vision of God more palatable. Why not say that God is One with all there is, that nature and man are modes of God, or participants in his being who do not have any independent agency of their own?

We must not be casual about this concept of God as The One, for it is proposed by careful monists (Paul Tillich is fresh in mind). They are not saying that everything there is, collectively, is God. This simply renames things as they appear. Nor do such monists say that God is equally in all things that participate in his being. God is indeed the One who is manifest in the many, and the One would not be what he is apart from the many. God is to be found in his different manifestations in different degrees, just as a man is to be found in his varied utterances even though none of them express all that he is.

Again, The One may be said to have many centres of his being. However we express it, on this view the continuity and unity observed among the myriad things in the world manifest, at different levels or in different dimensions, the unity and continuity that God is. While significant exponents of this view – Plotinus, Eckhardt, Spinoza, Tillich – have tended to think of this One as supra-Personal in the sense indicated above, this being has been held to be Mind or Spirit, as in the thought of Hegel, Lotze, Bradley, Royce, and W. E. Hocking.[1]

With such a galaxy of stars gloriously arraigned against him, why does the theistic personalist still maintain his creationist stand? First, he would point out that the *how* of this One-in-many is essentially no clearer than is the how of creation 'out of nothing'. There is no contest here, for it is mysterious to know how the infinite can be both infinite and finite, perfect and imperfect. But there is less that is opaque in this mysterious relation than there is in the contention of the dualist and pluralist mentioned earlier. Indeed, many idealistic personalistic theists, such as B. P. Bowne and E. S. Brightman, would even argue that while persons have delegated freedom and independence, beings of a physical and biological nature are direct expressions of the cosmic Person. The main personalistic objection to monism, accordingly, is not that Nature is unified with One but that man is unified with the One. Why?

Persons are not only self-conscious unified beings; they feel themselves to be free, and there is good reason to suppose that this feeling is not a delusion. However, this freedom is not self-instituted nor is this freedom without limits. The freedom

---

[1] Professor H. D. Lewis's treatment of Buber (see pp. 168–84) is an excellent presentation of the issue involved. At the same time Professor Lewis suggests a notion of 'the elusive self' and of interpersonal relations that reinforces the view of personhood suggested here.

of persons is the freedom to choose within the margins of their own possibilities in the world that surrounds them. But it is *their* freedom; it underlies their feeling of responsibility for much of what they do. If this is so, then they cannot be part of God, centres of His being. To express this crucial fact, the personalist calls for a doctrine of *creatio*.

It is important to emphasise here that the creationist theist will not allow any theory of the universe and of God to contradict or reduce to delusion the experience of free will. Human freedom, for good or ill, is limited, to be sure. But it is denied only at the cost of making human beings robots. To be sure, the exact scope of human freedom, and related matters, must be debated. But if man's actions are to be his, if they are to define his own individuality, he cannot be said to participate in God in any way that endangers this relative autonomy. If a person is a mode or a centre of another Being, *his* freedom, *his* individuality, is gone. Thus *creatio ex nihilo* now becomes the personalistic theist's way of saying that every attempt to explain how persons can be free and still be *parts* of, or *centres* of, a larger controlling Whole will not do.

There are many who will insist that the doctrine of human freedom is mysterious enough, for they think that a free act simply must mean arbitrary action unlinked to anything else past or present. Why then extend such mystery to horrendous, cosmic proportions, in a doctrine of divine creation of free persons?

The personalist stands firm and replies: If there is to be mystery in any world view, let this be where it is – namely, where it protects human finite unity and freedom, within limits to be determined in each instance. What is basically asserted in the doctrine of creation is that God can make what is not there before his act. This may be hard to imagine or picture, but it is defensible if theory is not to dictate to experienced personal unity and freedom.

Thus man is to be conceived of as a created co-creator. He has delegated responsibility for his own choices and sub-creations in God's world. This means that God is transcendent, for he has a Being for Himself. It also means that he is immanent not only by virtue of the dependence of the natural world upon him, but by virtue of his relationship to free persons. For God has created persons endowed with freedom to choose within the limits of their own capacities and of the rest of the world as God made it. It also means that he will join man in creating what is not possible without God and man in mutual response.

Of course this doctrine of the cosmic Person as creator of free persons who, having a place in God's purpose, yet are not *in* or *as* his Being, needs more defence. But since the monistic view of God is often defended on the grounds of the unity felt in mystical experience, one question may be raised here. What is love, or worship, if it does not involve the self-disciplined freedom of man to act in certain ways toward God and man? The personalist would argue that an adequate doctrine of sin, salvation, grace, prayer, worship, and immortality, is not forthcoming unless persons are created, free, co-creators with God.

Finally, is God the Person-Creator in fact arbitrary? The personalist finds no arbitrariness. For (on other grounds) he believes that God in his creating expresses the purposes of love and reason that constitute his intrinsic nature. God, the Creator-Person, creates the finite creator-person in accordance with his purpose that men should be free to choose which way their souls shall go. God's own purpose, as the personalist sees it, calls for a-community-of-responsive-responsible-persons as the norm of creation and history. The kingdom of God, on earth and in heaven, is a community of persons, dedicating themselves to each other as persons. The 'kingdom of heaven' is not the achievement of a benevolent despot; it is the qualitative growth of persons who find in their daily living that their freedom is most constructive and fruitful when it is expressed in creative and forgiving love.

The *person God is* – He is the Lover-Creator who expresses his love in the order of Nature without which man could not even exist. But the *person God is* – He is also the Lover-Creator who leaves man free to be a creator. The *person God is* – He makes it clear in the foundations of Nature and Man that only in mutual love unto forgiveness is there self-fulfilment for God or man. Only in mutual love is there that fellowship-in-

creativity-with-God that is God's highest goal for himself and
for every man.[1]

[1] In another place I have defended this view of human freedom and
argued that, contrary to the view theists usually have taken, its very nature
does provide us with finite instances of *creation* that involves bringing into
being what-is-not before the act of free creation. And I have also argued
that a temporalist view of God is involved when we see the consequences of
a fellowship of creative love. See 'Free Will, the Creativity of God, and
Order' in *Current Philosophical Issues* (*Essays in Honor of C. J. Ducasse*), ed.
F. Dommeyer (Illinois, 1966).

13

HELL

Ian Ramsey

In this paper I would like to consider Hell as a concept around which there cluster various different difficulties, and to see how and on what conditions some of these difficulties could be overcome, the whole paper illustrating, albeit by reference to a particular topic, and so with obvious restrictions, the character of theological argument, the nature of theological assertions, and the kind of empirical grounding that must be given to them.

Taking Hell in its most colourless, though popular, context, we may say briefly that it is the place, in a life after death, of endless punishment. About such a concept there arise three major difficulties – its moral repugnance; its logical inconsistency with other doctrines, not least in a Christian context; and cosmological difficulties which arise around its location. Let me develop these three difficulties in turn:

(1) *Its moral repugnance*: Quite plainly, there seems to be a head-on clash with ordinary moral insights. While it would obviously be granted by many that wrong-doing 'deserves' or merits punishment – this being the core of truth in the retributive theory – no one, it is said, could ever indulge in such wrong-doing as deserved punishment not only for ten years, not only for 'life', but for an unending period of time. In short, the doctrine of Hell is immoral.

We need not deny, of course, that what might be called the doctrine of a limited Hell might not only be morally viable, but some would say morally necessary for any theism. It might be said that far from being morally repugnant, some state of life after death where there could be a due balancing of 'reward and punishment' is morally necessary to balance the ostensible injustice about much human life on earth. Though I am far from thinking that the parable of Dives and Lazarus (Luke 16: 19–31) is designed to make precisely this point – and I shall have a little more to say on the significance of parables presently – nevertheless, the parable gains a certain initial credibility from representing poverty and misfortune here balanced by friendship and comfort hereafter, with social irresponsibilities and neglect being balanced by unhappiness and anguish. But a Hell of endless punishment strikes *no* moral balance and is morally repugnant.

(2) *The criticism of inconsistency*: In some ways this difficulty can be regarded as a rather more sophisticated version of the first. Whereas the first difficulty arose from a *prima facie* clash between natural moral insights and specifically Christian claims, this second kind of difficulty arises internally in relation to the whole array of Christian doctrine. The objection is that any notion of a place of endless punishment is inconsistent with those attributes of love and mercy, and especially love, which are distinctive of the Christian God. Perhaps I may quote from Professor Hick's book *Evil and the God of Love* (p. 120) where I have introduced a slight variation at the end in order, as I hope, to strengthen the main point: 'The contrast between the bad news of a God who deliberately makes creatures for whom He must also make a hell, and the good news of the God of Love heard in the parables and sayings of Jesus, is so great that I cannot regard them both as true; and every instinct of faith, hope and charity responds to Jesus' vision of the heavenly Father' rather than to that of the omnipotent insensitive Planner who deals so ruthlessly and 'cold-bloodedly with His finite creatures'.

It is true that there have been attempts, such as that of Augustine himself, to contain such a doctrine of Hell consistently within a Christian belief about God, and these attempts have tried to attach to Hell a certain fitness in so far as it has been argued, be it noted, on an aesthetic analogy, that the shades and blackness of Hell serve to set off the more strikingly the brightness and light of the rest of the universe,

the whole being aesthetically more attractive for having the
Hell there as a part. Professor Hick (p. 88) quotes Harnack:
'Augustine never tires of realising the beauty (pulchrum) and
fitness (aptum) of creation, of regarding the universe as an
ordered work of art. . . .'[1] As Augustine himself says: 'The black
colour in a picture may very well be beautiful if you take the
picture as a whole.'[2]

But plainly such an argument which came to have a central
place, for example, in eighteenth-century apologetic, does not
make the black less black, and it further presupposes that details
are somewhat neglected in the picture seen as a whole. In
other words, the presupposition of this aesthetic argument is
that God takes an overall point of view, and is only concerned
with details in so far as they contribute to the overall pattern.
In this sense the view certainly tends to conflict with the notion
of God's care being directed to each individual. Alternatively,
it implies that in the case of some individuals God has to
admit failure. In one way or another it certainly conflicts with a
theodicy in the sense of there being some all-embracing and
morally approvable purpose of God.

It is in this kind of context that the argument is sometimes
deployed, that since man is free he is therefore free to sin, and
since he is free to sin without limit, there must then be an
appropriate and balancing punishment without limit. But it
might well be argued that while man's freedom is something of
great value, if in fact there had to be a Hell as a condition of
creating man free, the whole project might well have been seen
as self-defeating from the start. In short, any kind of Hell seems
to point to a radical inconsistency in the concept of God, either
because it conflicts with the notion of God's individual care, or
because it demands a restriction on God's knowledge or God's
love or both.

(3) *Cosmological difficulties*: These difficulties can be expressed
as briefly as they are, in principle, crude. If there is a Hell in the
sense of some place in a life after death for endless punishment,

[1] C. G. A. Harnack, *History of Dogma* (trans. J. Millar), 3rd ed., vol. 5,
p. 114.
[2] *De Vera Religione*, xl, 76, quoted in Hick, *Evil and the God of Love* (London,
1966), p. 89.

where do we locate such a Hell? Further, so far as time goes, have we to suppose that its time series is continuous with the time which we know in human life? In other words, to be at all clear and effective as a doctrine, Hell presupposes a life *after* death largely continuous in time with life *before* death, and having very similar spatial features. Yet neither of these presuppositions seems at all antecedently plausible. Death would seem to be such a major spatio-temporal discontinuity, judging from what happens to the body at death, that there seems little reason to suppose that life after death is in a time series continuous with the present, or that it embodies spatial features which bear much resemblance to what we know now.

These are the cosmological difficulties which arise for any crude and literal account of Hell. But this is not of course to deny – to anticipate a point to which I shall return presently – that if the doctrine of Hell has any reliable point at all this point may have to be expressed in picture language which, as such, might well have to be constructed from the discourse of the world in which we live at present. To say this is to go no further necessarily than the cautious Joseph Butler, one-time Bishop of Durham, who argued in effect that if, as he believed, there is a 'serious apprehension' of a future state, then it will be somehow best talked about in terms of the same kind of 'righteous administration established in Nature' that we already discern here. In other words, while talk about life after death will always bristle with logical problems, nevertheless *faute de mieux* we must speak of it somehow or other in terms of such features of our present existence as seem to us most fundamental to human, and in particular (Butler would say) moral, existence. But to admit this, of course, is to grant that from the beginning talk about Hell is only talk 'after a fashion', 'as it were' talk, and once this point is granted the major cosmological problems clearly no longer arise.

Before dealing somewhat more constructively with the concept of Hell, I suggest that we might well ask ourselves at this point: Granting the difficulties which have been mentioned, why did anyone ever indulge in such unattractive themes? I think there are at least three answers to such a question:

(1) Undoubtedly, part of the answer is that these themes

were found in sacred literature taken as authoritative, and
not only authoritative but descriptive. In the Judaeo-Christian
tradition this remark of course relates to the Old and New
Testaments. I do not doubt that it was the detailed and colourful accounts of Hell, which can be found both in the Old and
New Testaments, that led to the doctrine being so commonly
accepted at a time when people were not as concerned as they
are now with the logical status of religious discourse. They did
not ask themselves what was the cash value of passages in
Jewish apocalyptic literature, or of some prophetical utterances,
or of particular parables, or of passages in the Apocalypse, or
doctrine of eschatology. Even so, I doubt whether an unquestioning attitude to sacred literature could by itself be a
complete reason for the great success of doctrines of Hell
winning men's acceptance. It seems to me that the doctrines
must in some way have matched some kind of antecedent
expectation, which brings me to my second point.

(2) I think that the attractiveness and centrality of a doctrine
of Hell goes back in part to the permanent significance which
men have often felt was attached to moral choice, in the sense
that men have believed that their moral and social actions
had some kind of abiding significance, involving God as he
who abides. There was also the associated moral insight (which
I mentioned earlier) that those who do wrong must inevitably
be punished; that wrong-doing brings with it a necessary demand for punishment. Or if it were thought that as a moral
insight this goes too far in being spelt out in terms of punishment,
I think that at least it would be generally agreed that wrong-
doing always seems to involve some kind of separation between
the wrong-doer and the person wronged. Wrong-doing, in
other words, creates some kind of gulf, and separation, between
persons. Such a state of separation may not always be a state of
unhappiness – which accounts for the popular comment that
some people would find perfect happiness in Hell – but it
would seem very likely to be a state leading to personal disintegration and destruction. It is interesting to recall that in the
Matthaean parable about the cup of cold water (Matt. 25:
31–46) the definitive remark is not about eternal punishment
or eternal life, but centres around the words 'come' and 'depart'

respectively, though it is true of course that the word 'depart' is contextualised in terms of a curse, eternal fire, the Devil and his angels, while 'come' is contextualised in terms of inheritance and a Kingdom long prepared and planned. But a point arises here to which I shall return later, viz., that very often in the doctrine of Hell we focus attention on words which are in fact logical ancillaries, and so blind our eyes to words which are logically more crucial. We are too prone to look at the countenance of a doctrine, instead of on its heart.

(3) The third reason why people have indulged in these unattractive themes seems to me that they have confused a natural reverential refusal to question God; with an indefensible logical refusal to question their own understandings of God. They have confused a matter of reverence and a matter of logic; they have given to doctrine an attitude which should be reserved for God. There is for them, as for all of us, a finality, an ultimacy about God. But to take God as authoritative does not commit us to taking doctrines of God as unquestionably true. Yet when some say that God is mysterious not only do they imply by this that we can never adequately understand God; they imply that (as they would put it) we must never 'judge' or 'question' God, by which they mean that we must never judge or question certain doctrines. Further, it seems to them to accord with human nature and to reflect its ruinous character that finite understandings of God are, as a matter of principle, not just inadequate, but logically scandalous, incoherent and the rest. In other words, the more repulsive a doctrine, the happier they will be. For those who would swallow camels such as these, Hell was a mere gnat, though they might enjoy straining at it.

A general reason for the surprising popularity of doctrines of Hell, and it is a reason which lies behind the acceptance of some other outrageous doctrines too, is that religious people have been only too ready to talk about God, to imagine themselves in the position of God, and to talk from God's point of view. When this propensity has been associated with an uncritical attitude to what has been said, when in other words, the two blunders have been married, the result has been disastrous. There has been no discourse too human, and no discourse too scandalous, to be used as a fully-fledged theology. We may take as an example of well-polished theology a relevant discussion in Professor Hick's book from which I have quoted before, and where he is discussing Dr Richard Downey's answer to the objection which, expressed in Dr Downey's words, is 'that if God foresaw, even though he did not positively forewill, the damnation of the wicked, nevertheless, as an infinitely good God, he ought to have abstained from creating such souls.'[1] Says Dr Downey:

> A little reflection, however, makes it clear that if God could be influenced in that way by a condition outside himself, the condition would be greater than he; he would be limited, constrained from without, and therefore not infinite, and not God. It would be as though the damned soul, whilst still only a mere possibility, could defy the Omnipotent to create it.[2]

Professor Hick comments:

> This argument rests upon the curious premise that God is only infinite and free if He does something the result of which He knows will be displeasing to Him! But why should it be considered a limitation upon God to refrain from self-frustrating activity? Surely it is a power rather than a weakness to be able to avoid defeating one's own ends. Indeed, presumably God has, in choosing to create the present universe, already chosen *not* to create other possible universes which would have been unacceptable to Him. But thus to choose the better rather than the worse does not indicate a restriction upon God's power. On the contrary, there *would* be limitation in being obliged to create a universe that the Creator did not want. And likewise it would be a limitation for God to be obliged to produce, simply because he *can* produce, free beings who He knows will, if created, fall away from Him and constitute a permanent stain upon His universe.

[1] *Evil and the God of Love*, p. 184.
[2] Richard Downey, 'Divine Providence', in *The Teaching of the Catholic Church* (ed. G. D. Smith) (rev. ed. London, 1952), vol. i, ch. vii, p. 245.

I do not particularly complain that as an *argumentum ad hominem*
Professor Hick stays in the material mode which Dr Downey
initiated. It shows how some fully-fledged theologies can continue in flight and never touch down. But if our purpose were
to assess the value of the whole argument, the first task would
be to convert it into the formal mode, and to grapple with the
issues *not* from the point of view as to whether God could or
could not do this, that, or the other, *but* as constituting a
problem in our talk about God. How do we use of God words
like 'produce', and phrases like 'choosing between universes'?
Here is theology in full flight, and our first demand must be
to know whence it cometh and whither it goeth. Too often
have men talked as if the way to solve theological problems was
by great familiarity with God, when what was needed was a
patient and thorough examination of the language being used
about him.

Perhaps, as a second example, I could comment on an
argument of my old friend Professor Journet, which is also
discussed by Professor Hick earlier in his book.[1] Journet remarks that there is 'a question that is hypothetical but nevertheless crucial for theodicy: could God, had he wished, have
exerted the irresistible influence of His grace within men's
souls in such a way as to bring *all* mankind freely to salvation?'
Journet continues:

> Could he always act thus? To ask this of him would be to
> expect from him a different world from the one he chose to
> make, in which the extraordinary would become the ordi-
> nary, and the exceptional would be changed into the rule. . . .
> But, at least, surely, the exceptions could be *more frequent*?
> Perhaps they could. But the real question lies elsewhere.
> Can we demand God to cause *even one single exception* to the
> ordinary rule of his subordinated power (i.e. his power
> within, and without altering, the structure of the universe
> which he had made)? Is the divine goodness, having showered
> its creatures with such help that, should they reject it, the
> fault should belong entirely to them . . . bound, under pain of
> ceasing to be infinite, to break down the resistance of one

[1] *Evil and the God of Love*, p. 118.

who freely wills to rebel against it? Not this question, but another is the one we find unanswerable: why does God sometimes do what he is in no way bound to do? And why does he do it for one person rather than for another? This is where we should listen to St Augustine: 'Do not judge, if you do not want to err.'[1]

Here is theology anxious to move in full flight, and to give us a display of the kind we have already had in our earlier example. But this time there is a difference. There is a sense that questions are being asked, which may be unanswerable. We see here very welcome evidence of a growing theological caution. My point would be that we need more caution and not less. In particular, before judging whether some questions are answerable or not, we might be well advised first to translate them into the formal mode when they would reveal their true character, and some might become no more, though no less, than logical questions of consistency and coherence.

All this is not to say that high-powered theological language such as we have quoted in these two examples above has no grounding in fact. But it is to say that in the form in which this and many other theological discussions are cast, logical questions and reference questions are most unedifyingly mixed and confused. It is only when we avoid speaking of God in too human terms that we shall avoid confounding these two sorts of question as well as the rather pointless difficulties which centre around what God can or cannot do, whether he fails and so on. Let us realise that we shall never be in a position to talk about God's intentions, and that in any case it is not what God can or cannot do, but rather what we can or cannot say about him. Recalling the quotation from Augustine: in all this we do *not* judge God, but only our understandings of, our discourse about God.

Before passing to some more positive suggestions let me illustrate this point, as well as making some others, by looking for a moment at one fully developed doctrine of Hell. It is a doctrine whose theological context incorporates themes of arbitrary election, and of redemption of sin which is then

---

[1] Charles Journet, *The Meaning of Evil* (London, 1963), pp. 168–9.

construed as *o felix culpa*. Because of the particular way in which
these doctrines are interwoven, the finished product is all the
more morally repugnant. It is a doctrine held, for example, by
Hugh of St Victor, and I will give it in terms that Professor
Hick uses in his book:

> In the writings of Hugh of St Victor we have presented with
> a total lack of reticence the monstrous moral paradox that
> God intends His creatures to sin (since it is better that there
> should be sin and redemption in the universe than that there
> should not), but that He nevertheless inflicts eternal punish-
> ment upon them when they do sin, though arbitrarily re-
> prieving some and granting to them the joy of His presence –
> a joy that is supposed not to be eclipsed, but on the contrary
> heightened, by their contemplation of the torments of
> others who were no more wicked than themselves, but who
> were left behind when the arbitrary divine decree lifted
> some out of the *massa perditionis*. This [says Professor Hick,
> and who could disagree?] is a morally repugnant set of
> ideas; and a theology cannot go unchallenged when it is
> repugnant to the moral sense that has been formed by the
> religious realities upon which this theology itself professes
> to be based.[1]

Professor Hick later comments more generally on the Augus-
tinian tradition:

> Now this doctrine of God's creation of beings whom He
> knows will fall and whom, having fallen, He does not intend
> to raise up again, is directly at variance with the thought
> that He permits sin only in order to bring out of it the
> greater and more glorious good of redemption. We can only
> claim that the second-order good of a redeemed humanity
> justifies the first-order evil of sin to the extent that sinners
> are in fact finally redeemed. So far as the rest of fallen
> humanity are concerned, no justification has been offered,
> but on the contrary the problem has been exacerbated by
> the appalling doctrine that God creates persons who He

[1] *Evil and the God of Love*, p. 98.

knows will merit damnation and who He is content should
be damned.[1]

We may say about this view what Professor Hick has already
said about Hugh of St Victor:

> It is without biblical warrant, and can be connected with
> the teaching of our Lord only by long speculative and theor-
> etical extensions and constructions. Not only are these theor-
> etical constructions the work of the human mind, rather than
> any kind of divinely revealed truths, but they are not
> among the more beautiful or morally elevated creations of
> human speculation. There is no reason why they should
> not be subjected to uninhibited Christian scrutiny; and in
> the light of this they may well have to be rejected as pro-
> ducts of a sinful imagination.[2]

I could not agree more; though in this paper I shall try to see
whether even theoretical constructions as offensive as this one,
nevertheless contain somewhere some insights worth preserving.
For it is, and will be, part of my case that these speculative
constructions arise, as does so much unsatisfactory theological
argument, from interweaving without due logical care various
themes each of which may be in and for itself reputable. But
if the interweaving is done without logical circumspection the
result can be incoherence, scandal and chaos.

For instance, in the appalling speculation of Hugh of St
Victor we can discern a number of themes, five of them at
least. First there is what might be called the 'Ultimacy of God'.
Here is a point which I have made earlier, and in one sense for
the theist it is unassailable. 'God' is for him an irreducible posit,
that by which he names the objective referent of his determining
commitment. But that does not mean that *our understanding*
of God is ultimate and cannot be questioned. There may be
some analytical assertions in this logical position, for instance
assertions which relate 'God' to other posits e.g. 'good', as
when we say 'Whatever God does is good'. But it is something
quite different to know, and to talk of, *what* God does, and

[1] Ibid., pp. 183, 184.   [2] Ibid., p. 98.

such discourse however constructed must be open to moral checking.

Secondly there are *biblical themes* incorporated in this fully fledged doctrine of Hell, and the mistake we have just discussed is seen at its worst in some attitudes to the Bible where biblical assertions are supposed to have the status of irreducible posits, of God himself. I have no doubt, for example, that the idea of the pleasures of heaven being heightened by the view of the torments of Hell has, for a part of its origin, Isaiah 65: 24 where Zion's future hope includes their going forth 'to look on the dead bodies of the men that have rebelled . . . for their worms shall not die, their fire shall not be quenched, and they shall be abhorrence to all flesh.' This has been taken to be plain description of the future state, subject in due course to a straight empirical verification. But what should we think of someone who having heard that Churchill was at the helm of the ship of state in 1942 said how suitable this was, seeing that the war-time Prime Minister was a member of Trinity House with a good sense of seamanship. Such a remark admittedly is not without its value. But if it was made we would suspect that our hearer had missed the point and had misconstrued the logic of our remarks. Equally do those misconstrue the logic of biblical narratives who take eschatology as plainly descriptive.

Thirdly, while we must for obvious reasons use human language about God, we must plainly *not* use it without logical qualification. We may speak, for example, of God's *decision* or *decree* or *choice*, and to speak of these as 'arbitrary' *may* be to use what I have called a qualifier,[1] and thus meet my first point. If so, all is well. But often it is taken as a logically straightforward adjective implying 'subject to no further examination'. The result then can be morally and intellectually disastrous.

Fourthly, there may be incorporated into theological discourse moral insights which cannot be faulted. For example, on a principle like Moore's principle of ethical organic unities, redemption may allow sin to be consistently incorporated into a morally approvable purpose which is then attributable to God.

[1] See, e.g., I. Ramsey, *Religious Language* (London, 1957), ch. ii.

I have already mentioned also the insight, if insight it be, that wrong-doing deserves punishment. But incoherence will arise when, after using such moral insights in our discourse, we then immunise the discourse from further moral criticism, and the disaster is even greater if this immunity from moral criticism occurs by injecting into the discourse a claim which originates in a logical howler such as I mentioned at the start.

Fifthly, as a matter of empirical fact and judging from our present experience it looks *prima facie* as if there will always be those who will never respond to the Christian gospel. But incoherence arises when this plausible judgement of fact is interwoven with plausible moral insights about punishment, the whole being then contextualised, however, in discourse which, besides misconstruing the Bible in a way at which I have already hinted above, commits the logical blunder about the priority and ultimacy of God. It is out of such indiscriminate interweaving that fully-fledged doctrines of Hell have often appeared.

Having now seen something of the complex character of doctrines of Hell, let me in conclusion make one or two suggestions as to how such doctrines may best be construed.

In the first place, let us realise that the Bible in general, and the New Testament in particular, has not to be taken as supplying us with descriptive pictures of a life after death. Such descriptions as we have of fire, brimstone and the gnashing of teeth have not to be taken as having any kind of easy direct relationship to foam extinguishers, the chemistry of sulphur, and dentists respectively. Rather are they images which suggest, and at first glance, destruction and even annihilation.

Let me say a little more about the image of fire. To do this let me go back to the word often used in this connection, Gehenna. Gehenna comes from the Greek equivalent of a Hebrew phrase for 'the Valley of Hinnom'. This was an area to the south of Jerusalem associated first with human sacrifices (cf. 2 Kgs. 16: 3 – 'the abominations of the heathen') and then foreshadowed by Jeremiah as the 'Valley of Slaughter' for the faithless, until it came to be regarded as a divinely appointed place of punishment. Some have suggested that the fire theme of Hell derives from the fires which, so it is said (though with no apparent authority before the thirteenth century), were continually burning there – possibly for the burning up of rubbish. But in any event it is easy to see how around this area could be associated the themes of fire, destruction and judgement, and how easily the model of fire developing in this context led to discourse about God. But that we need to be very careful before giving an over-simplified, descriptive logic to such discourse is evident from such a phrase as we find in Hebrews 10:27 where the reference to fire ('a fierceness of fire which shall devour the adversaries') – a fire-like fierceness – is plainly metaphorical.

Incidentally, I should be greatly interested to know for certain the cultural origin in this context of the image of brimstone, though it might well have to do with volcanic eruptions, and the major destruction which they brought with them. There are certainly hot sulphur springs in the region of Palestine, and volcanic deposits of sulphur might well, as I have said and for obvious reasons, be associated with destruction. Further, it may be that just as human sacrifices were often thrown into a pit of fire, sulphur springs were used as an alternative. There is also the interesting point that some sulphur springs of moderate temperature could be used alternatively as health-giving baths, so that we have again the ambiguity between destruction and purifying. But all this is conjecture and suggestion on my part. Nevertheless, it is interesting that commentators have been not at all certain as to what discourse this model of the brimstone lake licensed. The classical reference to the 'lake which burneth with fire and brimstone' is in Revelation 21: 8 (cf. 19: 20, 20: 10) where it is obvious imagery to talk of the 'second death'. Some commentators say that the fire here might be to destroy, or to punish, or to purify (H. B. Swete). Others have said that the punishment had to be fearful enough to deter those who might otherwise be persuaded to offer worship to the emperor, because of the torments which the civil authorities of the day would apply.

At this point, however, we may recall the well-known remark made by Jülicher about the parables, namely that we should see the parables as making one striking point, and one only. I

think that in the Matthaean parable for example, the main
point here is the one I have made already, that is, the permanent significance of moral behaviour and the need to see our
responses to the moral demands of society as an acceptance or
rejection of Christ. This acceptance and rejection theme is
undoubtedly pointed up and made the more emphatic by the
highly colourful and by no means inappropriate images
associated, for example, with the Valley of Hinnom, with fire
and lakes of brimstone, with which it is associated. But the
trouble is that believers and unbelievers alike are tempted to
extend the discourse in terms of its most colourful images, paying less and less attention to the moral point which is at its
heart. They forget that the further we go from the centre, the
more peripheral will be our religious discourse, whose one
and only subject is God. Fire, brimstone and teeth are all
peripheral to the discourse, and apocalyptic as well as parables
always need to be read around a particular point at which a
disclosure of God is claimed. To put it very crudely, most parables and most apocalyptic need reading backwards, back
into the disclosure of God which is at their heart and centre.
Once we recognise in this way the imaginative logic of eschatology and the parables, the great location difficulties of a
doctrine of Hell completely disappear, and we also see where,
and where not God comes in.

Now, one important principle lying behind the doctrine of
Hell seems to me to be, as I have said already, the cosmic
significance of moral decision, the view that the taking of
moral decisions involves an attitude to God so that an evil
decision alienates the agent from God, a condition to which
the images are meant to point. Let me now develop this
suggestion. At the human level, to do wrong is to opt for a
human 'hell' talked of in terms of punishment or, as I have
said already, at least in terms of separation. When this feature
of wrong-doing has been set in a cosmic perspective, which
occurs if, for example, we have been led to see all wrong-doing
as involving our relation to God, then the human models of
punishment or separation will need, as always, to be suitably
qualified to be adequate currency for the new context, and it is
in this context that the word 'eternal' is used. 'Eternal' is that

hint, that signpost, that reminder that in talking e.g. about punishment – 'eternal punishment' – we are using a model, viz. 'punishment', in such a way as to aim at a revelation of God; that we are using a model by which to point to that loneliness, despair, separation, and so on, in whose agony and anguish it is the claim of the Christian Gospel that God speaks. All this is spelt out very simply in relation to God in Whittier's hymn – 'To turn aside from thee is hell, to walk with thee is heaven'. On this view the word Hell and its cluster of associated images names 'eternal loneliness' as a condition in which God will, according to the Christian Gospel, disclose himself. Alternatively, we may say that any doctrine of Hell consistent with the Gospel must be such that, interpreting a situation of loneliness, or despair, it will lead from that situation to one of cosmic disclosure where God reveals himself.

There is of course the possibility of using other models for discourse about Hell besides the ones of moral separation and punishment, filled out by colourful geographical images, such as I have discussed so far. As is well known, 'Hell' in a non-theological context is often used to name what seems to be a surd or irrational element in life. This of course is its connotation where, as Sartre writes in *No Exit*: 'Hell is other people'. For (as he would say), I cannot avoid the fact that other people see me as an 'object', yet neither can I accept it. In other words, here are irrational features of contemporary life which might be used as models to provide an anchorage for doctrines of Hell, and so be transformed by a disclosure of God. For the believer in God, these are contemporary valleys of Hinnom around which may cluster imaginative pictures, this time from drama and literature, the whole array being a basis for a doctrine of Hell which points to a disclosure of God. One way of expressing the problem of Hell is to say that it is the problem of using these models to point to God, to talk of God, without running into discourse which is morally repugnant or blatantly inconsistent with other regions of religious discourse.

I have already mentioned in the course of this paper various mistakes and blunders to which we must be alert. At the moment, the one point I would like to make here is the need for logical qualifiers to remind us of the status of the model

The logic of the word 'eternal' is indeed meant to direct us to set these various experiences to which I have referred in what might be called a wider and deeper context so that God may be disclosed, and (the Christian would say) most characteristically disclosed. 'Eternal' is entirely misunderstood when it is translated descriptively as 'everlasting', as it is when this word is taken to represent temporal span whether sempiternal or otherwise.

Once 'eternal' is seen to be a qualifier whose logic is not that of the descriptive adjective 'everlasting', the major argument from moral repugnance collapses, since no one is committed to saying that God punishes over a temporal span which is without end. That would be to mistake the function of the qualifier. At the same time, the inconsistency with other Christian doctrines disappears in so far as the whole purpose of this discourse about Hell is not only to call attention to the Christian Gospel, but in doing that to reveal a loving and moral God which speaks to a man in his loneliness, despair and separation. This is the end-point which the picture of Hell must be designed to conjure up.

But we have not quite finished with the difficulties, and two remain, which I will treat quite briefly. First, we must realise that if we would avoid blatant inconsistencies with Christian doctrines, it will always be hazardous to talk about God punishing, not only because it makes God too human, and falls into the logical confusion I have mentioned above, but because the activity of punishment is one which always involves us as something less than persons, whether as punisher or punished. I suppose the bearing of all that on our present discussion is that I would myself opt, in a doctrine of Hell, for the model rather of separation than punishment.

Secondly a new point, though it is one which is implied in what I have said about doctrines of Hell as leading to a disclosure of a redeeming God. I entirely agree with Professor Hick that theological consistency demands in the end universalism at least in the sense of there being a final triumph of God's purposes of redemption, the triumph of his redeeming love. Nevertheless we have to be quite clear that because this is the most consistent theology it does not necessarily follow that it

is true. We still need to ask about the empirical grounding of
such a doctrine. That would demand a very different paper
from one on Hell, but it is relevant here to make one comment
in this connection. Undoubtedly, universalism has generally
been criticised because, it is said, if it were true it would take
the edge off any moral challenge. If universalism were true, it
has been said, we could all conclude that it would not matter
very much in the long run what we did. But if, in this way, we
did not bother about the challenge of a moral situation, it
would be to deny the very significance of the situation from
which the discourse started. Let me briefly develop that point.

If we accepted a doctrine of universalism in the sense of
believing in a final triumph of God's purposes and so, in a
phrase, in the final disappearance of Hell, it would be because we believed ourselves able to speak consistently *both*
of God and his love and his power, and *also* about the cosmic
significance of moral decision, the cosmic loneliness and
separation it involves and so on. But there could then be no
question of the doctrine denying part of the rock whence it was
hewn. I think that what I am saying is that while universalism
may have formal difficulties of the kind I mentioned earlier in
this section, the objection breaks down on what the logician
W. E. Johnson calls the epistemic conditions for the argument.
In other words, if we had in fact approached universalism in
the context in which we have in this paper approached it, we
could not, without denying the conditions under which we
gave utterance to the belief, claim at the same time that moral
decision did not matter.

Here, in a rather sophisticated area, the doctrine of universalism, we can see again how theological doctrines can all
too easily come to have a life of their own, when they break into
full flight, whereupon they inevitably raise difficulties which,
on the whole, are pseudo-difficulties, difficulties which can
certainly be avoided with sufficient logical circumspection and a
determination not to overlook the empirical anchorage of the
doctrine.

So my conclusion is that all the pictures which cluster around
the doctrine of Hell have their point when and only when they
recapture for us a disclosure of God's redeeming love, and this

they will do when they are set in the context of wrong-doing and punishment, or separation, or loneliness, when they are set in those particular strands of moral or existential discourse. The moral repugnance that there is to doctrines of Hell, and the cosmological difficulties that arise around them, arise largely from logical blunders in their construction, which only too readily encourage, where no encouragement is needed, logical blunders in their understanding. Doctrines of Hell provide a good example of the complex way in which theological discourse emerges as a multi-model, many-stranded discourse, some of the strands being derived from biblical images, and some from moral and existential insights. They also provide, as we saw earlier in the paper, a good example of how theology can be bedevilled by misundertandings of its point, its status and its character. Doctrines of Hell, like all other theistic doctrines, exist primarily to point to God who is, in the last resort, the single topic of all religious discourse. Doctrines of Hell, in other words, afford a particular example of the complex character of Christian discourse, and when various misunderstandings have been cleared up even these doctrines may help us to see in their own way the kind of situation in which all religious discourse is grounded, a 'cosmic disclosure' reached from the direction of separation, loneliness and despair where, the Christian would claim, God reveals himself.

14

THE CONCEPT OF HEAVEN

Ninian Smart

M y title is in a way misleading, for I want to show that there is a number of concepts of heaven. I want to explore these in the first part of this lecture. In the second part I shall comment on most of them, to see which, if any, seem to be viable.

I

Concepts of heaven have, of course, to be seen in context. There are two features of their religious context which it is especially important to note, for the purposes of this exploration of these concepts. First, schemes of religious belief are organic. By this I mean that it is impossible to understand a given religious utterance or belief without paying attention to the range of utterances or beliefs it goes with, and these in turn have to be understood in the milieu of religious practice, etc. For example, Christianity has traditionally affirmed that Christ is the Son of God. Obviously, this has to be seen in the context of the idea of God as expressed in a whole set of affirmations about the history of Israel and so forth; and equally obviously, the concept of God is the concept of a Being to whom worship is due, and which therefore has to be understood in the milieu of liturgical and other practical religious acts.

The second important point to note is that religious ideas undergo changes, and in particular the mythic or symbolic side of religious ideas is liable to suffer changes as a result of reflection upon them from later cultural standpoints. For instance, it is doubtful whether the question of Adam's being a historical or a symbolic figure (summing up something about mankind's relation to God) could properly be asked in the context in which the Genesis narratives were originally composed. For the mythic way of thinking eschews the distinctions which we are inclined to make. I shall therefore refer to certain ideas of heaven as mythic and others as doctrinal, to signalise the difference between two stages of thinking. For instance, God is mythically represented as dwelling in or beyond the sky, but it would be folly to suppose that this, at the mythic stage, is meant literally, as though God were like a Gagarin. Doctrinally, God is represented as transcendent, in such a way that *now* the language of heaven is treated as symolic of transcendence.

Perhaps the term 'doctrinal' is a little misleading, and I would utter a warning about it. Some may think that doctrines are simply descriptive, or supposedly descriptive, propositions about the nature of God, the world, etc. But it is worth seeing that doctrines, in their proper milieu, have a strong relevance to forms of piety and religious practice. For instance, the doctrine that God is continuous creator of the whole cosmos implies that God has a sort of presence everywhere: he is omnipresent, as we might rather barbarously say. But this omnipresence is tied in with the religious life, since it means that God is always here to be addressed in prayer, etc. In brief, I do not want to use 'doctrinal' as though it is an alternative word for 'metaphysical'. Religious affirmations may sometimes have philosophical roots, but their dominant source is religion itself.

I want, then, to insist on the following three preliminary points: first, that a sketch of a given idea of heaven has to take into account the organic milieu in which it has its life; second, that it is convenient to distinguish between mythic and doctrinal concepts of heaven; and third, that doctrinal concepts are as much to be seen in a living religious milieu as mythic ones. But as to the first point, it is not easy in a brief treatment such as we are now undertaking to fill in the organic milieu satisfactorily, so that sometimes I shall be leaving it to you to do so.

The first idea of heaven which I wish to consider is that of
heaven conceived as the place of God (or of the gods), as in
the opening words of the Lord's Prayer, 'Our father, which art
in heaven . . .'. There are, of course, a number of cultures in
which God's place is associated with the sky. Almost inevitably,
this mythic idea of God's location comes to be refined into a
doctrinal one: this is a way of protecting part of its significance
from hard-hearted criticisms of faith – criticisms which per-
sistently reduce the mythic concept in the other direction to a
literal one. *Of course* God is not literally in the sky, and yet this
is what the mythic concept seems to be saying, once we begin
to ask the literal-minded question. Though the substitution of
a doctrinal idea of God's place for the mythic one sacrifices
some of the poetic flavour of the latter, it is still possible to
retain the symbolism by continuing to use the mythology in
liturgy. By the 'poetic flavour', I mean that there are suggestions in the idea of God as dwelling in the sky, or beyond it,
which are relevant to religious experience and practice, but
which are not brought out in such a technical-sounding term as
'transcendence'. For example, the sky shines, it contains the
stars above, it is high: it thus hints at God's glory, majesty and
supreme holiness. How often do value-predicates connect up
with height – 'supreme', 'a high quality of . . .' and so on. A
religious tradition is liable to try to retain these suggestions,
by continuing to sing hymns about a sky-God, long after it has
introduced a severer and apparently more abstract account of
God's place. The tension, however, can be so great that liturgy
needs to be reshaped.

The doctrinal idea of God's place, i.e. the notion that God is
transcendent, can be explained briefly as follows. It ties in
with the context of the doctrine of Creation, as commonly
interpreted to mean that God continuously creates and sustains
the cosmos, which is thus at all points dependent upon him.
This belief implies that God and the cosmos are distinct. For
this and other reasons, God does not take spatial predicates
(except at the mythic level). Thus God is conceived as lying
beyond the cosmos – he transcends it – but not in such a way
that it makes sense to say that he is a thousand or a million
miles further on. There is an analogy in some of the talk we

have about human beings: thoughts and feelings are sometimes masked *behind* my overt behaviour, though it is nonsense to say that they are three inches behind my smile, or wherever. In giving this explanation of the idea of transcendence as applied to God, I am concentrating on the idea that God has, so to say, a transcendent place. There are other ways (sometimes confused ones) of using 'transcend' and its cognates but I do not remark on these here.[1]

So far, we have noted two concepts of heaven, both as being the 'place' of God. One is the mythic concept of heaven up there in or beyond the sky. The other is the doctrinal concept of God as transcendent. But as we have seen, the latter idea can be held side by side with the mythic concept of heaven, except that the latter has now been displaced as the central account of where God is, and is thus treated merely symbolically. When the mythic undergoes this displacement, it is convenient to refer to it as the symbolic concept of heaven. For it has indeed undergone a change – become a new concept, if you like – by virtue of the principle of the organic understanding of religious concepts and utterances described near the beginning of this lecture. Since a given concept has to be understood by reference to its organic milieu, some major change in that milieu creates a new concept, in effect. And this is what happens where the idea of the mythic heaven is no longer taken altogether seriously, but is in essence replaced by a doctrinal concept of heaven, and only retained as a symbolism which points us towards that which is more precisely described by means of the doctrinal concept. This, then, is an argument for distinguishing the original mythic concept of heaven from what we are now calling the symbolic concept.

Before moving to other ideas of heaven, I would like to make one major comment on the notion of transcendence as briefly outlined earlier. If transcendence in this sense means that God is not spatial, and yet is distinct from the cosmos, while sustaining it, so to say, from behind, then there is no strong reason to distinguish this account of transcendence from one main meaning of *immanence*. The belief that God works

[1] A fuller exposition of this concept of transcendence is to be found in my article 'Myth and Transcendence' in *The Monist* (October, 1966).

within all things merely uses a different spatial analogy from the belief that he is behind or beyond the cosmos.

So far, then, we may distinguish three forms of the idea of heaven considered as the place of God. Some religions, however, do not involve or do not necessarily involve belief in God, as commonly understood. Buddhism is one of these. Here the central concept is of transcendent nirvana, a state realisable through treading the Eightfold Path. It is true that Buddhism does not abandon the concept of heaven, but the heavenly state is inferior to nirvana: it belongs to the realm of the impermanent, while nirvana is the permanent abode. There is a certain ambiguity in the Pali Canon as to the status of heavens, just as there is an ambiguity about the gods. Sometimes the heavens are matched with meditational states, and it leads one to wonder whether they are not in the last resort simply symbols of psychological, contemplative stages. But it is unwise to insist too strictly on treating them as symbolic. What seems to have happened is that Buddhism consciously retained the mythic concept of heaven, but placed it firmly below nirvana in order of priority. The gods who are in the heavens themselves are much inferior in insight to the Buddhas and indeed to anyone who has gained nirvana in this life. The Buddhist way by-passes the gods, even the great god Brahmā. For this reason, it is not the case that, in the Theravadin tradition at least, the mythic concept of heaven comes to be treated as symbolic of nirvana. We see a different pattern from the development in theistic faiths, and this is not surprising since in many respects the whole structure of Buddhism is so different.

With these points in mind, it nevertheless is not too misleading to say that there is an analogy between the doctrinal concept of heaven as God's place and the doctrinal concept of nirvana as a transcendent state, beyond the impermanent world. But nirvana is neither the locus of God nor of souls: it is rather the transcendent place of liberation (though one should not ask what is *contained* in that place). We can thus distinguish a fourth idea of what loosely can come under the head of heaven, namely the idea of a transcendent place of liberation.

This brings us to a further notion: for in some religions (though not in Buddhism) there has been a theory of souls. It thus becomes possible to treat heaven as the place whither at least some souls are translated upon death. Not surprisingly, something depends upon the nature of beliefs about souls and persons. Thus it is possible to have a rather ill-defined belief in the persistence of personhood beyond the grave – a mythic picture of post-mortem existence; and this fits in with the mythic concept of heaven as the place of God (or the gods). People who go to God's presence thus can enjoy a mythic position close to him. But it is tempting, especially when there has been elaborated a doctrinal idea of God's transcendence, to have a doctrine of souls, constituting the eternal, non-spatial aspect of the person, which can in this way plausibly make the transition from the cosmos to the state lying beyond it. This concept of heaven can be summed up as the idea of a place of liberated souls.

It is worth commenting that there are schemes of belief which retain a form of soul-theory without entailing that there are many souls: thus notably for Shankara, in his exposition of Advaita Vedanta, there is only one atman, and this is identical with the one divine Being. Thus liberation does not involve translation of an individual soul to a heavenly state, but simply the shedding of those factors which obscure the self's true identity. There is thus an analogy with Buddhist nirvana, at least in the sense that there is a state of liberation, but no individual being who enjoys it.

One reason in theistic systems for the idea of a plurality of souls to be attractive is that theism implies a gap between the focus of worship and the worshipper. It would indeed be blasphemous and absurd, from this point of view, to identify the individual soul with God. There are, of course, other reasons why a plural soul-theory has entered into the Christian and other traditions.

It seems then that we have at least the following ideas of heaven to consider: heaven as the mythic place of God; heaven as the mythic place of liberation; heaven as the doctrinal place of God; heaven as the doctrinal place of liberated souls; heaven simply as the doctrinal place of liberation; heaven as the symbolic place of God; and by analogy heaven as the symbolic place of liberation.

Ideas of the so-called future life or last things are not exhausted by the forms mentioned above. For there is the faith
in the resurrection of the dead. This has its own form of ambiguity. The more natural interpretation of it in the Christian
tradition, for instance, is that it occurs upon earth, in this
world – it is a consummation of human history, etc. It is thus
not other-worldly in its emphasis, as many ideas of heaven are.
But it does not take much shift for the mythic concept of the
general resurrection, etc., to slide into the symbolic idea of
heaven. Thus some writers have treated the idea of a resurrection body as an unimaginable vehicle for personhood
in the next world. On the other hand, doctrinal elaboration of
the hope of the last things can replace the expectation of risings
from the dead as a consummation of human history, in which
the hope of heaven in a transcendent sphere is essentially
absent. The doctrine becomes a way of expressing hope about
the divine guidance of human history, etc. Though resurrection
of the body rather than immortality of the soul is probably the
dominant motif in New Testament hope, I shall not comment
further upon it, since it lies outside the discussion of the concept
of heaven, except in so far as it sometimes is collapsed into the
symbolic idea of heaven.

Finally, in this rapid account of beliefs about heaven, it is
worth mentioning a common form of ordinary hope, namely
that people survive death in some higher realm, but not
necessarily oriented towards God or concern for salvation or
liberation. Ordinary folk want to meet their loved ones in the
beyond, even if they are not specially concerned with religion,
worship, piety or contemplation. There is indeed often a
tension between religion and ordinary hopes: ordinary hopes
may be pointed towards simple continuation of life in company, but not particularly the company of God. Since traditional Christianity sometimes pictures heaven, the place of
liberated souls, as containing the realisation of the summit of
the contemplative life (the beatific vision of God in heaven only
has its foretastes in the mystical life here on earth), there is a
gap between ordinary concerns and those encouraged by
religion. The contemplative life tends to be for the few rather
than for the many. What men do not do here on earth they

may not feel called to do in heaven! There is, then, a popular concept of heaven as being simply the place of survival among loved ones.

Though the ideas we have considered have a rather other-worldly flavour, it should be recalled that in the living milieu of religion they can have a strong this-worldly significance. The transcendent state of nirvana can be 'seen' by the saint here and now. Eternal life can be possessed on earth, just as God can be encountered on earth, though his 'place' lies beyond it.

It is now time to comment on some of the various ideas of heaven, to see whether they are consistent and meaningful.

II

I shall argue in this section of the paper that a crucial, but peculiar, place is held by the doctrinal concept of heaven as God's place. But I shall not argue directly that *this* concept is free from contradiction, nor that it is necessary to the expression of theistic faith. This lack of directness here is partly due to the fact that I have elsewhere tried to show that the idea is free from contradiction.

But first, let us consider the mythic idea of heaven, as God's place. I think it is largely the case, in the major religions, that it has become deeply eroded by the very fact that the major religions have evolved theologies or schemes of doctrine which effectively reduce it to symbolic status. But in any event, it is almost inevitable that we should here treat the mythic idea as dead: for the very question as to its consistency requires us to ask such questions as whether it is possible to locate God in the sky, and such questions belong to a different cultural and intellectual milieu from that in which such a mythic idea had its genesis. I am far from saying that myths are unimportant: but we are not here concerned with the vital and underdeveloped project of gaining a deep insight into the nature of myths. As we shall see, there may be a way of consistently using the mythic idea of heaven, even within the framework of modern cosmology, etc., but only by using it in a parabolic way, which almost amounts to giving it symbolic status.

The symbolic idea of heaven, as such, need not detain us, in that when the mythology of heaven is reinterpreted in a doctrinal way, the symbolic concept of heaven merely serves to point to the transcendence of which the doctrine of the beyond speaks. By the same token, the idea of heaven as the symbolic place of liberation or salvation can be left for the moment on one side.

What can be said about heaven as the doctrinal place of souls? It will be recalled that a principal motive of this idea is that the soul is in theory non-spatial, though somehow connected with the spatial organism, which constitutes or, more mildly, at least expresses human personhood. The non-spatiality of the soul helps us to understand how it can be that there is a transition from this world to the world of transcendence. For indeed it makes little sense to ascribe my thoughts or feelings to a place a few inches to the left of my right ear, etc. (a point canvassed in Gilbert Ryle's *The Concept of Mind* and elsewhere). One can be grateful for the thesis that spatial predicates have a limited purview, even within the realms of space: electrons and minds behave oddly. But the gratitude is only for this – that it rids us of a too-standard view of the concepts we use. It does not warrant us in inferring that because spatial predicates do not typically apply to mental processes, therefore the mind or soul can make an easy transition to the hereafter. The reason why this remark is in order is that it is quite feasible to treat predicates about the mind, etc., as applying essentially to the whole organism. Though Ryle's treatment of the topic was in some ways rather crude, it remains quite possible to take over the basis of his analysis. This in itself is not a criticism of the crucial notion of God's transcendence, which also trades on the possibility of non-spatiality, since it is open to us to treat the cosmos as God's body – a doctrine which we find in Ramanuja's writings and which has the attraction of militating against a strongly two-worlds view. It is obvious, of course, that the cosmos does not *look like* the bodily manifestation of an organism. Ramanuja indeed produced a whole series of telling arguments against the Teleological Argument and of the argument from the likeness of the cosmos to an organic body (an argument only partially treated in Hume's famous *Dialogues*, written a few centuries later). But one must distinguish between the grounds of a belief and its conceptual viability. The conflation between the two can cause much trouble. In essence the recent tendency to condemn religious utterances as meaningless turned on the lack of ordinary sorts of grounds for them: in short, on the view that because groundless (i.e. according to some preconceived straitjacket of epistemology) therefore meaningless or without conceptual viability. Hence, even if the cosmos may not look like the body (to use only one analogy) of God it does not at all follow either that the idea is absurd or that it is false. Needless to say, the concept of a body here undergoes some change: but it is natural in religious discourse as elsewhere to use analogical terms.

However, the possibility of a consistent notion of heaven as the place of God does not guarantee the possibility of a consistent idea of the disembodied existence of the soul in the next world. It might be that the idea of transcendence is a necessary condition of the acceptability of belief in the existence of souls in a liberated state. But the latter idea, especially in the context of belief in God, has some notorious difficulties. First, it is an important sentiment within the context of worship that God and the worshipper are distinct (unlike the non-dualistic Hindu view to which we made reference). The notion of distinct, but non-spatial, entities is difficult, since there would be problems of how to identify separately such beings. That is, our present criteria of identity of persons are heavily bound up with bodily position, etc. It could be objected, from a Christian point of view, that the Trinity doctrine does indeed imply distinct (though also united) persons within the Godhead. But it would be reasonable to hold that identification here is through the different modes under which God manifests himself in salvation-history. As to the inner constitution of the Trinity, it is hard to know what can be said. By analogy, it might be argued that people could be identified here and now in the way in which we normally identify them, and this would somehow guarantee their separateness in a heavenly existence.

The second difficulty arises out of this, namely that the notion of an independent 'something' which can link an embodied person to a non-spatial existence does not, partly because of the thinness of the life which it might have, provide what is often required of people in immortality. That is, it is doubtful whether we could talk of the immortality of a *person*. It is true that some Indian schemes of religious belief would not find a difficulty here, in that liberation is conceived as a state where the person as an individual is transcended. As has been pointed out by some Buddhist writers in the Indian tradition, the Buddhist 'agnostic' belief in a liberated state constitutes as rich an account of liberation as such soul-theories, which effectively divorce the soul from the normal psychological and physiological aspects of the individual. It would therefore seem that the best that one could do in the way of a concept of liberation in a transcendent place would be to adopt an 'agnostic' view, that is one where no specific description of such a state can be given in terms of a soul theory.

However, the thinness of this account does not agree with the richer picture which is given, for instance, in the Christian tradition. Is it possible to use the mythic idea of heaven not just symbolically, which would imply that the picture described in images could be described *otherwise doctrinally*, but parabolically? By this I mean (in line with suggestions made by I. C. Crombie, T. R. Miles and others) that the picture of heaven would tell us something about the nature of heaven, but there would be no one–one correspondence between the details of the picture and the state which it depicts. In this way, the idea of heaven could be retained within the whole scheme of Christian belief and practice, but it would not be possible to spell out what it meant doctrinally. There are, however, difficulties about a *totally* parabolic account of a scheme of belief, since that which parables refer to becomes in essence indescribable; one ends up with the silence qualified by parables canvassed by T. R. Miles. There must be a richer doctrinal account of the object of reference so that it is possible to make sense of the notion that there is something for the parables to refer to. I would therefore conclude that one might accept a parabolic account of heaven, provided there was not also a totally parabolic account of God. This seems to be a further way in which the idea of heaven as a transcendent place of God is in its way crucial to a continued acceptance of the idea of heaven as a place of salvation.

Another way to avoid the difficulties of understanding any transition to a future life is to make the mythic idea symbolic of what happens here and now. I recall reading an account of a British visitor to a Tibetan home whose host invited some lamas to meet him. When they arrived they were laughing, as at some joke, and the visitor enquired what was so funny. The lamas replied that they had been discussing the question of whether heaven is a place or a state of mind. Certainly there are treatments of the conquest of death which imply that this is something to be attained here and now through facing it in some way (the way is sometimes treated opaquely, by existentialists). Is a kind of serenity and authenticity in the face of death what the idea of heaven refers to? There is something in this approach, by the very fact that eternal life, as we have said earlier, is, in religion, thought to be available to us now. However, this view also by implication denies the belief in a future life, and for this reason might be criticised as failing to take account of the predicament of those who die without having conquered death. This criticism can perhaps be by-passed by treating it simply as another aspect of the problem of evil; it is doubtful whether one should believe in heaven simply to redress the wrongs of the present world. This 'existentialist' solution to the problem of heaven is a possible one, but again it could hardly work as an account of religious belief if the concept of God is to be treated in the same manner, for then the focus of religious aspiration itself evaporates. That is, the 'existentialist' account has an analogy to the parabolic one, namely that its viability depends upon the retention of the idea of transcendence – unless, that is, one wishes to make a radical break with the traditional meaning of Christian faith. Putting it crudely, a sort of 'Christian' atheism is consistent, but it scarcely connects with the hitherto established sense of Christian language.

It is for these reasons that the notion of the transcendent place of God holds a crucial position. I have not here argued that this notion is consistent. But it may be useful to reflect briefly upon a non-philosophical objection which might be brought against it, namely that it implies a kind of split into two worlds, so that religion, by focusing on God or heaven, becomes other-worldly at the expense of the concerns of this world. It is not surprising if sometimes ideas of heaven have generated this attitude. However, there is no necessity about it. The idea of transcendence can be treated so that it is indistinguishable from the idea of immanence, that is, that God is working in everything. The world also can be looked upon as the self-expression of the Creator, so that there is no need to undervalue it or to flee from it (any more than one would wish to scrape away a person's smile or frown in the hope of penetrating to his true personality).

15

ETERNAL LIFE

John Wisdom

I FEAR you will be disappointed in what I have to say. For I am going to talk about those who, though they have said 'There is a way to eternal life', have then gone on to explain that what they mean does not imply that there is a way to a life that endures for ever or even a life after death. It is plain that those who do this take from the words 'There is a way to eternal life' a part of their meaning which has been and still is to very many people of very great importance. Nevertheless between those who when they speak of a way to eternal life are thinking of a life after death which endures for ever, and those who when they speak of eternal life give to their words a meaning which carries no implication as to whether there is a life after death, there is a link, in that both are seeking a remedy against a sort of despair which comes not merely from the thought of death but from a disappointment with life together with the thought that it ends in death.

Through the words of the author of Ecclesiastes runs a note of sadness. He is not suffering from a painful disease. He has all that money can buy. He has tried many things and has found some pleasure in some but never the contentment he was looking for. He no longer expects to find it. He sees all things under the shadow of death which he believes to be the end of a man. His despair is expressed in the refrain 'All is vanity'.

It is against such a pervasive despair that both those who when they speak of eternal life mean a life which endures for ever and those who when they speak of eternal life do not mean a life that endures for ever have sought to present a remedy. They have sought to present not just any remedy but what they would call 'a true remedy'. St Augustine at a time when he was very much depressed was walking with friends in the streets of Milan when he noticed one whom he describes as a poor beggar-man, half drunk, very jocund and pleasant upon the matter. St Augustine remarked to his friends that for the price of a penny or two this man was free from the depression which lay so heavily upon them. He nevertheless says that he would not change places with the beggar because the beggar's joy was not a true joy. I do not think he says the beggar had not reached a true joy merely because the beggar's joy was not lasting. I think he called the beggar's joy not a true joy because he believed that it did not arise from a true view of things, a view of things as they are. Those who have said 'There is a way to eternal life', whether or no they have meant a life of endless duration, have sought to combat despair by presenting a view of things which they regard as a truer view than any which generates despair, and also brings with it a sort of happiness which even the disappointments of life and the thought of death cannot take from us.

Those who have said that there is a life after death which can be of everlasting happiness have brought comfort to millions of people. But there have been and there are many who think that, at present at least, we have no sufficient foundation for belief in a life after death. And there are some who say that they do not know what is meant by those who say there is a life after death.

It will not do to say that no one has brought comfort to many unless he has said that there is a life after death. For the words of Buddha have brought comfort to very many and yet he says:

Accordingly, Malunkaputta, bear always in mind what it is that I have not elucidated and what it is that I have elucidated. . . . I have not elucidated, Malunkaputta, that the world is eternal, I have not elucidated that the world is not eternal. . . . I have not elucidated that the soul and the body are identical, I have not elucidated that the soul is one thing and the body another; I have not elucidated that the saint exists after death, I have not elucidated that the saint does not exist after death; I have not elucidated that the saint both exists and does not exist after death. . . . And what, Malunkaputta, have I elucidated? Misery, the origin of misery . . . the cessation of misery . . . the path leading to the cessation of misery have I elucidated.[1]

Those who have said such things as 'There is a way to eternal life' or 'We feel and know that we are eternal', without implying anything as to life's duration and without implying that there is a life after death, have been of help to very few people. Very few people have understood their words. It is not that none of them has made an effort to explain his meaning. Spinoza made a great effort to do so. He endeavours to make plain the nature of a certain kind of knowledge or consciousness of things from which arises a love of God. Our 'salvation, blessedness or liberty', he says, consists in 'the constant and eternal love for God or in the love of God for men. And this love or blessedness is called in the Scriptures "Glory" . . .'. In so far as a man has this sort of loving knowledge or consciousness of himself, God, and things, he has a mind which 'cannot be absolutely destroyed with the human body', he has a mind of which 'the greatest or principal part is eternal'. But Spinoza in the eighth of the definitions with which he begins the five books of his *Ethics* says: 'I understand Eternity to be existence itself, in so far as it is conceived to follow necessarily from the definition of an eternal thing.' He then adds: 'Explanation. For the existence of a thing as an eternal truth, is conceived to be the same as its essence, and therefore cannot be explained by duration or time, although duration can be conceived as wanting beginning and end.' For my part all I learn from his definition and explanation is that when he calls a thing 'eternal' he implies nothing as to its duration. From his definition and explanation I do not learn what he does mean by the words 'eternity' and 'eternal'. In the light of his explanatory note I am not surprised when he later says: 'The human mind cannot be absolutely destroyed with the human body, but there is some part of it that remains

[1] Quoted by Herbert Fingarette, *The Self in Transformation* (London, 1963), p. 221.

eternal'[1] and then says that eternity cannot be 'defined by time nor have any relation to time'. I am not surprised when he says 'But nevertheless we feel and know that we are eternal' and also says: 'If we pay attention to the common opinion of men, we shall see that they are conscious of the eternity of their minds: but they confuse eternity with duration . . .'.[2] His definition of eternity together with the explanatory note he adds to it prevent me from being surprised by what he says later, but they do not enable me to understand it. For while I gather that Spinoza would say that the more the mind understands things by what he calls the second and third kinds of knowledge the less it will fear death,[3] I do not understand when he tries to explain what kinds of knowledge he is thinking of. The examples Spinoza provides suggest to me that a person has knowledge of the second kind only when he knows a proposition to be true as a result of following a mathematical proof, and that a person has knowledge of the third kind only when he knows a proposition to be true because it is self-evident, as is the proposition that 6 is in the same proportion to 3 as 4 is to 2. But if this is so then a person's knowledge of himself, of God, and of things cannot be knowledge of the second kind or of the third kind. No one can know himself or any matter of fact about himself, or any matter of fact whatever, in the way that he knows a self-evident truth or a truth that can be deduced from self-evident truths.

Spinoza's words when he says that we feel and know that we are eternal, and when he speaks of seeing things under a species of eternity, may linger in one's mind even after one has been driven to admit that what he says by way of indicating what he means has left one still at a loss as to what he means and, perhaps, with a suspicion that he himself is not clear as to what he means. This may lead one along the following line of thought. There are occasions when a person engaged in an enquiry, perhaps a person trying to gain an understanding of certain bewildering phenomena in nature, finds in his mouth certain words, for example 'lines of force' or 'field of force', without yet knowing what he means by them. We know that in such circumstances it may happen that the words of which he may himself

---

[1] *Ethics*, pt. v, prop. xxiii.
[2] *Ethics*, pt. v, prop. xxxiv, note. [3] *Ethics*, pt. v, prop. xxxviii.

say that he doesn't yet know what he means by them nevertheless help him to grope his way towards a concept which turns
out to be just what he needs for that understanding of things
which he is struggling to attain.

It is worth thinking of a very clear instance of this so that we
are better prepared to recognise less clear instances of it.
Imagine a group of people who though they often speak of the
time it took a man or a camel to cover a certain distance and
even of the average speed at which a thing moved during a
certain time, never speak of the speed at which a thing was
moving at a certain moment. A party of these people are
crossing a hillside when a boulder from above them begins to
roll downwards towards them at a steadily increasing speed.
It passes close beside them and rolls on till it plunges into a
stream in the valley below. One of them finds in his mouth the
words 'At what speed was it moving at the moment it passed
us?' His companions say 'What do you mean "At what speed
was it moving at the moment it passed us?"? You don't know
what you mean by your own words.' The person who asked
the question may be discouraged not only by the clamour of
those around him who say 'You don't know what you mean by
your own words' but also by a voice within himself which says
'It's true. I didn't know what I meant, I don't know what I
meant by my own words.' He may be so much discouraged that
he quite abandons his own question as worthless. But he may
not be. He may say 'Nobody knows, I don't know, what my
question means. But I am sure I can find a meaning for it, form
a meaning for it. I am sure it can lead me to find, to form, some
concept worth having.' And he may go on thinking until he
discovers or creates the methods of the calculus and finds or
forms the concepts of speed at a moment, rate of change at an
instant – concepts which we now know to be of immense value
in gaining an understanding of nature.

Consider a somewhat different yet still similar case. Think of
someone who says:

> I no longer believe what the words 'There's a God above' used
> to mean to me when I was a child. I no longer believe what
> the words 'There's a God above' still mean to many. Indeed

the words 'God exists' no longer mean to me anything which
I believe. And yet I can't dismiss them from my mind. When
I look back on all that has been said about God then I feel
that though much of it has been false or doubtful or obscure,
still the words 'There is a God above' may yet with further
thought guide us to some truth which is still of great impor-
ance for our lives.

Perhaps William James was like this at the start of the
enquiry which he presents in *The Varieties of Religious Experience*.
For it may well be that when he began to assemble the great
variety of religious and mystical experience which he presents
in that book he had not yet formed that modified concept of
God which he tries to explain at the end of his book.

These reflections may lead someone to say something of this
sort. Those who read Spinoza feel that his words, though very
obscure, may nevertheless in conjunction with further thought
lead us to a new meaning for the words 'There is a way to
eternal life' – a new meaning in which they no longer carry any
implication as to life's duration and yet still convey a truth
which can save us from despair as it saved Spinoza, and bring
us that sort of happiness in things as they are to which it brought
him.

When this suggestion is made the question arises: 'What
further thought will take us from the unsatisfactory situation in
which one is saying "Although I don't understand these words
I feel that they can with further thought lead me to a knowledge
of a profoundly important truth" to the situation in which one
is saying "Now at last I can see the truth these words convey"?'

Other people beside Spinoza have felt driven to speak of
eternal life without implications as to life's duration. Can we by
considering what they have said reach a better understanding
of what he meant? Perhaps by comparing the philosopher,
Spinoza, whose words suggest that behind his philosophical
thought lies some mystical experience, with the words of some
mystics who have spoken of experiences in which they have felt
themselves to have an immortality which some have described
as timeless, we can gain a better understanding both of the
philosopher and the mystics.

William James in his chapter on Mysticism in *The Varieties of Religious Experience* speaks of 'the doctrine that eternity is timeless, that our "immortality", if we live in the eternal, is not so much future as already now and here.' (p. 413) As an example of one who presents such a doctrine he quotes a Dr R. M. Bucke. Professor Walter Stace in his book *Mysticism and Philosophy* also refers to Dr Bucke. I suppose that James and Stace regard Dr Bucke's words as being at least as understandable as those of anyone else who speaks of a timeless immortality.

James quotes Dr Bucke as follows:

I had spent the evening in a great city, with two friends, reading and discussing poetry and philosophy. We parted at midnight. I had a long drive in a hansom to my lodging. My mind, deeply under the influence of the ideas, images, and emotions called up by the reading and talk, was calm and peaceful. I was in a state of quiet, almost passive enjoyment, not actually thinking, but letting ideas, images, and emotions flow of themselves, as it were, through my mind. All at once, without warning of any kind, I found myself wrapped in a flame-colored cloud. For an instant I thought of fire, an immense conflagration somewhere close by in that great city; the next, I knew that the fire was within myself. Directly afterwards there came upon me a sense of exultation, of immense joyousness accompanied or immediately followed by an intellectual illumination impossible to describe. Among other things, I did not merely come to believe, but I saw that the universe is not composed of dead matter, but is, on the contrary, a living Presence; I became conscious in myself of eternal life. It was not a conviction that I would have eternal life, but a consciousness that I possessed eternal life then; I saw that all men are immortal; that the cosmic order is such that without any peradventure all things work together for the good of each and all; that the foundation principle of the world, of all the worlds, is what we call love, and that the happiness of each and all is in the long run absolutely certain. The vision lasted a few seconds and was gone, but the memory of it and the sense of the reality of what it taught has remained during the quarter of a century which has since elapsed. I knew that what the vision showed was true. I had attained to a point of view from which I saw that it must be true. That view, that conviction, I may say that consciousness, has never, even during periods of the deepest depression, been lost.[1]

Although William James speaks of the doctrine that 'eternity is timeless, that our "immortality", if we live in the eternal, is not so much future as already now and here', he does not claim to understand talk of this sort. On the contrary, he says 'We recognise the passwords to the mystical region as we hear them but we cannot use them ourselves.' Dr Bucke's words have not enlightened William James. And I am not surprised. For what Dr Bucke says is at critical places obscure. He does not take the precaution of separating what he says as to what his experience was like from what he says as to what interpretation he put upon that experience. He says 'I became conscious in myself of eternal life. It was not a conviction that I would have eternal life, but a consciousness that I possessed eternal life then.' What we want to know is the difference between a man who is convinced that he will never cease to exist and a man who is conscious that he possesses eternal life now. Dr Bucke's words do not make clear what that difference is.

Professor Walter Stace in his book *Mysticism and Philosophy* says 'Mystics unite in asserting that their experience is beyond time. And it is natural to surmise that the immortality which they feel themselves to have achieved is the immortality of the timeless moment.' No mystic is as insistent as Eckhart that the soul which has attained to the mystic state has passed beyond time into 'the eternal now'. Of the 'apex of the soul' wherein the mystical union with God takes place he tells us: 'It ranks so high that it communes with God face to face as He is. It . . . is unconscious of yesterday or the day before or of tomorrow or of the day after, for in eternity there is no yesterday nor any tomorrow but only Now.'[2]

Stace also refers to a quotation from Plotinus which runs as follows: 'They see all not in process of becoming, but in being,

[1] *The Varieties of Religious Experience* (London, 1902), pp. 390–1.
[2] *Mysticism and Philosophy* (London, 1961), p. 309.

and they see themselves in the other. Each being contains within itself the whole intelligible world. Therefore all is everywhere. Each is there all and all is each.'

It seems to me that the words of Spinoza, of Bucke, of Eckhart, of Plotinus and of others who use somewhat similar words, are so obscure that we cannot be sure that they refer to the same thing. Let us, however, imagine someone who is convinced that they do refer to the same thing and believes he knows what they mean and now presents the following explanation of what they mean. He says: 'I have occasionally been in a state of which I am now inclined to say "When I was in that state I felt myself to be eternal because in that state I saw things as having a sort of eternity or to use Spinoza's phrase 'as under a species of eternity'." I recall Traherne's words "By contemplating the eternal the soul becomes immortal." But let me try to make clearer what I mean by saying that on the occasions I am talking about I saw things as having a sort of eternity. You know that people sometimes in describing an experience say "Time seemed to stop" or "Time stopped". The words "Time stopped" taken as a statement as to what happened are, I agree, useless and bewildering but when they are used as a way of indicating what an experience was like then I think most of us have a fairly good idea of what is meant. Well, now, from time to time I have had a sort of experience of which I want to say "When I have that sort of experience then for me Time stops, things past, present and future no longer appear to me as things which have ceased to be, things which are, and things which are not yet, but as simultaneous parts of a changeless whole." Every performance of a musical work is a pattern in time. When one hears the earlier parts one is not yet hearing the later parts and when one hears the later parts one is not still hearing the earlier parts. And yet when one hears a musical work after having heard it several times then as one hears each part one's apprehension of that part is modified by one's knowledge of the other parts. Well, sometimes much more than at others, I see past, present and future that way. Think of a man who in the dark explores a large picture with a torch which illuminates only a small area at a time. He may come to have beliefs, or theories as one might say, about the picture. But that

is different from what happens when suddenly a big light shows
him the whole and each part in relation to every other part.
There have been times when in an extraordinary degree I have
seen things in that way. At such times I have felt a joy, a
contentment, which no regrets for the past nor fears for the
future could take from me.'

One who says something like this has had an experience
which he regards as having brought him some sort of knowledge
or enlightenment. He does something towards indicating what
that experience was like. But what truth, over and above the
truth that he has had a certain sort of experience, did he learn
from that experience? What truth is he trying to convey to us?

I can't say. I don't know.

Some people have tried to make more understandable the
fact that mystics claim to have learned something and yet
remain unable to say what they have learned, by saying that the
truth or truths which mystics come to recognise are 'ineffable
truths', truths which cannot be, could not be, put into words.
Others have said that the truths which mystics come to recognise
are 'truths beyond the understanding'. Mystics themselves have
said this sort of thing about their situation.

But do such phrases as 'come to know an ineffable truth' and
'come to know a truth beyond the understanding' help us to
understand when someone is speaking of what he believes to be
some knowledge or enlightenment he has reached, but cannot
say 'This is the truth I learned and want to convey'? I don't
think they do help us. I think they encourage a tendency to
forget that a change in a person's apprehension is not always a
matter of his learning a truth or coming to believe that this or
that is so. I will try to make clear what I am referring to by
describing in outline an occasion when I was hindered by this
tendency.

A friend of mine, Mr Kollerstrom by name, sent me the
typescript of a book he had written. In the last four essays of this
book he presents what he describes as 'a new way of thinking
about eternity and all that we locate in the eternal'. It was
very soon clear to me that such words as 'There is a way to
eternal life' or 'We feel and know that we are eternal' would not
for Mr Kollerstrom have a meaning with an implication as to

life's duration. But when I asked myself the question: 'What meaning would Mr Kollerstrom give to the words "There is a way to eternal life"?' I was in difficulty. At first I thought of my difficulty as like that of one who is confident that someone has given a new meaning to old words but is not clear what that new meaning is. This idea about the nature of my difficulty was not, I think, all wrong but I soon found it inadequate. I next thought of my difficulty as like that of one who is trying to understand someone who is using old words but is still groping his way towards a new meaning for them. This idea about the nature of my difficulty in learning what Mr Kollerstrom wished to convey and his difficulty in making clear what he wished to convey was also, I think, not all wrong. But it was still inadequate.

I would not have found the situation so bewildering had I been able to say 'This man's words convey nothing to me', but I could not say that. His words did convey something to me. But when I asked myself 'What do they convey?' and 'What, if he is right, is the truth that he presents?' I could not answer. I tried again and again to formulate some proposition of which I could say 'This is what he believes to be the truth'. In the course of my efforts to do this I re-read a passage in which he describes in outline a dream or sequence of dreams he once had and speaks of the enlightenment which this experience brought him, in some degree at the time of his dream and more so later in conjunction with further experience and further thought.

Mr Kollerstrom had the dream he speaks of within the very few minutes between the time someone with him left the room he was in and the time when he returned and woke him. Of the first part of the dream Mr Kollerstrom says: 'I dreamed my whole life over again, but backwards, like reading a novel starting with the last chapter and working backwards chapter by chapter.' The experience was one of disturbing frustration. In the second part of his dream he lived a life starting from his position at the time he dreamed and ending in his committing a murder and dying of disease in a condemned cell tormented by guilt. In a third part of his dream he again experienced, 'in full details' he says, another possible life which started from his then actual age and ended in lonely squalor and suicide. In the last part of his dream he lived a life of success and happiness and love, purged of guilt and bitterness – a life in which his deepest desires were fulfilled.

Speaking of his life after the dream, he says that it took him years to digest the experience, to discover himself and regrow his being. He also says: 'But everything that is spiritually my own, everything of true worth that I have found for myself, derives from that great dream. Still it enriches and instructs me; without it my life would have been a husk. Though the gifts of the gods may blast or wither us, if we can at last bear them, they will transform us.'

When I read this I felt inclined to say: 'It's the old story. It is true that though Mr Kollerstrom's dream was somewhat extraordinary I have some idea of what it was like. But does it provide evidence for some truth, some doctrine, some proposition? And, if so, how so? And what is the truth, or what he regards as the truth, for which he thinks it provides evidence?'

But then I said to myself: 'Do his words really convey to you so little? You know, we know, that occasionally what happens in a dream throws suddenly a light on one's life, on the life of another, on some range of reality small or great. Someone in a dream may say what he or she has never said and now perhaps will never say, which gives one an apprehension of what in years of experience one has been blind to. What happens in a dream, what happens in a play presented on the stage, what happens in real life, sometimes is such that for the rest of one's life one sees things differently.'

[*Unfinished*]

INDEX

251